PLEASURES OF BENTHAMISM

Frontispiece. *Calico Printing*, engraving from a drawing by Thomas Allom, in Sir Edward Baines, *History of the Cotton Manufacture in Great Britain*, London, 1835. © V & A Images, Victoria and Albert Museum, London

Pleasures of Benthamism

*Victorian Literature, Utility,
Political Economy*

KATHLEEN BLAKE

OXFORD
UNIVERSITY PRESS

OXFORD
UNIVERSITY PRESS

Great Clarendon Street, Oxford OX2 6DP

Oxford University Press is a department of the University of Oxford.
It furthers the University's objective of excellence in research, scholarship,
and education by publishing worldwide in

Oxford New York

Auckland Cape Town Dar es Salaam Hong Kong Karachi
Kuala Lumpur Madrid Melbourne Mexico City Nairobi
New Delhi Shanghai Taipei Toronto

With offices in

Argentina Austria Brazil Chile Czech Republic France Greece
Guatemala Hungary Italy Japan Poland Portugal Singapore
South Korea Switzerland Thailand Turkey Ukraine Vietnam

Oxford is a registered trade mark of Oxford University Press
in the UK and in certain other countries

Published in the United States
by Oxford University Press Inc., New York

British Library Cataloguing in Publication Data

Data available

Library of Congress Cataloging in Publication Data

Data available

Typeset by SPI Publisher Services, Pondicherry, India
Printed in Great Britain
on acid-free paper by
the MPG Books Group, Bodmin and King's Lynn

ISBN 978-0-19-956326-5

3 5 7 9 10 8 6 4

Acknowledgements

I would like to thank these colleagues for their astute and helpful readings of chapters and grant and prospectus materials—Mona Modiano, Marshall Brown, and Henry Staten, Lauren Goodlad, Ann Banfield and Michael Rogin, and Christine Rose. I am grateful to Annette Federico for putting together the panels at which I first presented my ideas on Bentham and pleasure. These were at the Modern Language Association conference, December 2000 in New York, and the 'Locating the Victorians' Interdisciplinary Conference for the Sesquicentenary of the Great Exhibition, July 2001 in London. I am also grateful to Regenia Gagnier for her interest and encouragement at key points in the course of writing the book. I thank the librarians and staff of the University of Washington Libraries and the Bentham Library at University College London. Research support from the University of Washington has been invaluable, including Sabbatical leave, a Royalty Research Fellowship, and travel funding from the Graduate School. I have gained a great deal from the laboratory of the classroom and from my students in Victorian literature and culture. Additional thanks go to Christine Rose—not only colleague and reader of my work, but friend and companion in a regime of walking that has helped both of us see through our book projects. To my son Colin Blake—thank you for deepening my love of literature, language, and ideas by growing up to love them, too. To my husband Jon Blake—thank you for everything, your interest, your thoughts, your reading of drafts and practical help of every kind, and, throughout, your steady good judgement and good and happy spirit.

Further, I am grateful for permission to draw on materials from two articles of mine in *Victorian Literature and Culture*, published by Cambridge University Press: '*Bleak House*, Political Economy, Victorian Studies', 25/1 (1997): 1–27, and 'Between Economies in *The Mill on the Floss*: Loans versus Gifts, or, Auditing Mr. Tulliver's Accounts', 33/1 (2005), 219–37.

K.B.

Seattle
Autumn 2008

Contents

1

Victorian Literature, Utility, Political Economy

The Case of *Bleak House*

INTRODUCTION

Charles Dickens is not known as a Utilitarian or political economist. Neither are most others on the roster of major writers within Victorian literary and cultural studies, except John Stuart Mill. For that matter, a few sharp remarks of Mill's on Jeremy Bentham are often cited to suggest a parting of the ways between himself and Utilitarianism. This is so even though Mill remains Utilitarianism's champion in his late essay so named and is the authoritative spokesman for political economy in two volumes that receive little mention. Dickens's *Oliver Twist* is known for its exposé of workhouse abuses made topical by Utilitarian Poor Law reform. His *Hard Times* is known for its caricature of the disciple of political economy Mr Gradgrind, who names his sons Adam Smith and Malthus Gradgrind. The mid-twentieth-century promoter of the 'great tradition' in literature, F. R. Leavis, counts Dickens in, but certainly not Bentham, certainly not political economists. Leavis reads *Hard Times* as a condemnation of 'The World of Bentham'. This world encompasses the Utilitarian doctrine of Jeremy Bentham and the capitalist economics of Adam Smith and such followers as Thomas Malthus and J. S. Mill. Also identified under the names of 'philosophic radicalism' and the 'classical school' of economics, and closely interlinked, as Leavis says, these two schemes of thought achieved grand-scale 'philosophic' and 'classic' articulation and saw massive application in the period. They may indeed be said to set forth a 'world'.[1]

My own encompassing designation is Utilitarian political economy, though I sometimes find it more exact, or just a convenient shorthand, to use one half of the label or the other. Cognate terms are Benthamism and capitalism. An affiliated term is liberalism. Of course, this is looser. Those who might be deemed liberal or allied with liberalism include parliamentary Radicals, Reformers, liberal Whigs, members of the post-Whig Liberal party, and Gladstonians. There are odder crossovers like liberal Tories, Christian political economists, and liberal-conservative Peelites. Then, too, there are supporters of signature causes like democratized suffrage and free trade. And, very broadly, there are the bourgeois or middle classes, 'philistines', reform-minded questioners of one sort of establishment or another, ralliers to ideals of liberty, self-help, self-government, and personal and social improvement, and participants in industrial market culture.

For Leavis, the world of Bentham, home to Gradgrind, is hard, inhumane, inflexible, constrictive, and repellant. Such a judgement carries forward into the twenty-first century, especially owing to the influence of the social theorist Michel Foucault, another harsh commentator on Bentham. For Foucault, the world of Bentham is prison-like; it is the Panopticon. In a trendsetting application of Foucauldian theory to literary criticism, D. A. Miller reads Dickens's *Bleak House* as a dark rendering of a panoptical world.[2]

But *Bleak House* presents an interesting case. It prompts me to reopen the question of how to understand Utilitarian political economy in its bearings on this novel, and, within the scope of the book, on a broad range of Victorian writing. Among authors I discuss, Dickens and Thomas Carlyle are, by most lights, the evident opponents of Utilitarian political economy, and Bentham, Smith, Malthus, David Ricardo, and James and J. S. Mill its evident proponents. Anthony Trollope, George Eliot, Elizabeth Gaskell, and Rabindranath Tagore write further away from seeming alignment. Still, I believe all are touched and pervaded by a powerful force in the culture, and powerfully represent it.

There is a passage in *Bleak House* where Mr Skimpole declares his family to be 'all wrong in point of political economy' (p. 454). One of Skimpole's daughters marries young and takes a husband who is another child. They are improvident, have children, and bring them home to Skimpole's, as he thinks his other daughters and their husbands are likely to do, though none of them knows how the family is to get on.

Skimpole is exposed in the course of the novel as one of its worst characters. For a bribe and to save himself from infection he turns the smallpox-stricken Jo out into the night. He cadges loans from those who can't afford to make them. He encourages Richard in his fatal false hopes of a Chancery settlement for a payback to himself for helping the lawyer Mr Vholes to a client. The novel's heroine, Esther Summerson, ultimately condemns him, and her kind guardian, Mr Jarndyce, breaks with him. If Skimpole is all wrong in point of political economy, can there be something all right in political economy for Dickens?

It is rare to answer yes. Closer to Dickens's day Sir Henry Maine could say:

> It does not seem to me a fantastic assertion that the ideas of one of the great novelists of the last generation may be traced to Bentham....Dickens, who spent his early manhood among the politicians of 1832 trained in Bentham's school, hardly ever wrote a novel without attacking an abuse. The procedures of the Court of Chancery and of the Ecclesiastical Courts, the delays of the Public Offices, the costliness of divorce, the state of the dwellings of the poor, and the condition of the cheap schools in the North of England, furnished him with ... the true moral of a series of fictions.[3]

There is biographical evidence of Dickens's Benthamite connections, including his parliamentary reporting for the *Morning Chronicle* under the editorship of John Black, a friend of James Mill imbued with many of Bentham's ideas. J. S. Mill published here, and Dickens joined the staff in 1834. Dickens had associations with Harriet Martineau, popularizer of Utilitarian political economy and writer for Dickens's journal *Household Words* from 1850 to 1853. And he had associations with such generally Benthamite figures as Southwood Smith, Poor Law Commissioner and sanitation reformer and Dickens's companion in slum walking tours; Charles Knight, statistician and publisher for the Society for the Diffusion of Useful Knowledge and early contributor to *Household Words*; and Henry Cole, director of the Department of Practical Art, with whom Dickens sat on the Committee of the Society of Arts that proposed the Great Exhibition. A degree of alignment can be traced between Dickens as advocate for popular education and William Ellis, a friend of J. S. Mill, and founder of the Birkbeck Schools that won some approval in *Household Words*, though made an object of satire in *Hard Times*.[4]

Critics have researched the particular targets in *Hard Times* in large measure in order to sustain Leavis's idea of Dickens as an anti-Gradgrindian, an enemy of Bentham and his world. Sometimes this means contesting John Holloway's charge that Dickens is not systematic *enough* as an anti-Benthamite in *Hard Times*.[5] Alternatively, critics sound a note of disapproval like Holloway's of 'elements of compromise' and a 'philistine' streak (p. 165) in the novel. Patrick Brantlinger is one such, suggesting that Dickens falls short of his critical aim and appears no better than 'the ultimate capitalist-with-heart-of-gold'.[6] Catherine Gallagher perhaps mutes such disapproval, being one of a handful of critics who are 'now more curious and tolerant about economic logic than [critics have been] at any time in the twentieth century'. Still, in *Hard Times* she discerns a harsh ethic of work that to her signals Dickens's 'unwitting' if uneasy adherence to Bentham and the economists.[7]

I find it fruitful here to turn to Raymond Williams. He says that

in its mood, rather than in all of its detailed tenets and procedures, utilitarianism profoundly influenced all radical thought, and in ways not only not different from Dickens but in some respects very like him; he too would have accepted happiness or pleasure as an absolute criterion, as against the emphases of most other contemporary religious and philosophic systems.[8]

Williams sees a basic commonality between Dickens and Utilitarianism. Far from pointing to something severe in mood (like a harsh work ethic), he points to a shared commitment to pleasure. And he points to a shared 'radical' reformist bent. For Williams, Dickens may be the abettor and not only the critic of Utilitarian causes. But he says it has been difficult for commentators to recognize any such possibility—and I very much agree with him—because of a very confused idea of what Utilitarianism was, as a reforming movement.

So Marjorie Stone's essay on Dickens's and Bentham's common judicial concerns has little company. Stone maintains that Dickens was 'an enthusiastic and consistent supporter of Benthamism in the field where Bentham scored his greatest triumphs: the field of law'.[9] She focuses on the issue of legal fictions, which Bentham opposed for protecting wrongdoers from justice while providing lawyers and judges with a convenient and lucrative tool. Mill wrote against legal fictions in the *Morning Chronicle* and arranged Bentham's castigation of these and other devices of the law in the *Rationale of Judicial Evidence*. In

Household Words Eliza Lynn and W. H. Wills attack legal fictions, and Dickens satirizes them in 'Legal and Equitable Jokes' and in novels from *Pickwick Papers* on. The Chancery suit Jarndyce and Jarndyce in *Bleak House* is a notorious showcase for 'every masterly fiction' (p. 15). Stone points out critics' inattention to the Benthamite implications of Dickens's attack on this point of law.[10]

There is just such inattention to the Benthamite implications of the attack on the Court of Chancery in *Bleak House*. We see this in Miller's interpretation. His chapter on the novel in *The Novel and the Police* presents the police in Foucauldian fashion as a characteristically modern institution of discipline by surveillance. This is said to find its type in Bentham's plan for a prison, the Panopticon, where the prisoners never know when they may come under the eye of the unseen overseer in the central observation tower and so are socially disciplined into self-protective self-regulation. While it is worth considering the detective police in *Bleak House* in terms of aspects of this model (Bentham contributed ideas towards establishing the metropolitan police in *Memoirs*, x. 329), it is most un-historical to associate Chancery with the police as a panoptical institution (p. 64). The two are far more fundamentally opposed than aligned. The police are called modern in the novel; Chancery is immemorially old. It is not a recent creation of reform, but in need of reform. It is not panoptically all-seeing, but overwhelmingly befogged and befogging.

Not only superimposing the Panopticon on Chancery, Miller superimposes Foucault's Panopticon, ignoring aspects of Bentham's. Emphasizing one-way surveillance, Foucault focuses on the overseer who remains unseen. He notes only briefly that the overseer can also be seen, not by the prisoners but by prison inspectors and the general public.[11] In Bentham this is a major feature. It insures openness to official and public scrutiny of an institution that by its panoptic sight-lines reveals all its practices at a glance. A Utilitarian economics attends this openness to review. The prison is run on a business basis. The relation that maximizes the greatest happiness of the greatest number with least cost in pain and money is one that identifies the interests of guard and prisoners and situates the guard to profit by the well-being rather than the misery of his charges. Better supervised to make them more self-regulating, they endure fewer restraints and punishments, and the warden saves in time, trouble, and expense. The prisoners work for their food. The better they work, the better they eat, and the more the return to the warden. Even bad workers are not to be starved. The warden must pay if a prisoner dies. To assure all this, the monitor too must be monitored. In his calculus of pleasures and pains Bentham gives full weight to the moral sanction. This operates through people's concern for what others think of them, and there is a parallel here with Adam Smith on the impartial spectator.[12] Thus officials are as interested as other people are in how they are seen, and this makes oversight a powerful force for influencing and controlling those in power.

So hard and carceral has panopticism come to seem via Foucault that we might forget its broad purpose of benefiting humanity. Karl Marx expresses appreciation for England's 'factory inspectors, her medical reporters on public health, her commissioners of inquiry into the exploitation of women and children, into housing and food'.[13] Panoptical knowledge provided material for radical critique, as in *Capital*, and opportunity for many reforms.

So dogmatic has panopticism come to seem that we might forget its tie to critical thinking and freedom of thought, such as Mill champions in 'On Liberty'. Utilitarians defended freedom of the press and argued for extension of democratic representation; as Radicals they made common cause with Reformers and liberal Whigs to bring in the watershed 1832 Reform Bill. Power of the vote added a political sanction to the moral one, each operating effectively only to the extent that the public could look into affairs.[14]

We might also forget Bentham's own critical attention to dangers and limit cases in formulating his ideas. In his proposal for the Panopticon he points out problems in transposing the system to other environments, such as to a school. If pervasively monitored, might the students gain in happiness through increased learning with reduced misbehaviour and liability to punishment, but at the same time might they lose in liberty? In his proposal for a house for unmarried mothers he guards the women's privacy by providing a means for them to screen their visitors. In his proposal for the electoral franchise he guards the voters' privacy—on behalf of their free critical thought and power to advance the good as they see it—in the secret ballot.[15]

In following sections I will give my own Benthamite rather than Foucauldian, or Leavisite, reading of *Bleak House*. At stake are some main claims of the book. Reading literary texts in relation to texts of

Utilitarianism and political economy and in context of associated historical developments alters perception of Victorian writing and Victorian times. Literature does not appear so much to challenge or else unwittingly collude with bourgeois philistinism. Theoretical and topical writings on the 'philistine' side appear more compelling than expected and less like an anti-literature. Many fresh readings emerge. While, text to text, I attend to differences, strains, and shifts in position, I am most interested in expanding awareness of commonalities across leading expressions of the age. A view takes shape of a broadly Benthamite, capitalist, and liberal age in pursuit of utility alike in commerce and industry and in socio-economic-political reforms, in good measure favourable to freedom and levelling in terms of class and gender.

My reading of *Bleak House*, moreover, allows me to introduce main principles of Utilitarianism and political economy and associated practices and policies that will be explored further in subsequent chapters for their importance to Victorian literature and culture. Following a conceptual rather than a chronological order of texts, Chapters 2–6 take up these principles in turn, contextualizing them historically in terms of practical, often reformist applications, and tracing their expression in representative theoretical/topical and literary texts. Chapter 2 focuses on utility, the principle of pleasure, Chapters 3 and 4 on the principle of pain in relation to pleasure, especially the pain of work and the pain of capital savings and investment, sometimes linked to the pain of sexual abstinence. Chapter 5 focuses on the principle of liberty, and Chapter 6 on the temporal principle, which, if less theoretically discrete, is pervasive. There is a shift in Chapter 6 to step up attention to principles in historical practice in an arena of particular importance—the textile industry, the lead industry of the Industrial Revolution and the product and driver of worldwide trade and empire, notably in India. Chapter 7 also gives sustained attention to principles in practice and presses further into the arena of British imperialism in India.

Distinctive aspects of my approach are to treat Utilitarianism along with political economy, and to treat texts in these traditions, as well as literary texts, for their expressive power—as eloquent and shaping articulations of a 'world'. In these respects, my attention to Bentham particularly stands out. Another distinctive aspect is to follow through from theoretical principles to historical practice. It may seem that I overindulge in glossing *Bleak House* and other works in terms of

theoretical and historical details of Utilitarianism and political economy. But I see no other way while the confusion that Raymond Williams speaks of remains. This confusion concerns theory and historical
developments as well. Many such developments are movements of
reform that carry liberal implications for class and gender. But then,
too, there is the development of British imperialism in the period. After
all, James and J. S. Mill were officials of the East India Company.
A further distinctive aspect of my approach is to address the apparent
contradiction of theory, or violation of principles, in 'liberal imperialism'. Thus my concluding chapter treats writings on India by Bentham,
with parallels in Smith, and by the elder and younger Mill. It revisits the
principle of liberty, placed in the light of other main principles and
many practices and policies, and confronts the difficult question of how
to recognize a character of liberalism in a Utilitarian, capitalist age that
is also an age of empire.

At the end of the present chapter I will say more to sum up and
explore reasons for the long-standing neglect and bias in Victorian
studies concerning Utilitarianism and political economy. And I will
survey revisionist trends, to which I hope to contribute. But now for
more on *Bleak House*.

CHANCERY

Dickens hated Chancery. He was a victorious plaintiff in five Chancery
suits against pirating publishers but was unable to recover his costs.[16] He
published two *Household Words* pieces on 'The Martyrs of Chancery'
(Alfred Whaley Cole, 7 Dec. 1850, 15 Feb. 1851). Bentham hated
Chancery. In his 'Indications Respecting Lord Eldon' he accuses the
high Tory Lord Chancellor of shoring up and extending a 'project of
plunderage' (p. 215). In his 'Equity Dispatch Court Proposal', he remarks
to the suffering suitors that 'to convince you of your *affliction*, words
would be thrown away... that which you have need of, is *relief*' (p. 299).

In Bentham's attack on the Equity Courts in the *Rationale of Judicial
Evidence* connections may be seen to the rest of his thinking on the law
and to his general philosophy. Chancery is a legacy from medieval times.
It takes its name from the Lord Chancellor, who was to preside over a
new jurisdiction—the Court of Equity—set up in contradistinction to

the Courts of Common Law. Chancery is royal—instituted by the king—and of ecclesiastical dye, for the king set his first minister, the Lord Chancellor, to run it, and he was a bishop. Its ancient lineage and monarchical and clerical derivation lend Chancery no charm to the modernizing, democratic, anti-Church, anti-Christian—more specifically, anti-Pauline—Bentham. The Lord Chancellor looked to 'Roman law, the seat of monarchical despotism' (vii. 297). He presumed that 'whatsoever a bishop did, was for the good of men's souls: whatsoever a lord chancellor did was for equity'—hence the name, though for Bentham it is an unmeaning denomination chosen only for its sanctimonious sound, and though 'ecclesiastics, the sons of the church, were liable like other men to be fools—like other men to be knaves—like other men to be liars' (vii. 293–6). In like manner Dickens satirizes the court's following of ancient 'precedent and usage' (*Bleak House*, 6), its lordly highness under the Lord High Chancellor, and its pretensions to offer God's own judgement under a great seal that (to the mad suitor Miss Flite) seems equivalent to the sixth seal of Revelation. Dickens also satirizes the court's baseless self-satisfaction in its name. Says Conversation Kenge: 'This is a very great country, a very great country. Its system of equity is a very great system, a very great system. Really, really!' (p. 638).

According to Bentham, 'by Roman law, though everything had been done badly, everything had been done' (vii. 297). What specially needed doing was something Common Law Courts did poorly because they depended on juries, which sat for a limited period. A way was needed to handle cases involving long-term inquiries and administration such as dispositions of property bound up in trusts and legacies. Here equity judges and lawyers saw 'a gold mine—a rich mine in *business*', says Bentham (vii. 294). This finds an echo in Dickens, who says: 'the one great principle of the English law is to make business for itself' (p. 416). Equity took advantage of a leading feature also found in other jurisdictions, the technical or fee-gathering system whereby court functionaries are paid for each service rendered. This system depends on a law built by tradition and precedent, hoary and backward-looking, lawyer-made rather than legislated, without a written code. A code would simplify the law and make it easier for all to understand. It would reduce the power of men of law to add technicality to technicality year after year and create a monopoly on knowledge that places them as the well-paid guides to obscure regions of their own making for their own profit.

The more services over the longest stretch, the more profit. Thus for Bentham—as for Dickens—'Chancery an open delay shop' (vii. 216). At the optimum all goes in costs, as in Jarndyce and Jarndyce. The court's slow pace shows its small concern for the principle of time. A symbol of the delay that enriches men of law is the long vacation. Bentham says:

Cruelty, negligence, dissipation, imbecility have not their long vacation. But the *custodes morum*, the judges, had, and resolved to have, *their* long vacation; not one week of it would they part with: the wife might be plagued to death, the child corrupted, the property consumed and wasted,—it was no concern of theirs. (vii. 293–4)

Dickens has a field day with the satisfaction taken in the long vacation by the English bar holidaying in Switzerland, at French watering-places, at Constantinople, on the canals of Venice, beside the cataracts of the Nile, in the baths of Germany, and upon the sands of the English coast, while clerks lounge in Chancery Lane and suitors wait.

One of the most significant sources of delay is the requirement for written documents. These are the bills—or plaintiff's statements—with new ones constantly being written upon the deaths and births of litigants, and the dispositions from witnesses composed in a technical language and published with a price at each stage. Bentham calls for freer use of oral evidence and much less dependence on writing in court procedures. Dickens gives a grotesque description of the 'bundles in bags, bundles too large to be got into any bags, immense masses of paper' (p. 655) carried out of the court at suit's end.

Even with all this documentation the facts are never to be fully viewed because of exclusionary rules of evidence. These come under heavy fire in Bentham's *Rationale of Judicial Evidence*.[17] Exclusion of evidence figures in *Bleak House* when the Man from Shropshire cannot be heard from in court when he attempts to speak on his own behalf. Nor behind its aristocratic and Christian prestige and fine old name and amidst its masses of paper and maze of technicalities is Chancery itself open to review as Bentham would wish. Bentham notes Lord Chancellor Eldon's ability to 'wrap his misery-breeding meaning up in clouds' when answering to parliament or others ('Indications Respecting Lord Eldon', 262). Dickens notes Chancery lawyer Kenge's inquiry-defeating responses before a parliamentary investigative committee (p. 416).

Chancery structurally divides rather than identifies the interests of court and suitors. It is a sinister interest in Bentham's term, and Dickens frequently shows the solidarity of the whole legal profession as an interest—judge, clerk, and lawyer on either side of a case 'making hay of the grass which is flesh' (p. 416).

Thus Chancery is as far as possible from panoptical. It is a centuries-old establishment, aristocratic, quasi-ecclesiastic, time-wasting, uneconomical, uncomprehensive in view, closed to inspection, and self-serving at the expense of those it serves. Chancery was, in fact, a prime target of Benthamite-spearheaded legal reform through the Chancery Commission Report of 1826, the Court of Chancery Act of 1850, the Chancery Procedure Acts of 1852, and the Judicature Act of 1873, which integrated the equity with the common-law system.

But Chancery in *Bleak House* broaches issues beyond the strictly legal. This is commonly understood, though a common idea is that the court represents forces of the modern, a newly bureaucratic state, industrialization, and market capitalism under attack by Dickens. D. A. Miller joins a long-standing critical tradition that identifies Chancery in such ways and passes on a Foucauldian variant in his influential reading. A Millerite/Foucauldian understanding of Chancery carries forward in criticism.[18] However, this mistakes the social criticism of the novel. Itself an ancient inheritance, Chancery presides over the Jarndyce inheritance case. Aristocratic in provenance, it is specially prized by the great hereditary landlord Sir Leicester Dedlock. Christian in provenance, it is a standard-bearer for Christian values such as those specially recommended to the low-born, portionless, feminine figure of Esther Summerson. The novel's anti-Chancery stance sets it against structures of inheritance, against class norms, Christian norms, and gender norms that work in combination to preserve the highness of the high and the lowness of the low. In all this we should recognize common cause with Utilitarianism and political economy, just as in the indictment of the court itself.

INHERITANCE

Dickens is not inclined to revere legacies from the past. The false book backs in his library bear the titles: The Wisdom of Our Ancestors:

I. Ignorance. II. Superstition. III. The Block. IV. The Stake. V. The Rack. VI. Dirt. VII. Disease.[19] Bentham calls the proverb about speaking only good of the dead 'flattery bestowed upon dead tyrants' (*Memoirs*, x. 4). Utilitarians and political economists challenge many legacies, among them legacy law. They oppose primogeniture and entail and favour the breaking up of estates among children or others as a means of greater equalization of property and expansion of the middle class.[20] A passage in Mill's *Principles of Political Economy* bears close comparison with *Bleak House*. Mill considers

what is due to children. . . . Whatever fortune a parent may have inherited, or still more, may have acquired, I cannot admit that he owes to his children, merely because they are his children, to leave them rich, without the necessity of any exertion. I could not admit it, even if to be so left were always, and certainly, for the good of the children themselves. But this is in the highest degree uncertain.

What parents owe to children is education

as will enable them to start with a fair chance of achieving by their own exertions a successful life. To this every child has a claim; and I cannot admit, that as a child he has a claim to more. There is a case in which these obligations present themselves in their true light, without any extrinsic circumstances to disguise or confuse them: it is that of an illegitimate child. (ii. 221)

In Jo we see an illegitimate child (Jo is parentless and darkly suspected by Mrs Snagsby of being her husband's illicit offspring) with all claims unmet, with no chance to know more than 'nothink' and no chance to 'move on' to any success in life. Esther, the illegitimate daughter of Lady Dedlock and No One (Nemo), presents the terms by which such a child can succeed. It is not birth, not inheritance, that legitimates her. Esther is less materially deprived than Jo, for Mr Jarndyce funds her schooling and 'the acquisition of those accomplishments, upon the exercise of which she will ultimately be dependent' (p. 16). She studies at Greenleaf School and begins to teach there. She prepares to be a governess but then takes a position as Mr Jarndyce's housekeeper and companion to his wards Ada and Richard. Later she teaches Charley and Caddy— reading and housekeeping—and these characters provide further evidence of the value of education. So do Mr Rouncewell's children, educated to fill a higher station than their parents, and so does

Mr Rouncewell's son's betrothed, a servant whose education will enable her to join her husband on an equal footing.

From early on Esther commits herself to exertions despite the 'fault' of her birth. She resolves to 'strive as I grew up to be industrious, contented, and kind-hearted, and to do some good to some one, and win some love to myself if I could' (pp. 13–14). Busy Bee, Dame Durden, jingling her household keys, she is not just an object of Jarndyce's philanthropy but earns her way in some sense in his employ. She also saves and has money to lend (though she becomes wary of bad risks like Skimpole). Esther is the counter to Skimpole with his Drone philosophy. He is a debtor rather than a worker or saver, living as luxuriously as he can in indolence and proposing that Esther and Jarndyce 'live upon your practical wisdom, and let [the Skimpoles] live upon you!' (p. 453). And Esther is the counter to Richard, a non-saver who runs through his small fortune, failing to exert himself in studying for medicine, the law, or the army because he is waiting for a judgment in Chancery and a legacy that will cancel the need for education, work, or saving. Skimpole is repudiated in the novel, and Richard comes to grief and dies.

Education, work, and the saving and investing of capital are much promoted by Utilitarian political economy, as they are by *Bleak House*. All in the Smith–Bentham tradition press for extension of public education. As indicated regarding *Hard Times*, whatever disagreements Dickens may have with Benthamites over pedagogical particulars, he shares in their support of popular education.[21] In *Hard Times*, nothing suggests that Sissy Jupe should have stayed with the circus and not gone to school. In *Bleak House*, Esther rises in the world by means of education.

As for work, Smith, Ricardo, Mill, and also Marx powerfully articulate a labour theory of value. Labour is in principle a pain, a price paid to gain a larger payback on the pleasure side. Mill, as much as Dickens through the example of Skimpole, warns of the temptations of indolence, which he thinks socialists underestimate (*Political Economy*, iii. 795). Mr Jarndyce is a generous guardian, but he gives Esther household work to do, and he certainly wants Richard to work. Political economists go beyond justifying labour as a painful cost traded off for a benefit to strike a note of admiration or awe at its ability to create value. This comes across in Smith's passage on the pin factory (*Wealth of Nations*, i. 14–15) and in Mill's description of the chain of labour

(ii. 31–2). According to the theory, an object's value in exchange is tightly proportional to the labour that goes into it—though for Marx the labourer is bilked of his fair share of the price paid. For all the importance of capital accumulation and investment in political economy, Mill insists on the even more fundamental importance of present labour: 'The greater part, in value, of the wealth now existing in England has been produced by human hands within the last twelve months' or at most the last ten years (ii. 73). Mill does not consider it a child's due to receive an inheritance beyond provision for education enabling work. He is close to Dickens.

As for capital, this is labour-created value stored up, the 'accumulated stock of the produce of labour' (ii. 55). In principle it is a pain to save capital, by 'abstinence from present consumption for the sake of a future good' (ii. 160). Political economists, sans Marx, urge capital accumulation and investment by individuals. They would approve of Mrs Bagnet, who saved the capital to start the Bagnet business, and would condemn Richard's prodigal spending. Yet the point is not hoarding but investment. This is because 'everything which is produced perishes, and most things very quickly'. 'Capital is kept up, not by preservation, but by perpetual reproduction' (ii. 74, 73). Taking account of the principle of time, the capitalist is one who bewares the decay of value in delay of use.[22] Investment means immediate consumption by workers and later consumption by capitalists and society at large of what workers produce. So some temporal postponement has its place in capitalism. This applies to lending as a form of investing, and Bentham even defends usury. But carrying too much debt like Trooper George is not good. Neither is the practice of lenders and debtors like Jarndyce and Skimpole, between whom loans are more properly gifts, being held to no defined repayment schedule. Though Mr Jarndyce is a kindly gift-giver to Skimpole, Dickens presents this as ill-advised. Jarndyce himself does not want his wards to give money to a man who is unconcerned about ever paying it back. All this makes Chancery-time the capitalist's nightmare in which the waiting is never over till all has gone in costs.

Malthus introduced the population problem into political economy with his postulation of a faster growth rate in population than in food production. Foreseeing dire consequences, Utilitarians and political economists—in closer or looser alliance with parliamentary Radicals like John Roebuck, liberal Reform Whigs like Henry Brougham,

Christian economists like Thomas Chalmers, liberal Tories like Sir Robert Peel[23]—backed the 1834 New Poor Law as one countermeasure. The law instituted commitment to workhouses instead of outdoor relief as a disincentive to reliance on charity, that is, charity functioning to subsidize large family size. This was bitter medicine. More palatably, with more evident humanity, Utilitarians and political economists— along with Free-Traders like Richard Cobden and John Bright, also Liberals, also Peelites[24]—backed the 1846 Corn Law Repeal that increased the supply of cheap food through free-trade policy, or laissez- faire. And—with exceptions and reservations—they, along with Rad- icals-turned-Liberals like Lord Durham,[25] countenanced emigration as a palliative for surplus population, enabling people to pursue oppor- tunities abroad opened up by trade and colonialism. But the surest solution lies in individuals' choice of Malthusian 'moral restraint', another pain of calculated postponement like the saving and investing of capital. Moral restraint results in late marriages and smaller fam- ilies.[26] Mill's *Political Economy* reads practically like an extended birth- control tract. I would not go quite so far as to say that about *Bleak House*. However, the Skimpole marriages in which improvident children bring ill-provisioned children into the world are all wrong in point of political economy and all wrong according to Dickens. True, the Small- weeds make the practice of early to go out and late to marry look mean. Still, Mr Jarndyce advises Richard and Ada not to marry until Richard has education and a job.

It is relevant here to consider the brickmakers' families. Jenny's child dies, and when her friend has a child, she can almost wish that hers too had died rather than grow up to a life of deprivation that may make him 'stray wild' and become 'hard and changed' (p. 238). This echoes the proposition from Miss Barbary that it would have been better if Esther had never been born. Indeed there is a symbolic consonance between Jenny and Lady Dedlock. The plot so has it that Lady Dedlock is dressed in Jenny's clothes when Mr Bucket and Esther track her to where she lies dead. Esther first takes her for 'the mother of the dead child' (p. 614). But there are means available to Esther, and these matter more than her illegitimacy, while means are sadly lacking to the brick- maker's child. What is due to a child is not to be born without means to live, learn, work, save, even invest, and better her condition, and that is due to every child. Bentham approves of sexual pleasure, as he approves of pleasures generally. His unpublished 'Sextus' makes this remarkably explicit. Malthus repeatedly acknowledges the strength and benefits of sexual passion (under moral restraint). Malthusians can seem hard and prudish in urging restraint on population-control grounds, as when Mill inveighs against 'degrading slavery to a brute instinct'. But taking a cue from Malthus as to the advantages to women from moral restraint, Mill is pressing a feminist point about women's slavery to men in service of the instinct. Thus a 'helpless submission to a revolting abuse of power' is part of the population problem (*Political Economy*, ii. 352). Not to make out Dickens to be Mill, still the brickmakers' wives carry bruises from their husbands, whom they call 'masters'. The novel gives some suggestion that it is not the due of children to be conceived on such a condition of abuse, any more than on condition of living to be abused or to abuse others.

Something better is to be passed to children, but not by Chancery. Esther's mother is in the suit, but Esther isn't because the line of inheritance doesn't reach to the illegitimate. If she could be an heir, she might be worse off, like Richard, a prodigal content to wait for later enrichment, rather than exerting herself through learning, work, saving, and prudent timing in marriage. Chancery only spectacularly prolongs the unproductive waiting integral to all dependence on legacies.

LANDLORDS

Esther's lack of inheritance keeps her out of Chancery; Sir Leicester's inheritance as a great landlord makes him Chancery's loyal defender. His landed estate resembles the court as a realm of old precedent and usage; the rain of the one resembles the fog of the other (p. 6). For Sir Leicester Chancery is a great national bulwark against 'levelling'. It is allied to everything that resists the opening of floodgates and the obliteration of landmarks. Sir Leicester's class is served by lawyers like Mr Tulkinghorn, a Chancery solicitor and 'butler of the legal cellar, of the Dedlocks' (p. 9). The property we see in Chancery is land. Chancery has 'its decaying houses and its blighted lands in every shire' (p. 2). The London property of Tom All Alone's, where Jo lives so wretchedly, is in Chancery. It is going to rack and ruin. Bleak House itself is not in

Chancery, but in the time of Tom Jarndyce, who was, it too became dilapidated and decayed.

Krook, the weird double and namesake of the Lord Chancellor, is a landlord. He rents out rooms to Nemo, Miss Flite, and Jobling. We may identify him with his Rag and Bottle Warehouse, but this place has little to do with commerce. Rags, bones, kitchen-stuff, old iron, waste paper, clothes, and ladies' hair are bought, but 'everything seemed to be bought, and nothing to be sold there' (p. 38). Everything slowly accumulates, like the papers in Chancery, like the estates that Chancery is so slow to disperse. An atmosphere of darkness, confusion, fog, dirt, damp, delay, decay, and deadlock characterizes Krook's establishment as it does Chancery and the lands and houses in Chancery. Krook's reluctance to part with anything is of a piece with his reluctance to clean or make repairs. His lack of concern for commercial circulation or investment in upkeep identifies him with the Lord Chancellor and the landlord class. There is a rapacity to Krook; his cat is hungry to eat Miss Flite's birds and, it seems, needs to be kept away from Krook's own remains upon his grisly demise. But Krook's is not peculiarly a trades-man's greed for profit. It might have been a good thing had he sold his papers, bringing the valid Jarndyce will into circulation and helping to end the suit sooner. As he sells nothing, he lives off his rents. The rooms he lets are described in the deadliest terms, rooms where Nemo dies and Jobling suffers the horrors. When Krook's decaying existence ends in spontaneous combustion, the walls run with his own combusted fleshly effluvia. Much better are commercial establishments that produce a living such as the Bagnet musical instrument shop, the Turveydrop dancing academy, and Trooper George's shooting gallery (though it could stand to turn more profit).

But the most vivid counter-image to Krook's house—symbolically Chancery—is Bleak House itself, as seen under the care of Mr Jarndyce and Esther (pp. 50–1). It bears an odd resemblance to what it counters. Its rooms are full of a variety, even a jumble of things. They present a certain confusing endlessness, for the floor plan is irregular and you can find yourself going round in a circle. But they escape the suggestion of wasteful accumulation because they are clean and bright. Things are not dark and mouldering; they can be seen and used. The endlessness of these rooms is not that of deadlock but circulation. The circulation is not commercial for a neat opposite to the non-circulation in Krook's non-shop. Still, world and colonial trade has contributed to the decor, which includes a Native Hindoo chair, chintz textiles, a china-closet, and depictions by Chinese artists of the preparation of tea. Such details are worth mentioning because Dickens is often taken to oppose commercial-colonial expansion through his satire of Mrs Jellyby's philanthropic/business/emigration scheme for Borrioboola-Gha, which causes her to neglect her family. Still, Dr Woodcourt, good enough to deserve to marry Esther, goes off to India to advance his medical career. In this dark book it is a notably light passage that describes the fog lifting at the port of Deal, revealing the ships in the sun, especially an Indiaman, amidst a beautiful bustle of commercial life (pp. 468–9).

Industrial manufacturing for commerce is endorsed by the Rouncewell contingent in the novel. Dickens approves of the Rouncewell rise from the station of domestic servants to the gentry. Mrs Rouncewell is Sir Leicester's housekeeper, and her elder son becomes an Iron Master in the north of England. His is a progress by means of steam engines, hydraulic pressure, and power looms (p. 64), not inheritance, not land, and he expects his son to advance by education and his own work. These anti-Chancery values belong to the anti-inheriting, anti-landed classes. Sir Leicester divines a rebellious Wat Tyler in Mr Rouncewell, just as he does in anyone who objects to Chancery (pp. 64, 10). Rouncewell's son is named Watt. James Watt, inventor of the steam engine (patented 1769) and Wat Tyler, leader of the fourteenth-century Peasant Rebellion, represent middle- and working-class advance men for the principle of liberty posing revolutionary threats to the landlord class.[27]

Next to the 1832 Reform Bill that challenged aristocratic power by extending the franchise, the strongest, most epochal policy cause of Utilitarians and political economists was Corn Law Repeal, which abolished protective tariffs on grain. These had favoured the landed gentry by keeping up the cost of food for the middle and working classes, a particular hardship for the poor. Like the democratic vote, free-trade laissez-faire invoked liberty and bore against landlords. The ground of Anti-Corn Law arguments was the doctrine of rent formulated by Ricardo in the light of Malthus's law of population. For Ricardo, proceeds to landlords come by something like monopoly control of a natural resource, the land, which grows scarcer and more valuable as population grows. Rent does not reward labour or capital conceived as the accumulation of past labour. Unlike labour and capital so conceived, the landlord does not create value, and that is the nub of the objection.[28] The doctrine launched fighting words. Ricardo: '[Rent] adds nothing to the resources of a country'. 'The interest of the landlord is always opposed to that of the consumer and manufacturer' (*Principles of Political Economy and Taxation*, 400, 335). Mill: 'No man made the land. It is the original inheritance of the whole species. . . . The claim of the landowners to the land is altogether subordinate to the general policy of the state' (*Political Economy*, ii. 230). Mill's least favourite landowners are Irish rack-renters; his favourites are peasant proprietors with incentive to work, save, and invest in their property. In his last years he drew on the doctrine of rent and his East India Company experience to propose a radical next step beyond the challenge to landlords of Corn Law Repeal. He became an advocate for a levelling land-tenure policy. Landholding dissociated from work and investment leads to dirt, disrepair, waste. This is what we see in the lands and houses in Chancery, in Tom All Alone's, and in Krook's 'shop'. Esther's housekeeping belongs to an opposite economics.

There is something odd, though, in Esther's being the one to embody capitalist propensities. As a woman she is removed from the market. She does not work, save, invest, turn a profit in the classic sense. She is not a Rouncewell. Still the counter-image to Krook's dirty, profitless place of business is not a clean, thriving one, say the shop Mrs Bagnet runs, but Bleak House, a domestic interior. Much criticism of the novel has turned on the idea of a Victorian domestic ideology in Dickens that separates the private sphere of home from the public sphere of industry, marketplace, politics, and bureaucratic systems and validates the private as the ideal alternative or corrective to the public. But, after all, Dickens called his journal covering every issue of the day *Household Words*. And for classical-school economists, households are part of the widest socio-economic-political class dynamic as a rising domestic standard of living drives economic endeavour and growth.[29] I join others who study the implication of the private in the public sphere, though I am less inclined to construe this as collaboration with new or old forms of domination.[30]

The landlord class under assault by Utilitarian political economy is 'levelled' in *Bleak House* by a woman. Sir Leicester, defender of Chancery and all inherited ways, including inheritance law, is felled by marital disaster leading to a stroke. He is childless; his house begins to moulder into decline. As he goes down, the Rouncewell family that began in his service goes upward to middle-class industrial prosperity. Sir Leicester does not die, but his legal butler, the Chancery solicitor Tulkinghorn, is murdered. Tulkinghorn has enigmatically voiced the view that women are at the bottom of most trouble (pp. 444–5). He is killed by a woman, Lady Dedlock's former maid Hortense. While Hortense's animus might seem narrowly personal—Tulkinghorn was rough to her and did not reward her for helping him to information to put her lady in his power—she is oddly politicized by her characterization as a Frenchwoman, a revolutionary, a 'woman from the streets of Paris in the reign of terror' (p. 243). It is not a Wat Tyler but a female Jacobin who strikes the blow. Hortense's blow against Tulkinghorn is by indirection Lady Dedlock's against Sir Leicester. It is suspicions of murder directed against his wife on top of the scandal of her love affair and illegitimate child that overwhelm him. What gives Tulkinghorn power—to threaten to expose Lady Dedlock's past—is the code of 'Sir Leicester and his ancestors and his patrimony' (p. 440). The lawyer declares his loyalty to this code and invokes it against Lady Dedlock. This might be enough to motivate her resistance, whether against Sir Leicester or his minion. In fact, Lady Dedlock uses no violence against either. However, she is persistently associated with a symbolism of violent rebellion through the story of the ghost that is to be heard pacing at Sir Leicester's house.

This ghost is such as only haunts the upper classes, says Mrs Rouncewell. It is the ghost of a woman. She was from a commoner class and a rebel. At the time of the Civil War Sir Morbury Dedlock had a wife with no family blood who supported the enemies of the king. Her brother was killed on the rebel side, and the lady's hatred of the Dedlocks turned violent. She lamed horses ready to ride out in the king's cause, and her husband lamed her. Her lamed tread is what is heard on the Ghost's Walk. Childless, she did not contribute to the Dedlock line but will haunt it 'until the pride of this house is humbled' (pp. 68–9). The contemporary Lady Dedlock comes from a lower class—she is said to lack family, and what property she brought is valueless, being in Jarndyce and Jarndyce. In a veiled allusion Tulkinghorn refers to her as 'the commonest of commoners' (p. 435). She is childless (her illegitimate daughter not counting). She humbles the house by violation of its patrimonial code.

Laws of aristocratic landed inheritance are at stake in Sir Leicester's patrimony as they were in the English Civil War that disinherited and beheaded a king and in the French Revolution that did the same. Prerogatives of gender link to those of class in patrimony, as women are subordinated in marriage to serve inheritance through the male line, this being of utmost importance to the property-passing class. Free female sexual action like Lady Dedlock's, with the bearing of a child out of wedlock, is a direct threat to patrimony. It is rebellion.

It is interesting to consider Lady Dedlock's avatars in the novel. They descend the class hierarchy to the lowest level. The rebellious lady ghost is her namesake. The working-class Jacobin Hortense dresses up in her clothes. Jo is greatly confused between her and 't'other one', whether Hortense, or at another point Esther, the illegitimate daughter who resembles her mother. The poor brickmaker's wife Jenny, in whose clothes Lady Dedlock is found at the time of her death, is the mother of the dead child, just as Lady Dedlock is the mother of a child better dead in the light of patrimonial inheritance, and just as she is, in this light, a wife subordinated to a 'master'.

While gender subordination is most evidently integral to the land-lord class whose bloodlines are lines of property transmission, Dickens shows that such subordination does not stop with the upper class. Likewise Mill associates gender tyranny with royal and aristocratic tyranny but also shows it extending down the social scale ('Subjection of Women', 267–70, 287). Such an issue of gender is not typically looked for in Dickens, yet suggests another tie to the Smith–Bentham tradition. Still, at this point the tie is clearer to see in the class critique. Esther, the illegitimate child, comes to know that she is as innocent of her birth as a queen is of hers, and that she should no more be punished for it than a queen should be rewarded (p. 391). She has no need of a pedigree to marry the well-descended Woodcourt. Sir Leicester, when he forgives his wife and bears his losses well, has a worth that is the same whether found in the commonest mechanic or the best-born gentleman (p. 601).

THE CHRISTIAN—AND THE FEMININE

Dickens's gender critique becomes clearer, along with its connection to his class critique, if we turn attention to another aspect of Chancery, its Christian association. Dickens, like Bentham, characterizes Chancery as

a Church-sanctified institution. It features a biblical great seal, and its
Christian authority is repeatedly represented by Miss Flite's expectation of
a judgment as good as apocalyptic, though any such expectation is shown
to be delusional. Beyond the court itself are other Christian targets, for
instance the oily minister Mr Chadband. But the most serious criticism is
directed at the Christian teachings to which Esther is subjected.

For Esther's aunt Miss Barbary the child of sin has no claim on life.
She inherits disgrace, which she is to feel as her own fault. Miss Barbary,
a 'good' woman who goes to church three times on Sunday and to
morning prayers on Wednesdays and Fridays, tells Esther that she fills 'a
place in her house which ought to have been empty' (p. 14). In the last
of her daily Bible readings with Esther, when Miss Barbary is fatally
stricken, she turns the passage in St John on the woman taken in
adultery (8: 3–7), which is forgiving in itself, into a baleful message of
the Second Coming and Judgement Day (Mark 13: 35–7). Such a
Christian turn towards obsession with desire as sin provokes the deepest
resistance in Dickens, as it does in Bentham.

Bentham's *Not Paul, but Jesus* criticizes the Church's following of
the asceticism of Paul. The associated 'Sextus' manuscript challenges
Pauline devaluation of sexuality in particular. As its first principle,
Utilitarianism values pleasure—satisfaction of desire subject only to a
cost–benefit analysis of the trade-off with pain. It accepts self-interest. It
is anti-ascetic and antagonistic to Christian morality in a Pauline strain
that 'make[s] it a matter of merit and of duty to court pain' (*Principles of
Morals and Legislation*, 18). Mill sets the doctrine of 'doing as we like' in
contrast to the Christian creed that makes an 'idol of asceticism' and
preaches that blessed are the poor and humble, the ill-used who love
their neighbours as themselves and give away what they have. For Mill
virtues of self-abnegation and selfless giving are more honoured in the
breach than the observance, and they are often foisted on others for
unadmitted purposes of self-interest ('On Liberty', 226, 255, 248–9). In
particular, he says they are foisted on women. He lambastes the morality
that enslaves women's minds to 'meekness, submissiveness, and resignation of all individual will' ('Subjection of Women', 271–2). Women are
to be self-sacrificing and live for others, to the advantage of men.
Esther's Christian aunt enjoins her to 'submission' and 'self-denial'
(p. 13). A figure for a self who is to claim nothing for itself would be
a girl, especially one with no patrimony.

Not that a boy cannot share her plight. Jo and Esther are sharers in smallpox, and Jo succumbs to what threatens Esther: a sense of having nothing to claim and being nothing but a fault. Ill because ill-cared for by the world, Jo suffers not only from the disease that leads to his death but from the guilt of having passed his sickness on. Neither Jo nor Esther is helped by Christian teachings—from Mr Chadband or Miss Barbary. Esther's situation doubles Jo's. Class and gender compound to make her a person born to have no self. Dickens says through Esther's narration how almost impossible it is to penetrate the consciousness of the poor (p. 83), and Jo is the poorest of the poor.[31] But knowing more than 'nothink', literate enough to use as a narrator, Esther through her motherless-fatherless girl's voice can represent what it might be to be nothing.

Bleak House has been thought to make light of 'Woman's wrongs' under 'her Tyrant, Man' via satire of Miss Wisk and of Mrs Jellyby when she takes up the cause of women's right to sit in Parliament (pp. 322, 664). Still the symbolism of a chain of women suffering from and resisting forces identified with Chancery gives one pause in interpreting the novel as anti-feminist, as does the accrual of meaning from Jo to Esther, and her importance as a representative figure and means of representation though her narration.

It would seem by her very language that Esther presents a feminine epitome of Christian selflessness. This is a heroine who begins by telling us she is not clever, apologizing for whatever might appear to be vanity on her part, and justifying any mention of herself by its necessity in getting other people's stories told. But I disagree with the view that *Bleak House* supports Christian values through a self-abnegating Esther.[32] Rather, I belong with those who have re-examined Esther as an unreliable narrator whose meekness may be more symptomatic than exemplary and less than total.[33] In Mr Bucket's words, Esther is 'as game as she's mild' (p. 606). Feminist criticism has tended to sharpen attention to her game side.

Nina Auerbach notes the myriad faces of this seemingly self-effacing girl, and though on balance Suzanne Graver finds Esther disappointing in feminist terms, she observes her critical intelligence and double-edged voice, which can show up the shortcomings of Skimpole and Richard pretty sharply.[34] John Kucich calls Esther 'perhaps the most complexly, ambiguously self-effacing character in the Dickens canon'.[35] Critics sometimes acknowledge a limited power of voice in her, sometimes a narrative power that grows in the novel.[36] Timothy Peltason presses us to recognize a will and even sexual assertiveness that work by indirection. Alexander Welsh calls Esther self-aggrandizing to a point 'even dangerous to her friends'.[37]

For me, the most telling instance of Esther's turn from denial to assertion of the claims of self comes in her response to meeting her mother after she has been ill. She experiences a 'terror of myself' (p. 389), seeming to confirm Miss Barbary's dictum that it would have been better if she had never been born. At the extreme of self-effacement is her thankfulness for being defaced by smallpox, for if she no longer looks like her mother, she cannot give her away. But Esther comes to a 'better condition' (p. 391)—she can regret rather than be glad of defacement. This can only come from self-interest. The interest is that of keeping Ada's love, which she fears may cool if she cannot recognize the old Esther. There is a subtle rendering of Esther's displacement of other erotic feelings onto her feelings for Ada, so that another interest is implied, that of keeping Woodcourt's love. From her earliest days Esther has resolved to 'win some love to myself if I could'. I take this in an active sense to go with the language of striving in her resolution. In winning love there is an interest in it for herself. And it is the sharpest token of self-interest that in a case of direct conflict it takes precedence over another's interest—here daughter's over mother's.

This is Bentham's definition of utility:

benefit, advantage, pleasure, good or happiness [or, which comes to the same thing, prevention of] mischief, pain, evil, or unhappiness to the party whose interest is considered. (*Introduction to the Principles of Morals and Legislation*, 12)

And this is his declaration of the primacy of each party's interest in its own utility:

The general predominance of personal interest over every other interest . . . is a principle not only not capable of being done away, but which for the good of mankind there exists no sufficient reason for endeavouring, for wishing, to do away: since it is upon this general predominance that . . . the continuance of the whole species—of every individual belonging to it, will be found to depend. Bad as the consequences sometimes are of an over-anxiety on the part of each individual for his own welfare; yet, if the chief object of each man's anxiety were placed without himself—without the sphere of his own knowledge and experience, the consequences would be much worse. (*Rationale of Judicial Evidence*, vii. 329)

There are those, like Graver, who take Esther's concern for her looks as Victorian-womanly overdependence on others' views. But Bentham, like Smith, declares the interest for the self of other people's good regard. As I read the last page of the novel, Esther has won love and a capital-letter, twice-repeated sense of Me. Her last rather arch words suggest that she is pleased to hear from Woodcourt that she may still be pretty after all. Or if that is not the cause of her gratification, it is that her family 'can very well do without much beauty in me—even supposing—'. It comes across that she now feels she has enough to offer regardless of her looks (no terror of herself, no thought that she should never have been born). She is happy to have a good-looking family though they may miss out on seeing beauty in her, but if anyone is to 'do without' it can very well be others.

The preference for one's own over others' interests takes a mild form here, compared to Esther's prior preference for keeping her face over giving it up to help her mother, or compared to the violence against what subjects them, symbolized through the chain of doubles to Lady Dedlock. In this regard Hortense, with her motivations for murder concerning money, mistreatment, and a job, does not seem to measure up as a figure of a rebel upholding her own claims. Yet there is something striking in representing a perfectly worldly and violent self-interest in a working woman, reminding us that self-interest may well extend down the line of class and gender hierarchies to the less powerful and supposedly meek. In a woman, and one of humble station, an un-Christian ethos goes on exhibit for being unlooked for. Dickens contrasts the 'self-unmade' to the 'self-made' man with reference to Trooper George and Mr Rouncewell (p. 568), and the latter wins by the comparison. Nobody could seem at times so self-unmaking as Esther, but ultimately she is self-making. She needs to receive enough from the past to be educated and to learn to exert herself, but it is not by inheritance, not by high class, not by Christian—at their epitome feminine—values that she progresses. She is not in Chancery.

UTILITARIAN POLITICAL ECONOMY AND VICTORIAN LITERARY AND CULTURAL STUDIES

Why has *Bleak House* been cast more as opponent than proponent of Utilitarianism and political economy? There are complications or contradictions in Dickens's work. In the Smallweeds he caricatures what he also celebrates in the novel: self-interest, work, saving, investing, late marriages, business, turning a profit. Dickens is not doctrinaire. He disagreed with the workings of the Benthamite New Poor Law and with particulars of semi-Benthamite pedagogy. He did not hold with women's suffrage as Bentham did in theory and Mill in fact.[38] *Hard Times* criticizes aspects of the Gradgrind school gone too far. As Dickens remarks:

I often say to Mr. Gradgrind that there is reason and good intention in much that he does—in fact, in all that he does—but that he overdoes it. Perhaps by dint of his going his way and my going mine, we shall meet at last. (To Henry Cole, 17 June 1854)[39]

The problem is that present readers are better taught to recognize the divergence than the reconvergence between Dickens and the Gradgrind school, the world of Bentham, which they know mostly through its critics. In Victorian studies Dickens, Carlyle (in the usual readings of their works), Ruskin, Arnold, Shaw, Marx, and Engels are more attended to than Smith, Bentham, Malthus, Ricardo, Mill—or Mill's 'On Liberty' and 'The Subjection of Women' than his 'Utilitarianism' and *Political Economy*. Economics as the 'dismal science'[40] comes more readily to mind than the signification of pleasure in the word 'utility'. Foucault's Panopticon is better known than Bentham's.

Victorian studies exhibits a high-cultural leaning in the modern period and in the postmodern period a leaning towards ideology critique, whether right or left, largely oppositional to Utilitarian, capitalist, liberal, bourgeois values. The older critical tradition is one of distaste for middle-class, Benthamite attributes. This goes back to Leavis.[41] In Leavis Terry Eagleton sees a petty bourgeois reaching for a more elite ground of humanism from which to look down on sordid, brutal capitalism.[42] Richard Altick's still much-used handbook carries forward Leavis-like judgements. The world of Bentham is 'hard', 'dogmatic', 'repellently mechanical', 'narrow', full of 'fanaticism', 'glib rationalizations', 'dreary materialism', and 'moral myopia'.[43] It is too allied with facts, machines, and money, too literal-minded, calculating, scientific, secular, too overbearing and unselfcritical, too unfeeling, unimaginative, unaesthetic, too progressive and modern—one might say unelite, ungenteel. In more recent criticism, comparable middle-class attributes are observed with comparable distaste but now judged to be not progressive and modern enough, too elite, too genteel, or at any rate too privileged and entrenched. Raymond Williams traces an early Marxist embrace of Romantic values perceived to be humanist/anti-capitalist in thrust.[44] Eagleton thinks Williams himself passes along such 'Left-Leavisism'.[45] Foucauldian criticism picks up on this, and Foucault has deeply marked the whole field of Victorian studies. Besides figuring frequently in discussions of *Bleak House*, references abound to carceral implications of sundry forms of disciplinary self-governance in Victorian literature generally.[46] Nancy Armstrong invokes panopticism in this unflattering sense. What she sees is a force of middle-class social control, disciplinary not liberatory, working 'to contain forms of political resistance within liberal discourse'.[47]

To cite current handbooks on Victorian literature and culture, Robin Gilmour finds it hard to understand how ideas as 'crude' as Bentham's could inspire a political movement,[48] James Nelson characterizes Utilitarian political economy by reference to Gradgrind (plus Bounderby) as a 'heartless' and 'stultifying' philosophy.[49] For information indexed to Bentham, Athena Vrettos and Audrey Jaffe give us Gradgrind and his fact-bound schoolroom and the Panopticon according to Foucault.[50] Covering Bentham, David Newsome features Gradgrind and facts, facts, facts, and the Panopticon, that 'nightmare of a penal institution'.[51] Then too, Francis O'Gorman's collection *A Concise Companion to the Victorian Novel* doesn't cover Bentham at all.

It remains a common view, as expressed by Herbert Sussman, that most great Victorian writers joined in a 'counter-revolution' against a new industrial age.[52] 'The age of capital was thick with detractors', says Jeff Nunokawa.[53] Victorian literary works are collectively anti-industrial, according to Elaine Freedgood.[54] James Nelson positions Dickens and Carlyle as opponents of Gradgrindery.[55] For the economist David Levy, to speak on behalf of Smith and Mill is to defend them against Dickens and Carlyle, against Ruskin, and against the main body of Victorian literary criticism.[56] Paul Delany admits to having some respect for economics himself, but he describes the literature of the period as 'largely hostile to commerce and industry', and ensuing literary criticism likewise.[57] Mary Poovey conveys fascination with the period's financial as well as literary writings but presents these as genres ultimately so estranged that literature 'denies virtually every relation except

critique between imaginative writing and the market' and passes this on
to become a credo of literary criticism.[58] Expressing a variant on the
common view, Josephine Guy describes Dickens and other social-problem novelists as would-be challengers of bourgeois market culture but
unable to formulate satisfactory alternatives, being limited by some
sharing of perspective. Claudia Klaver says something similar regarding
Dickens.[59] Guy's and Klaver's stance resembles Holloway's, Brantlinger's, and Gallagher's on *Hard Times* and D. A. Miller's on *Bleak House*.
Miller believes *Bleak House* attacks a panoptical power in attacking
Chancery, yet is ultimately complicit with what it attacks: 'the argument
is never free from the utilitarianism that Dickens' sentimentality about
the family rationalizes rather than resists'.[60]

In *The Industrial Reformation of English Fiction* Catherine Gallagher
argues that the values of industrial capitalism held only brief sway in
Victorian literature. In her view, self-interested, self-making economic
motivations got discredited in favour of gentry values (pp. 266–7). It
would seem that in *The Body Economic* Gallagher tells a different tale of
Victorian novelists' engagement with economics. However, pleasure
plays a subordinate role to pain in her account of economic theory,
and reforms aimed at the bettering of condition mainly fall out of sight.
She ends up emphasizing a quasi-sacredness attaching to suffering,
sacrifice, and guilt—values 'full of disdain for bourgeois pieties'
(pp. 183–4). Nancy Armstrong refers to an ongoing liberal discourse;
however, she characterizes it as one that turned defensive against working-class aspirations.[61] In these accounts, the middle class settled in as a
ruling class, whether by affiliating itself with the class above and re-
nouncing its self-interested, self-making ideology, or by disaffiliating
itself from the class below and discountenancing working-class self-
interest and self-making that might threaten its own class standing.
Gallagher and Armstrong date to the mid-century this abandonment
or betrayal of the liberal, the progressive, the insurgent, in middle-class
values.

I am not convinced that the insurgency was spent so soon. In our
minds we often set too early a date for an end to the contest with the
ancien régime and are too quick to presume that the division that matters
is between the middle and working classes. We need the reminder from
historians that the backbone of power remained with the great landlords
till late in the century.[62] Dedlocks and Chancery were not so soon

levelled. And we need the reminder from Williams cited at the outset of this chapter of the 'radicalism' that we miss because of our 'very confused idea of what utilitarianism was, as a reforming movement'.

Writing in *Blackwood's Magazine* in 1855 with reference to *Bleak House*, Margaret Oliphant calls Dickens above all a '*class* writer', 'a man of very liberal sentiments', spokesman for the middle class of England, for 'every man for himself', winning his own bread and his own fortune.[63] Miller portrays Dickens as attacking yet subtly upholding a Chancery that Miller mistakes as panoptical. This is blind to the simpler, solider proposition that in attacking Chancery Dickens aligns himself with Utilitarianism and political economy in the open and in good faith. The novel contends against deadlocking hereditary land-lords and the class and gender prerogatives they exercise under the law and under Christian auspices. At the most basic level it validates satisfaction of self-interest, and it extends portrayals of self-interest, self-making, and rebellion from middle to working class and from male to female figures.

Criticism is giving increasing attention to issues germane to my study. There are commentaries focusing on the individual in both literature and economics;[64] on themes of credit, debt, and finance, on the prob-lematics of saving, on economic risk, bankruptcy, banking panic, and desire for domestic security in the face of market insecurity;[65] and on semiotic representations, most notably writing, found in money and credit and language and fiction, along with differences in such repre-sentations that mark out genre divisions and hierarchies.[66] New atten-tion is being paid to the financial press, and to pro-industrial voices in debates on manufacturing.[67] In addition, there are studies of the literary market as a market.[68] And studies of liberalism, and of liberalism in relation to imperialism.[69] There are some signs of increased 'tolerance' of capitalist economics and less 'knee-jerk recoil' from the commercial and industrial cast of the times,[70] and some calls for reduced reliance on Foucauldian paradigms, most notably the panoptical idea.[71]

Of special value to me are works by Martha Woodmansee and Mark Osteen, Regenia Gagnier, Catherine Gallagher, and Philip Connell. Woodmansee's and Osteen's collection *The New Economic Criticism* gives visibility to a cross-disciplinary approach to literature and eco-nomics that I embrace. In *The Insatiability of Human Wants: Economics and Aesthetics in Market Society* Gagnier sets a standard for thoroughness of grounding in economics that, as she rightly suggests, is not always met by critics who invoke economic principles.[72] Gagnier is most interested in the late nineteenth-century adaptation of classical economics, the 'neoclassical school', and *fin de siècle* and twentieth-century literature and other cultural forms. She holds that there was a significant break between the late century and earlier, marked by de-emphasis on the role of labour and new emphasis on consumer desire. Gallagher, in *The Body Economic: Life, Death, and Sensation in Political Economy and the Victorian Novel*, is most interested in the classical economist Malthus and post-Malthusian thinking in the classical and neoclassical schools and in nineteenth-century evolutionary life sciences and anthropology as these inform Dickens's and Eliot's novels and are passed on to twentieth-century modernism. Gallagher does not perceive the waning concern with labour that Gagnier does, nor waxing belief in consumption. To the contrary, she highlights undiminished painfulness in work and diminishing returns of pleasure in consumption. Connell, like Gallagher, is most interested in Malthus and, in his case, Romanticism. He argues in *Romanticism, Economics, and the Question of 'Culture'* that Romanticism was at points more interwoven than has been acknowledged with classical economics, also with its Christian side branch, as well as with philosophic radicalism, liberal Whiggism, and liberal Toryism.[73] He points towards revisionist implications for Victorian Studies as well.[74] While he registers the dismay forming part of the Romantic response to Malthus, he also lays out a historical record that shows overlap of reform causes, especially emphasizing educational reform. Though Gallagher addresses reform on occasion,[75] she is not much concerned with it or its historical trajectory, and she conveys little overall sense of an 'improving' impulse and developments along that line. Gagnier names a number of practical reformist aims of the classical school, while implications of economics for aesthetics concern her more, and, similarly, Gallagher emphasizes novelists' attention to economic issues relevant to their own experience as writers for a market.

Gallagher might be speaking for most new economic critics when she notes spending far less time analysing 'authorial effects' in economic than in literary texts.[76] For me, this constitutes a call to seek a better balance of close reading.[77] By contrast to Gagnier, I do not identify 'insatiability' so particularly with neoclassical theory and the late century, but rather make out a longer-term bourgeois capitalist culture that premisses strong, driving desire, believes in possibilities for net gains over costs for the individual and the larger society, and produces considerably happier results than Gallagher describes. With Connell, I pay attention to historical, reformist, often radically reformist, liberalism. I portray a liberalism that is powerful and authentic, especially in implications for class and gender. At the same time I raise the matter of empire. This is not a keynote for the new economic critics I have been discussing. There are postcolonial critics who address liberalism in the vein of the Mills, but typically at some remove from economics and practical and policy specifics.[78] Indeed such a liberalism, with its ties to empire, seems to jeopardize any claim to a liberal title. Still I uphold that claim and that title as I probe the paradox of liberalism's development *as* liberalism alongside and even partly through its imperial connection. I treat the mainline classical school from Smith to Mill and a range of mainly 'high Victorian' literature.

In addition I treat Bentham. Benthamite Utilitarianism, close philosophic kin to political economy, is even more poorly understood and poorly regarded, and this is true even among new economic critics.[79] Literary critics' attention to Bentham—of any sort—remains scanty in extent and substance. This makes me welcome remarks by Robert Newsom naming Benthamites alongside Dickens as critics of Chancery, and, in fact, voicing an idea like Raymond Williams's, and like mine, that with the value he places on pleasure, Dickens moves in the direction of a Utilitarian ethics.[80] The most noteworthy literary critical engagement with Utilitarianism I have encountered in recent years appears in the rather unexpected form of a book on pornography by Frances Ferguson. This is her *Pornography, the Theory: What Utilitarianism Did to Action*. Still making use of Foucault on the Panopticon (pp. 18–22), Ferguson searches out implications that lead from the carceral to the pornographic. She has valuable insights into the functioning of panoptical sightlines to produce feelings and motivations. However, pleasure comes in more secondarily than one might think likely, given the subject of pornography, and of Utilitarianism, and it comes in under a cloud. My view is not so shaded. I give pride of place in my book's title to 'pleasures of Benthamism'. I consider utility, the primal pleasure principle of Utilitarianism, to be the theoretical starting point for political economy as well, and for a great deal in Victorian literature and culture.

NOTES

1. Leavis, ' "Hard Times": The World of Bentham'.
2. Miller, 'Discipline in Different Voices: Bureaucracy, Police, Family, and *Bleak House*', in *The Novel and the Police*, 58–106.
3. Maine, *Popular Government* (1885), quoted in House, *The Dickens World*, 36. Overlapping circles brought Bentham and Dickens into proximity. Leigh Hunt, the original of Skimpole and friend of Keats and Shelley, was visited by Bentham while in prison for libel against the king in 1812. In 1835–6 John Bowring, Bentham's editor, joined Carlyle in efforts to get the impecunious Hunt a government pension. In the 1830s the *Monthly Repository* circle around William James Fox included Hunt, Carlyle, J. S. Mill, Harriet Taylor, the Benthamite Southwood Smith, Harriet Martineau, John Forster, and Dickens (Blainey, *Immortal Boy*, 68, 167–9). There is verbal evidence of Dickens's familiarity with Bentham's work in a play on the phrase 'the greatest happiness of the greatest number' in *The Mystery of Edwin Drood* (ch. 16, p. 198). For a verbal echo carried through Sidney Smith's 1825 *Edinburgh Review* piece on 'Bentham's Book of Fallacies' to Dickens's 'Legal and Equitable Jokes' in *Household Words*, 23 Sept. 1854, see Stone, 'Dickens, Bentham, and the Fictions of the Law', 145 n. 49. According to Shatto (*Companion to Bleak House*, 124), Smith's review fed Dickens's caricature of Noodle, a Tory anti-reform MP, in an 1849 *Examiner* article, and of Boodle, Coodle, Doodle, Foodle, and Noodle, Tory insiders and patronage recipients, in *Bleak House*.
4. Edgar Johnson, *Charles Dickens*, 73–4; Mill, *Autobiography*, 90; Mill's *Morning Chronicle* letter of 5 Jan. 1824 signed 'An Enemy of Legal Fictions' (cited by Stone, 'Dickens, Bentham, and the Fictions of the Law', 131). It must be added that Martineau left *Household Words* in 1853, having sharp differences with Dickens over his presentation of workhouses, Mrs Jellyby, and factory legislation (Fielding and Smith, '*Hard Times* and the Factory Controversy'). See Coles, 'The Politics of *Hard Times*', 150–2 and Gilmour, 'The Gradgrind School', 213 n. 11, 219, citing Henry Morley, 'Rational Schools', *Household Words*, 25 Dec. 1852.
5. Holloway, '*Hard Times*: A History and a Criticism'.
6. Brantlinger, *Fictions of State*, 170.
7. Gallagher, *Body Economic*, 192, 66, 80–4.
8. Raymond Williams, 'Dickens and Social Ideas', 88–9.
9. Stone, 'Dickens, Bentham, and the Fictions of the Law', 126.

10. Citing Mill, *Morning Chronicle*, letter of 5 Jan. 1824 and 'One of Our Legal Fictions', 'A Legal Fiction', and 'Legal and Equitable Jokes', *Household Words*, 29 Apr. 1854, 21 July 1855, 23 Sept. 1854 (pp. 131, 136, 139, 151–2). See Schramm on a Benthamite background to Dickens's critical treatment of exclusion of evidence in legal proceedings in *Bleak House* (*Testimony and Advocacy in Victorian Law*, 103, 118–19, 134–5).

11. Foucault, *Discipline and Punish*, 204, 207.

12. See Bentham, 'Panopticon', and also *Introduction to the Principles of Morals and Legislation*, 35, and Adam Smith, *Theory of Moral Sentiments*, 134–8.

13. Marx, *Capital*, 'Preface' to the 1st German edn., p. xxiv.

14. Halévy, *Growth of Philosophic Radicalism*, 256, 415–16, 431; Schofield, *Utility and Democracy*, 250–1, 266–77, ch. 6.

15. Williford, 'Bentham on the Rights of Women', 172–3; Semple, *Bentham's Prison*, 293; Schofield, *Utility and Democracy*, 334–5.

16. Holdsworth, *Charles Dickens as a Legal Historian*, 80.

17. Halévy, *Growth of Philosophic Radicalism*, 376–403 summarizes recommendations for court procedures: less exclusion of evidence on technicalities and more power to the judge to hear from all parties, not only in prepared statements but under cross-examination. See also Schramm, *Testimony and Advocacy*, 103, 118–19, 134–6.

18. Older criticism includes Grahame Smith, *Dickens, Money, and Society*, 130; Goldberg, *Carlyle and Dickens*, 73; James Brown, *Dickens: Novelist in the Marketplace*, 62. See reprints of Miller's chapter on *Bleak House* in Connor (ed.), *Charles Dickens*; Tambling (ed.) *Bleak House: New Casebooks*; and corroborating citations of his *Novel and the Police* by Schor, Cheadle, and Waters and as recommended reading by J. Hillis Miller in Jordan (ed.), *Cambridge Companion to Charles Dickens*, 72, 80, 128, 62. Millerite/Foucauldian interpretations of Chancery include Tambling, *Dickens, Violence and the Modern State*, 71, 76, 81; Danahay, 'Housekeeping and Hegemony', 14–15; Waters, *Dickens and the Politics of Family*, 113; McLaughlin, 'Losing One's Place', 239; Polloczec, *Literature and Legal Discourse*, 138–9; Morris, '*Bleak House* and the Struggle for the State Domain', 689; Bigelow, *Fiction, Famine, and the Rise of Economics* (here with Chancery as market capitalism), 79, 86–90, 108; Keep, 'Technology and Information', 143, 151.

19. House, *The Dickens World*, 35.

20. Halévy, *Growth of Philosophic Radicalism*, 49–51.

21. Economists' commitment to popular education goes back to Smith, *Wealth of Nations*, ii. 758–814, and James Mill and Bentham write on

behalf of it, e.g. in 'Schools for All, in Preference to Schools for Churchmen Only' and *Chrestomathia*. Philip Connell points to the importance of popular education to the Lake School poets as evidence of their links to radical and liberal culture; this applies even to Robert Southey, far to the conservative pole of Romanticism (*Romanticism, Economics, and the Question of 'Culture'*, 68–9, 126, 131–5, 272). For a comprehensive view of extension of popular education in the period see Smelser, *Social Paralysis and Social Change*. The particular pedagogy of Gradgrind's school is Benthamite-leaning but not altogether easy to peg. It does not conform to the monitorial system of the early part of the century, such as that of Joseph Lancaster, hailed by James Mill ('Schools for All', 124) and an influence on Bentham (*Chrestomathia*, pp. xi–xiii). In this system older students taught younger ones in small groups. The secular subject matter of the Gradgrind school does bear some stamp of the Lancaster system, which downplayed religion insofar as it was non-denominational. But the Gradgrind school does not feature a particularly panoptical, all-seeing teacher nor high visibility for students' rank in class as advocated by Bentham in *Chrestomathia* (see below, Ch. 2). It appears to be a matter of impersonality rather than ranking when Sissy is called girl number 20. Lessons in political economy and other practical subjects compare to those in the Birkbeck schools founded by William Ellis in 1848 (see Gilmour, 'The Gradgrind School', 213–24). Dickens's teacher M'Choakumchild is clearly a product of the Teacher Training Colleges instituted in 1839 by James Kay-Shuttleworth. Kay-Shuttleworth was a disciple of the Christian political economist Thomas Chalmers, and he was a Poor Law Commissioner interested in pauper schools, secretary of the first operative central education ministry, and an important leader in the professionalization of teaching for the poor and working classes. By an 1846 ruling, what had been untrained student monitors could gain grants for five-year apprenticeships as pupil-teachers, then compete for Queen's Scholarships at the new training colleges. (On Chalmers see Hilton, *Age of Atonement*, 55–70, and Waterman, ch. 6. On Kay-Shuttleworth see Alton, 'Education in Victorian Fact and Fiction' and Goodlad, *Victorian Literature and the Victorian State*, 48–9, 168–73, and also Smelser, *Social Paralysis and Social Change*). Birkbeck and Kay-Shuttleworth precepts opposed rote learning in favour of learning from concrete examples and experience and were against corporal punishment. Kay-Shuttleworth precepts supported positive role modelling and rapport between teacher and students. According to Alton (p. 67), despite his satire in *Hard Times*, Dickens 'does not absolutely disagree with Kay-Shuttleworth's attempt to improve England's educational system'. See Ch. 2 n. 30.

22. A view divergent from Nunokawa's in *Afterlife of Property*, which holds that Dickens is disturbed by hazard in economic exchange and circulation—because to acquire property shows the possibility of losing it—and offers fantasies of static, secure possession not involving acquisition.

23. William Thomas, *Philosophic Radicals*, 235–6, 357; Hilton, *Age of Atonement*, 57–60, 86, 225; Waterman, *Revolution, Economics, and Religion*, 230.

24. Parry, *Rise and Fall of Liberal Government*, 163–5.

25. William Thomas, *Philosophic Radicals*, 378–83, 387.

26. 'Moral restraint' is a term and emphasis in Malthus's 1803 casting of *Essay on the Principle of Population* (pp. 207–16). As seen in *Wealth of Nations* and Bentham's 'Emancipate Your Colonies!', political economists and Utilitarians are not imperialists from fundamental principles, though both Mills worked in service of empire in East India House. Mill says emigration, like free trade, provides breathing space for dealing with the population problem but that the real solution is Malthusianism (*Political Economy*, ii. 378–9 (1865, 1871 edn.), 351–2). See below, Ch. 7.

27. In a passage cancelled in the first corrected proofs Dickens makes the Wat Tyler–James Watt connection even more evident by having Sir Leicester remark on it. Wat Tyler was current as an insurgent's name, being the nickname for a Chartist leader notorious for disturbances in 1848 (Shatto, *Companion to Bleak House*, 75–6, 44).

28. Labourers produce; the farmer is the capitalist, renting from the landlord. Worse land comes into cultivation to meet larger demand, it is harder to work, and corn sells at a higher price according to the labour theory of value. By this price the landlord gains a higher return—rent—for every acre with better yield than the break-even for cost of production. Rent doctrine concerns agriculture, though Ricardo applies it to mines and house rent.

29. The root meaning of the word economy is household management (ancient Greek οἰκονομία). Smith uses household goods—'building, dress, equipage, and household furniture'—to illustrate objects of virtually limitless desire. Desire for such objects prompts to expense and present enjoyment, while also to saving in service of the desire of 'bettering our condition' over time (*Wealth of Nations*, i. 181, 341). These precepts have applications across the classes, while Malthus (*Essay* (1803), 267, 321), Ricardo (*On the Principles of Political Economy*, 100), and J. S. Mill (*Political Economy*, ii. 341–2, and see 66–8) note the signal potential in expanding consumer demand within the working class. Most explicitly, Mill correlates working-class habituation to 'an improved scale of comfort' and new norms limiting family size. Such an economics is very evidently household-based.

30. D. A. Miller, *The Novel and the Police*, 103–5; Armstrong, *Desire and Domestic Fiction*, 24–6; Poovey, *Uneven Developments*, 122; Danahay, 'Housekeeping and Hegemony', 14–15; McClintock, *Imperial Leather*, 32–6; Kieran Dolin, *Fiction and the Law*, 93; Newsom, *Charles Dickens Revisited*, 125–6; Bigelow, *Fiction, Famine*, 93–108. Dolin stands out for implicating the family in old- rather than new-style social control; in this reading Dickens actually values the ancient ideal of paternal guardianship in Chancery, if this could be reclaimed from corruption, and holds a similarly paternalistic domestic ideal.

31. Chris Vanden Bossche observes a partial limitation to Dickens's representation of popular agency in making Jo inarticulate ('Class, Discourse, and Popular Agency', 26–7).

32. Jahn, 'Fit to Survive'.

33. Readings initiated by Zwerdling, 'Esther Summerson Rehabilitated'.

34. Auerbach, 'Alluring Vacancies'; Graver, 'Writing in a "Womanly Way"'.

35. Kucich, *Repression in Victorian Fiction*, 214.

36. Budd, 'Language Couples', 217; Sawicki, '"The mere truth won't do it"'.

37. Peltason, 'Esther's Will'; Welsh, *Dickens Redressed*, 145.

38. In *Oliver Twist* Dickens exposes workhouse abuses from periods both before and after institution of the 1834 Benthamite New Poor Law. We may draw the message that reform was needed but achieved too little. On women's suffrage see Bentham, *First Principles Preparatory to Constitutional Code*, 97–100; Boralevi, *Bentham and the Oppressed*, 14–19; Schofield, *Utility and Democracy*, 149–50; and Mill, 'Considerations on Representative Government', 479–81. Also as an MP Mill (unsuccessfully) proposed an amendment to the 1867 Second Reform Bill to give votes to women. Introduced under a Liberal government in 1866, the 1867 Bill actually came in under the Tories following convoluted party manoeuvring that yielded an extension of democracy more radical than the main body of Tories, or Liberals, had intended (see Parry, *Rise and Fall of Liberal Government*, 214–19).

39. Repr. in *Hard Times*, Norton edn., 274.

40. A phrase from Carlyle's 'The Nigger Question' (*Works*, xxix. 354), hardly an authoritative or even reputable source in many eyes, though the piece is possibly more ironic and equivocal in meaning than it is usually taken to be. One Dr Phelim M'Quirk reports upon a lecture delivered by an unnamed lecturer. There is a running thread of humour concerning escalating audience outrage at what they take to be a diatribe. The essay's thrust is to cast doubt on humane visions for Jamaican ex-slaves coming from economists and evangelical philanthropists, instead declaring that if these people won't work, they must be made to. It is actually not too

'dismal' but too rosy visions that are being challenged. See below, Ch. 3 and n. 6.

41. Even before that to Louis Cazamian at the turn of the century (*Carlyle*, 275; *The Social Novel in England*, 32–3, 115–16).

42. Eagleton, *Criticism and Ideology*, 12–14.

43. Altick, *Victorian People and Ideas*, 114–15, 135, 137, 144.

44. Williams, *Culture and Society* 263, 271.

45. Eagleton, *Criticism and Ideology*, 22, 25, and cf. David Levy, *How the Dismal Science Got its Name*, 67, 71; Philip Connell (*Romanticism, Economics*, 279–80) tags Williams with 'left-culturalism' (in Alan Sinfield's phrase, *Literature, Politics and Culture*, 241–5); Joseph Bizup (*Manufacturing Culture*, 6) speaks of Williams's identification with a Romantic tradition of culture for its anti-capitalist stance. However, I observe that Williams expresses concern at the widespread misunderstanding of Utilitarianism in 19th-c. literary studies and calls for better recognition of its radical reformist agenda.

46. Armstrong, *Desire and Domestic Fiction*, 22–3, 226, 190, 90–1 and *Fiction in the Age of Photography*, 24–5, 145–6, 169–70; Coles, 'Politics of *Hard Times*', 157; Tambling, 'Prison Bound: Dickens and Foucault (*Great Expectations*)', 118–21; Waters, *Dickens and the Politics of the Family*, 113; Colligan, 'Raising the House-Tops', 100; Schor, 'Novels of the 1850's', 70; McClintock, *Imperial Leather*, 32–6, 39, 56–61, 122–3; Thoms, *Detection and its Designs*, 36, 77; Flint, *Victorians and the Visual Imagination*, 7–8, 13; Levine, intro. to *Cambridge Companion to George Eliot*, 12–13, 15; Ulrich, *Signs of their Times*, 96–8. More generally, Joyce and Kent ('Victorian Studies Now') observe Foucault's wide influence in Victorian studies. Kieran Dolin calls Foucault the leading light of law-and-literature studies of the 19th c. and after (*Fiction and the Law*, 6–7). Clare Pettitt says something similar and observes Foucault's great importance across English studies ('Legal Subjects', 74). In political science, Stephen Engelmann says Foucault's commentary on the Panopticon has lent new impetus to a 'misreading' that contributes to 'a dominant illiberal image of Bentham' (*Imagining Interest in Political Thought*, 9).

47. Armstrong, *Desire and Domestic Fiction*, 226, 26.

48. Gilmour, *Victorian Period*, 153.

49. Nelson, 'Victorian Social Problem Novel', 192–3.

50. Vrettos, 'Victorian Psychology', 72–3, and Jaffe, 'Modern and Postmodern Theories of Fiction', 433–4.

51. Newsome, *Victorian World Picture*, 53.

52. Sussman, 'Industrial', 253–4.

53. Nunokawa, *Afterlife of Property*, 4.

54. Freedgood (ed.), *Factory Production*, 9.
55. Nelson, 'Victorian Social Problem Novel', 192–3.
56. Levy, *How the Dismal Science Got its Name*, e.g. citing various 'students of Victorian literature who hold that culture ought to trump markets' (p. 75).
57. Delany, *Literature, Money*, 7, 14, 15.
58. Poovey, *Genres of the Credit Economy*, 418. Another formulation is Tim Dolin's that 'mainstream [Victorian] novelists routinely condemned the incompatibility of mechanistic economic values and human values' though without directly blaming the capitalist system or offering alternatives (*George Eliot*, 132). Another is Franklin's that mid-century novelists express a 'utopian anticapitalism' that is mere fairy-tale consolation; or a more authentic transcendence of capitalism but one operative only in an artistic separate sphere; or a 'rear-guard' stance not denying the hegemony of economism but privileging exchange involving social/cultural versus economic capital ('Anthony Trollope Meets Pierre Bourdieu', 517–19).
59. Josephine Guy, *Victorian Social-Problem Novel*, 92, 115; Klaver, *A/Moral Economics*, 100–3.
60. D. A. Miller, *Novel and the Police*, 103, a position still built on by Gordon Bigelow (*Fiction, Famine*, 108).
61. Armstrong, *Desire and Domestic Fiction*, 26.
62. Rubinstein, *Britain's Century*, 297; Cannadine, *Decline and Fall*, 15.
63. Collins (ed.), *Dickens: The Critical Heritage*, 327–9.
64. Josephine Guy, *Victorian Social-Problem Novel*; Gagnier, *Insatiability of Human Wants*.
65. Finn, *Character of Credit*; Knezevic, *Figures of Finance Capitalism*; O'Gorman (ed.), *Victorian Literature and Finance*; Kreisel, 'Superfluity and Suction'; Freedgood, *Victorian Writing about Risk*; Weiss, *Hell of the English*; Houston, *From Dickens to Dracula*; Nunokawa, *Afterlife of Property*.
66. Brantlinger, *Fictions of State*; Bigelow, *Fiction, Famine*; Poovey, *Genres of the Credit Economy*.
67. Poovey, *Genres of the Credit Economy*; Bizup, *Manufacturing Culture*.
68. Erickson, *Economy of Literary Form*; Seville, *Literary Copyright Reform*; Guy and Small, *Oscar Wilde's Profession*; Delany, *Literature, Money*; Pettitt, *Patent Inventions*; Alison Chapman, Josephine Guy, and Seville in O'Gorman (ed.), *Victorian Literature and Finance*.
69. Eisenach (ed.), *Mill and the Moral Character of Liberalism*; Anderson, *Tainted Souls* and *Powers of Distance*; Goodlad, *Victorian Literature*; Thomas, *Cultivating Victorians*; Majeed, *Ungoverned Imaginings* and 'James Mill's *The History of British India*'; Mehta, *Liberalism and Empire*; Chakrabarty, *Provincializing Europe*; Pitts, *Turn to Empire*.

70. Gallagher, *Body Economic*, 192; Wicke, 'Commercial', 265. Francis O'Gorman describes his collection *Victorian Literature and Finance* as 'neither in love with the market, nor hostile to it'. He backs away from calling capitalism 'good for Victorian literature' (p. 9). Such is the provocative idea floated by Jonathan Rose in a review essay on studies of the literary market, 'Was Capitalism Good for Victorian Literature?'. However, 'critics of capitalism' have hardly been overtaken by 'capitalist critics' (pp. 489–90). To my mind, Susan Zlotnick and Nancy Henry stand out as exceptional for attention to the positive in fictional representations of industrialization (Zlotnick, *Women, Writing*) and investment (Henry, ' "Ladies do it?" '), in both cases treating implications of capitalism for women. Zlotnick argues that women writers were more apt than their male counterparts to present the benefits of capitalist industry; Henry observes women writers' own expanded earning and investment opportunities and says this perhaps explains why they 'were more tempered in their critiques of capitalism' (p. 121). Also exceptional is Joseph Bizup's study of discursive-prose vindications of industry, e.g. by Charles Babbage (*Manufacturing Culture*). And note: Josephine Guy includes economic selections from Ricardo, Mill, Jevons, etc. in her anthology of Victorian sources, *Victorian Age*. Mary Poovey provides an intellectual history of acounting/statistical representation in *History of the Modern Fact* and is general editor of the Victorian Archives series, where her collection of 19th-c. writings on the financial system appears, as does Elaine Freedgood's collection of 19th-c. writings on factory production.

71. Wicke, 'Commercial', 271; Pettitt, 'Legal Subjects', 74–5. Paul Delany expresses dissatisfaction with a Foucauldian viewpoint that deflects attention away from authors as subjects active in the literary market by envisaging them in inevitably subordinated positions within literary culture as an impersonal discursive field (*Literature, Money*, 4, 6). Lauren Goodlad reads Bentham himself next to Foucault on the Panopticon, which very few critics do, and she observes important discrepancies. She proposes moving 'beyond the Panopticon' in interpretation of Victorian literature and culture. Actually, she moves beyond Foucault's Panopticon to Foucault's later ideas on 'governmentality' ('Governmentality', 'The Subject and Power', in *Victorian Literature*, 8–16).

72. Gagnier and Dupré, 'Reply to Amariglio', 402; see also Erickson, *Economy of Literary Form*, 17.

73. See e.g. his detailing of personal/social relations linking Bentham and Benthamites, Shelley, Byron, and the Hunt circle, despite significant tensions (*Romanticism, Economics*, 214–19).

74. 'The Romantic component of nineteenth-century social criticism, as well as Victorian middle-class values, is still described in terms of an anti-industrial "culture and society tradition", which has in turn often been reliant upon a reductive opposition between Romanticism, on the one hand, and the impoverished, "bourgeois" ideologies of utilitarianism and political economy, on the other' (Connell, *Romanticism, Economics*, 283–4).

75. See her discussion of sanitary reform in *Body Economic* re Dickens's *Our Mutual Friend*.

76. Gallagher, *Body Economic*, 5.

77. I do find good models in Christopher Herbert's close rhetorical analyses of Smith and Malthus (*Culture and Anomie*) and Joseph Bizup's of 19th-c. pro-industrial texts (*Manufacturing Culture*). Claudia Klaver analyses Ricardo's discourse with an emphasis on stylistic abstraction, and is rare among literary critics in attending in some detail to Mill's economic writing (*A/Moral Economics*). Mary Poovey (*Genres of the Credit Economy*) identifies generic markers of economic writing as it evolves in the 18th and 19th cc. and agrees with Klaver in emphasizing abstraction in Ricardo and after. She finds abstraction emerging in Smith as well, to whom she devotes several pages of close reading. She closely scrutinizes contributory, intermediary, and/or popularizing texts, not part of generically consolidated political economic theory, such as texts by Thomas Bridges, J. R. McCulloch, Harriet Martineau, and Walter Bagehot. The economic historian Emma Rothschild addresses Smith's style, for instance, organizing a whole chapter around his image of the invisible hand (*Economic Sentiments*).

78. Some new economic critics treat empire, e.g. Henry (*George Eliot and the British Empire*) and Bigelow (*Fiction, Famine*). And note Bigelow, Blake, and Goodlad conference papers. For postcolonialists on liberalism see Mehta, *Liberalism and Empire*; Chakrabarty, *Provincializing Europe*; Pitts, *Turn to Empire*; Majeed stands as an exception for treating practical policy specifics in *Ungoverned Imagining* and 'James Mill's *The History of British India*'.

79. Bentham appears in a note in Woodmansee and Osteen's collection, *New Economic Criticism*, and is quite lightly touched on by Gagnier in *Insatiability of Human Wants*. In *Body Economic* Gallagher gives most play to the Bentham text 'Table of the Springs of Action' for its representation of labour as pain (p. 65), not balancing this with comparable specifics from Bentham's writings on pleasure, though pleasure is of primary importance in Benthamism. Bentham is rather minimized or disavowed by Connell in *Romanticism, Economics*. He speaks of him as an 'eccentric writer' whose 'personal reputation' has encouraged an idea of liberal hostility to

imagination. He alludes to 'ideological eccentricities of doctrinaire Benthamism' and conveys the idea that middle-class liberalism is centred elsewhere and is considerably more flexible than what we find in Bentham. He suggests that liberalism is wrongly censured as if it were more Benthamite than it is, protesting 'the alleged closure of a whole class within a narrow utilitarian discourse' (pp. 106, 100, 102–3, citing Seed, 'Unitarianism', 1). Bentham drops out of view in books by Kaufmann on Romantic novels and classical economics (*Business of Common Life*), Bigelow on Romantic trends in 19th-c. literature and neoclassical economics (*Fiction, Famine*), and Lewis on 18th- and 19th-c. British and American novels and neoclassical economics (*Coincidence of Wants*). He is notable for his absence or very small showing in Weiss, *Hell of the English*; Herbert, *Culture and Anomie*; Nunokawa, *Afterlife of Property*; Brantlinger, *Fictions of State*; Freedgood, *Victorian Writing about Risk*; Delany, *Literature, Money*; Finn, *Character of Credit*; Klaver, *A/Moral Economics*; Knezevic, *Figures of Finance Capitalism*; Houston, *From Dickens to Dracula*; O'Gorman (ed.), *Victorian Literature and Finance*; Poovey, *Genres of the Credit Economy*. Studies of Mill do address his Benthamite heritage.

80. Newsom, 'Administrative', 218; *Charles Dickens Revisited*, 179, though to my mind Newsom speaks in general terms. He does not baulk at Miller's yoking of Chancery to panoptical Benthamism and goes along with Miller's interpretation of *Bleak House*. He yokes 'Chancery or Gradgrindery' in a phrase, echoing Millerite/Foucauldian and Leavisite keynotes (*Charles Dickens Revisited*, 125, 138). Annette Federico links Dickens to a liberal belief in pursuit of happiness that she broadly associates with utilitarianism, individualism, utopianism, consumerism, and competition, while at the same time she distances Dickens from 'rigid utilitarian formulas' ('*David Copperfield*', 71). On the law, Stone ('Dickens, Bentham') remains important; re Schramm see above, nn. 10, 17; see Seville on Benthamites on copyright law (*Literary Copyright Reform*, 22, 45–6, 52, 60–3, 146). Peter Stokes counters vilification of Bentham on the workhouse and sentimentalization of Dickens ('Bentham, Dickens'). John Whale gives some commentary on Bentham, framed in familiar, negative terms (*Imagination under Pressure*). He holds that Utilitarian devaluation of imagination and literature put pressure on Romantics to reconceptualize and reaffirm imagination and its literary role (pp. 98–109). Josephine Guy includes a Bentham selection in her anthology *Victorian Age*.

2

Pleasures of Benthamism—Utility,
or, 'People mutht be amuthed'

Bentham and *Hard Times*

It is worth going back to Bentham to take fuller measure of utility, the pleasure principle. Bentham has been identified with hard Gradgrindery and carceral panopticism. But to the contrary, let us consider him as a spokesman for pleasures of all sorts and in works that are, in their own way, a pleasure to read. I will begin with key statements on utility, moving back and forth between Bentham and Smith, with interspersed commentary by Mill, then proceed to sections on Bentham's memoirs and correspondence and his discourses on prisons, usury, and sex. The final sections of the chapter suggest that Dickens's philosopher of the circus, Mr Sleary, might be speaking as a Benthamite in teaching that 'People mutht be amuthed'. This calls to mind the Bentham of Mill's account, defender of frivolous pastimes who teaches that 'push-pin is as good as poetry' ('Bentham', 113).

UTILITY

For Bentham utility is 'benefit, advantage, pleasure, good, or happiness' or, alternatively, prevention of 'mischief, pain, evil, or unhappiness to the party whose interest is considered' (*An Introduction to the Principles of Morals and Legislation*, 12). In political economy utility is value-in-use, in Mill's definition, invoking Smith, 'capacity to satisfy a desire' (*Principles of Political Economy*, iii. 456, and see *Wealth of Nations*, i. 44–5). Smith pronounces consumption to be the sole end of production, and he calls 'every man ... rich or poor according to the degree in which he can afford to enjoy the necessaries, conveniencies, and amusements of human life' (ii. 660, i. 47). Smith sees no limit to desire. While 'the desire of food is limited in every man by the narrow capacity of the human stomach ... the desire of the conveniencies and ornaments of building, dress, equipage, and household furniture, seems to have no limit or certain boundary' (i. 181).[1]

Utility or value-in-use as satisfaction of desire, as consumption, enjoyment, amusement, may or may not bear a price on the market and carry second-level value-in-exchange. But utility or value-in-use is primary. Bentham conceives of himself as a student and ally of Smith. He warmly and repeatedly acknowledges Smith in his 'Manual of Political Economy' and ends 'Defence of Usury' with 'A Letter to Adam Smith'. In the former he verbally echoes Smith's language on boundless desire (p. 37). Smith and Bentham join in their insistence on self-interest. 'It is not from the benevolence of the butcher, the brewer, or the baker, that we expect our dinner, but from their regard to their own interest', says Smith (i. 26–7). Bentham's analysis is wider, encompassing applications beyond market exchange. He asserts 'the general predominance of personal interest over every other interest' (*Rationale of Judicial Evidence*, vii. 329), as this motivates the seeking of value-in-use, utility, pleasure.

Utility or value-in-use connotes avoiding pain as part and parcel of gaining pleasure. The greatest happiness principle involves a perpetual cost–benefit analysis. To calculation on behalf of each individual add calculation of the greatest happiness of the greatest number. The more happiness and the less unhappiness the better—in one, and all. '*Sum up*', says Bentham in *The Principles of Morals and Legislation* (p. 40). There is a democratic and egalitarian reckoning here, as every person's happiness or the lack of it counts in the sum of welfare.

So Bentham's philosophy rejects asceticism, or 'to think it meritorious to fall in love with pain' (*Morals and Legislation*, 21). In his 'Table of the Springs of Action' Bentham does not count as interests to go hungry, to be poor, or to be celibate. But the table shows the influence that asceticism has exerted in the culture and that Bentham tirelessly combats. Asceticism has shaped much of the language by which people speak of desires. Bentham lists the large number of censorious terms attached to desires for food and drink or money: gluttony, voracity,

greediness, ravenousness, craving, hankering, cramming, stuffing, gour-
mandizing, drunkenness, sottishness, tippling, toping, swilling, covetousness, cupidity, avarice, rapacity, miserliness, stinginess, niggardliness,
parsimoniousness. He gives smaller lists of positive terms.

One object of the table is to lay out neutral terms under which desires
may be acknowledged rather than denigrated or euphemistically veiled.
With characteristic linguistic creativity Bentham dubs negative language
'dyslogistic', for an opposite to 'eulogistic'. When it comes to sex he
notes that there are ten dyslogistic terms from venery to salaciousness,
but only one that is neutral—sexual desire—and no eulogistic terms
at all.

The pleasures and their corollary pains run the gamut from those of
taste, sexuality, and the other senses to those of wealth, power, curiosity,
the goodwill of others, reputation, religion, sympathy towards others,
antipathy towards others, leisure versus work, life versus death. They are
not all materialistic, nor all self-regarding. Thus the pleasure and pain of
sympathy appear on the table. It is important to recognize that sympathy is not absent but of lesser force than self-regard in the Benthamite
view of human nature. It is not to be too heavily counted on for the
functioning of institutions and laws, which are Bentham's main concern
as a social analyst and reformer.[2] There is a tally here with Smith's idea
of sympathy in *The Theory of Moral Sentiments*. For Smith, sympathy is
a significant motivator but also a significantly weaker one than 'the
selfish and original passions of human nature [according to which] the
loss or gain of a very small interest of our own, appears to be of vastly
more importance, excites a much more passionate joy or sorrow, a much
more ardent desire or aversion, than the greatest concern of another
with whom we have no particular connection' (p. 135).

Smith's account of sympathy brings forward the further point that
other-regarding sympathy relates to desire for others' other-regarding
sympathy for ourselves, and thus circles back to self-interest.[3] Smith
analyses the elaborate mental process of envisaging how other people see
us. They feel much lesser joy or sorrow regarding our experience than
they feel regarding their own. Because of this Smith postulates that we
all of us moderate the expression of our passions and even the intensity
with which we feel them so as to hold them at a pitch at which they can
call forth fellow-feeling. In this process we must imagine ourselves as
but one locus of self, one self-interest among many, 'but one of the

multitude, in no respect better than any other in it'. We must imagine the view that an 'impartial spectator' would take of ourselves, just as of other people. Doing so, we must limit the otherwise limitless presumptuousness of self-interest in the self-interest of winning the sympathy, the approval, of the impartial spectator, whom we may suppose to be embodied in actual spectators of our actions, or to whom we may address ourselves as a purely disembodied mental figment. 'It is not the love of our neighbour, it is not the love of mankind, which upon many occasions prompts us to the practice of those divine virtues [of moral sentiments]. It is a stronger love, a more powerful affection . . . the love of what is honourable and noble, of the grandeur, and dignity, and superiority of our own characters' (p. 137).

In like manner Bentham gives full weight in his 'Table of the Springs of Action' to the pleasure or pain of the goodwill or disapproval of others and the pleasure or pain of reputation. This explains the importance of the 'moral sanction' throughout his thought. It is one of the four sanctions laid out in *The Principles of Morals and Legislation*. People calculating the odds of pleasure and pain in a given action take into account the physical, political, religious, and moral consequences that may operate as positive or negative sanctions. There may be a benefit or price to pay according to bodily repercussions, the support or punishment of the law, or of God (if one is a believer), and a benefit or price to pay according to others' approval or the lack of it—the moral sanction. This sanction counts for a great deal in Bentham, as in Smith. It explains the reliance Bentham places in his legal, political, and social theory on public opinion as this operates on those in power as a security for individual and general welfare.

Theorized here is transference of point of view, a self-reflexivity suggesting more of a role for imagination than we generally expect in the model of mind of a Bentham or Smith. It is possible to cite other instances where imagination is acknowledged. Bentham describes the part played by imagination in the complex mental dynamics of enjoying a country scene (*Morals and Legislation* 45, 49–50). He makes much of mental projections in time. Feelings of pleasure and pain are measured not only by intensity but by duration, degree of certainty in expectation, 'propinquity' or time until realization, and 'fecundity' or power of generating future pleasures and pains. Such judgements depend on imagining experience beyond the moment as part of presently felt reality (pp. 38–41). Still, awareness of viewpoints outside ourselves cast back on us in sympathetic or unsympathetic judgement, when this judgement is understood to constitute a crucial utility—to me this is the action of imagination on which Bentham and Smith most dwell. Such conceptualization of distinct and often enough conflicting self-interests in interaction spurs very active processes of critical thinking. Critical thinking formulates possible trade-offs, reciprocities, and compromises. It connects to the time-sense; it is forward-looking and developmental; it aids the cultivation of enjoyments that will prove 'fecund'. In the largest scope, it formulates prospects for the greatest happiness of the greatest number. There is sophisticated psychological insight here. The Benthamite, Smithian mentality should not be conceived, as it often is, as devoid of sympathy, unfeeling, unimaginative, oblivious of others and their interests, and narrowly egotistical.[4]

But I do not want to sophisticate and widen the meaning of self-interest until it seems to disappear in talk of sympathy, feelings, imagination, moral sentiments, the moral sanction, aesthetic appreciation, sense of time, self-reflexivity, critical thinking, and the greatest happiness of the greatest number. Bentham refuses to be squeamish about human motivations. Thus it is typical for him to include pleasures and pains of antipathy as well as pleasures and pains of sympathy on the 'Table of the Springs of Action'. People can very well enjoy their dislike and anger—call it eulogistically righteous indignation or dyslogistically ill-will, spite, or spleen. What Bentham's layout here and elsewhere on the table makes clear is that there are many words connoting judgements of our motivating springs of action but that we will reach deeper understanding and more satisfactory results if we acknowledge them in neutral terms.

So it typifies Bentham's thought to count all pleasures and pains equally, whether presentable in fine words or not, or, in an additional proviso, whether shared by everyone or not. *The Principles of Morals and Legislation* shows Bentham expecting people's proclivities to differ on an individual basis and according to age, sex, rank, wealth, and education, and also, as he puts it, according to climate, plus race and lineage, and according to institutions of government and religion. Another instance of the way he takes individual circumstances into account is in making a different assessment of the same quantum change in fortune depending on whether it produces gain or loss. He often stresses the greater intensity of pain from losing what one has or losing out on expectations as compared to the intensity of pleasure from gaining more ('Manual of Political Economy', 81). Derived from this is the importance of security because security makes pleasures lasting or lends confidence to expectation and renders anticipation itself a pleasure.[5] It is true that proclivities fall into broadly generalizable categories. But, constructing a theory of human nature to ground thinking about reforms in general structures of society, Bentham takes it as adequate to his purpose to generalize quite broadly. Still, though they may be common or less common and may operate with different force in relation to different circumstances and time-frames, he holds that it is proclivities that universally drive motivation. The individualism in Utilitarian theory is often lost sight of in view of its universalist claims, but we should not forget that in pleasures and pains the 'proportion will in different minds be different' (*Morals and Legislation*, 51).[6]

It is for this reason that Bentham becomes a proponent of full-scale representative democracy, as detailed in his *Constitutional Code*, with its call for virtually universal suffrage. He holds that each man or woman is motivated by individual interests in pursuing an individual proportioning of utilities and that all individual pleasures—as most favourably balanced against pains—add up to the greatest happiness of the greatest number.

Over and over again Bentham, like Smith, insists that each person has interests that are unique, and also that he or she is usually best positioned to know what those interests are. This two-part precept joins Bentham's democratic political doctrine to his political economy. He says in the 'Manual of Political Economy' that 'generally speaking, there is no one who knows what is for your interest, so well as yourself' (p. 33). This goes back to Smith's faith in leaving markets largely uncontrolled save by the 'invisible hand', for 'every individual, it is evident, can, in his local situation, judge much better than any statesman or lawgiver can do for him' (*Wealth of Nations*, i. 456). Further, people feel more intensely as concerns their own interests than others do on their behalf. As Mill sums it up: 'people understand their own business and their own interests better, and care for them more, than the government does, or can be expected to do' (*Political Economy*, iii. 942). With the best knowledge of personal interests goes the most eagerness, and therefore, very likely, the most effectiveness in pursuing them.

So Bentham tots up human nature in a table, but different minds are different, and we can hardly miss this as we read him. His writing conveys individuality, indeed a tang of idiosyncrasy. It does not seem to set him outside the realm of pleasures and pains that he analyses.

MEMOIRS AND CORRESPONDENCE

Bentham does not hide his face like the inspector in the Panopticon nor seem like an impersonal, joyless Mr Gradgrind. Mill describes him as being, with Coleridge, one of the two great seminal minds of the age. He calls him an original speculator, a critical and boldly subversive thinker, the great questioner of things established, an enemy of abuses, with an intensely practical turn of mind, indefatigable, systematic down to the smallest details, and in his early writings and many parts of his later ones possessed of a 'light, playful, and popular style'—though his scrupulously precise definitions, interjected qualifications, and exhaustive analytical breakdowns make some late works intricate, involved, and 'for the student only'. But through it all, early and late, he sports a 'sanguine and almost boyish fancy' ('Bentham', 114, 88).

This is a keynote for John Bowring, the compiler of Bentham's *Memoirs and Correspondence*. Bowring takes his estimate from personal interactions in the course of editing Bentham's work and from friendship and conversation. He presents Bentham's spoken reminiscences and reflections as the philosopher's 'self-drawn sketches', which, along with his letters, loom large in the narrative (xi. 76). For Bowring, Bentham appears to be 'the most gay and joyous of men'. 'The tenor of existence, from first to last, was in the broad way of felicity' (x. 5, 25). Bentham is typified by his fondness for a people like the French, with their 'vivacity, courtesy, and aptitude for enjoyment, [which] responded to all the tendencies of his own character'. And he is typified by his lack of fondness for a figure like Samuel Johnson, whose mind was essentially ascetic in Bentham's view (x. 47, 22). Bentham was the lover of gardens and flowers, good housekeeping and good food, though a moderate partaker of the pleasures of the bottle. He learned to moderate a too ready penchant for laughter. He loved his grandmothers' houses in the country when he was a boy, especially remembering the paradise of Browning Hill, a beautiful place which held 'always to him the interest of a novel, in which the principal characters were women, and those women preëminently excellent ones' (x. 8). 'I had indeed been struck by the kindness and fondness of women' (x. 10). Bentham describes himself as a sponge for affection from childhood. From boyhood he was also highly sensitive to reproach (x. 10, 15), in both respects showing the importance he gives to the regard of others. He recounts his delight in books of fairy tales and the romance of *Telemachus* 'as if he were still the impassioned boy' (x. 10). He did not forget his childhood ecstasy at seeing his first play, in which cherubim descended from the sky, nor forget being fascinated by puppets, including being afraid of a devil's imp in a Punch and Judy show. A memory remained to him of economical domestic management at Browning Hill that yielded a very pleasant prosperity. His grandmother, great-aunt, and aunt were able to live in comfort, and the bailiff, too, was able to have a good house and shop, build his trade, and become a timber merchant amassing thousands of pounds. Bentham enjoyed the amiable company of pretty women in his great-house-visiting days as a younger man at the estate of Lord Shelburne (later Lord Lansdowne) at Bowood, but he endured the loss of his first love through his father's disapproval and the rejection of a proposal of marriage that he made. In later life he became a lover of company in the form of small gatherings of friends in the after hours of work at his own home, having a shyness of temper despite polished, courteous manners and coming to consider himself a hermit withdrawn from the formal social world. He was a warm admirer of music, especially the solemn music of Handel. Here Bowring says it was not light and frivolous airs that pleased him (xi. 79). Bowring calls him sportive and amusing, with a 'perpetual playfulness of manner and of expression' and 'gaiety of heart' (x. 78, 93). The *Memoirs* offer charming, offbeat vignettes of Bentham. He insisted on whisking friends around his garden before dinner in 'ante-prandial circumgyration[s]' (xi. 81). He would call later in the evening for the sacred teapot Dick to be brought in. I have not found that he was a special devotee of push-pin, but he played cards and chess. An anecdote I like concerns his visit to Leigh Hunt in a Surrey jail, where Hunt was imprisoned for libel against the King—Bentham would deplore such muzzling of free political speech. The two of them played battledore in the garden.[7]

Bentham had a weakness for animals. His animal stories include one about keeping a cat who rejoiced in the name of Sir John Langborn when he was young and used to lure light and giddy young females of his species into the garden, but who, when he grew older and more sedate, was redubbed the Revd John Langborn. Ultimately a Doctor's degree was conferred on him. At the same time Bentham encouraged the mice to play about his workroom, though Bowring records the difficulty of reconciling affections for both cats and mice.

Bentham was 'to a high degree imaginative and inventive' (xi. 77). I have been showing the light side of his also, of course, serious thought. In an account of the long, frustrating course of Bentham's efforts to see his Panopticon built—this is in a study that is very unusual for the sympathy it expresses towards Bentham and his prison—Janet Semple speaks of the edge and passion of his ideas, developed out of practical worldly struggles and in the face of losing out to vested interests. She is rather impatient with Mill's and Bowring's picture of a Bentham who was playful into old age.[8]

Indeed, Bowring also shows that Bentham's wit could grow vehement and break out in 'bitter animadversion' (xi. 77) because he could not bear to contemplate the infliction of useless suffering, usually by the strong and few on the weak and many. In a letter to Lord Lansdowne he calls himself a mongrel philosopher, something between epicurean and cynic (x. 245). Even before his many disappointments in finding favour for the Panopticon, he felt let down by Lord Lansdowne in the promised backing for a place in Parliament. He had experience of receiving a 'bite' 'on pretense of an embrace' and could respond by 'snarling' (x. 230, 245). In one example of his snarling humour he says: 'if the lower orders have been called the dregs of the population, the higher may, by a much clearer title, be termed the scum of it' (x. 82). He sounds like no lapdog in a sketch of remarks to electors: 'I gave up my ambitious views of mixing with the great—I relapsed into what Nature designed me for—a low man—and one of the people' (x. 245). He made a career of lighting into lawyers, not least Chancery lawyers. He espied in lawyers a professional interest, a sinister interest, in shoring up the status quo. Blackstone is his favourite bad example. In an extract from his Commonplace Book: '[Blackstone] carries the disingenuousness of the hireling Advocate into the chair of the Professor. He is the dupe of every prejudice, and the abettor of every abuse. No sound principles can be expected from that writer whose first object is to defend a system' (x. 141).

Bentham knew what pain was by suffering it, such as in his failure to advance by means of men in high places as his father would have wished, in receiving a refusal of his offer of marriage, and in the slow destruction of his hopes for the Panopticon. He knew pain by having caused it. He felt that his Panopticon failure was hard not only on himself but on his younger brother's prospects attaching to the enterprise.[9] To return to animal incidents, Bentham recalls a rebuke to himself as a boy for putting earwigs in the flame of a candle. The servant 'asked me, how I should like to be so used myself?' And he recounts a story of having thrown a cat out the window out of curiosity to see whether, with its nine lives, it was sure to land on its feet. It didn't and gave a look and mewed at the future philosopher of the greatest happiness of the greatest number (x. 17; xi. 81).

Bowring says Bentham not only taught but lived by utility. He salutes Bentham's 'cultivation', his 'husbandry', of happiness. He speaks of 'pleasures which are cumulative, the very capacity for enjoying them continually increasing with the indulgence' and conveys a sense of Bentham as a conscious nurturer of fecund felicities, whether these are 'higher' or humbler ones. His life shows 'how the felicity of the individual might draw its habitual element from the felicity of the multitude,—how one man might, in the happiness of all men, seek and find his own highest happiness'. At the same time, his is a morality that does not 'despise one pleasure because it not another [nor] despise a smaller pleasure because it is not a greater' (xi. 76, 91). Therefore, despite a good many annoyances and discouragements, 'as age advanced, everything grew bright within and around him' (xi. 78).

So Bentham actually values pleasure—and avoidance of its opposite—at a personal level, grounding his philosophy and his style.[10] I will turn now to the piece by which Foucault has made us see everything painful and carceral in Bentham, his plan for the Panopticon prison, and the last place we might think to look to find the pleasures of Benthamism.

'PANOPTICON; OR, THE INSPECTION-HOUSE'

Bentham drew the first notion of the Panopticon from among the 'whimsies' of his brother Samuel and 'dressed [it] up in a little tinsel of my own' (*Memoirs*, x. 167, 165). In the exposition published in 1791 he uses the form of a series of letters to a reader whom he addresses in personal terms. He strikes the note of man who sets forth a bright idea. He invites the reader to entertain and be entertained by his idea, while he also anticipates some resistance. Like all his writing, 'Panopticon; or, the Inspection-House' seeks to serve utility or happiness. But Bentham notes that 'happiness is a very pretty thing to feel, but very dry to talk about' so his approach is 'to alleviate the tedium of a dry discussion' (pp. 64, 40). His main object is to present a plan for a prison in practical detail, but he also expands upon the concept in a manner of increasingly fanciful speculation as he sketches possible adaptations for other institutions such as manufactories, madhouses, hospitals, and schools. He calls his concluding section on schools a 'sort of *jeu d'esprit*', offered 'under the flow of spirits which the charms of novelty are apt enough to inspire', and he expects his proposals here to be lightly received, as they are given, and perhaps to bring a smile to the reader's countenance (pp. 40, 66).

There is wordplay in his invention of the name Panopticon. Bentham relishes odd coinages like this (Bowring notes that some have stuck with us, like maximize, minimize, international, forthcomingness, and codification; x. 68). Bentham says his prison might also be called the Elaboratory. In other diverse papers on the project he titles additional institutions to be placed on the grounds: the Metasylum, a house for discharged prisoners given continued work through the prison if they could secure no other; the Sotimion, a house for expectant, unmarried mothers (soter: saviour); and the Paedotrophium, a house for their infants and other infants in need (paedo: child; tropho: nourishment).[11]

As described in Chapter 1, the Panopticon is designed to position an inspector at a centre point from which he can see into a rotunda of individually partitioned cells. Due to a clever placement of screens and light sources, he can see but not be seen. Not knowing when they will come under a watchful eye, the prisoners prefer, in their own interest, to discipline themselves rather than risk discovery and subjection to external discipline for infractions. External discipline will be far rarer and may be made lighter in proportion to the sense of its inevitability. The scheme thus envisages unshackling from heavy irons, release from Newgate dungeons, decommissioning of prison hulks, cancellation of deportations to Botany Bay, and an end to merely punitive, time-wasting, and unproductive hard labour like beating hemp. The sum of inmates' happiness is to increase, as will that of the prison staff, whose work will become more efficient and easier. It may not flatter human nature but should not be ignored or left unharnessed for utility that people are curious about others, so Bentham expects the inspector to take an interest, beyond that of doing his job, in looking out his window. He will even be joined by his family, who will find the view 'not altogether an unamusing one' (p. 45). Bentham shows a cheerful satisfaction in planning the prison's economics. As the inspector contracts to run the prison with a profit for himself from the prisoners' work, he reaps an advantage in ability to dispense with superfluous overlookers. Bentham draws on homely models of domestic economy (as if from Browning Hill) and animal imagery (such as he often favours) to make his point: 'The greatest part of *his* science comes to *him* in maxims from his grand-mother; and amongst the foremost of those maxims is that which stigmatizes as unfrugal practice, the keeping of more cats than will catch mice' (p. 58). The plan further ensures that the inspector profits from the inmates' welfare (avoiding a penalty charge if they die). And the public gains a better, more humane prison at less expense.

Though the prisoners cannot see the inspector in his tower, Bentham stresses the visibility of the whole place to visiting prison monitors, to the press, and even to curious members of the public, 'the great *open committee* of the tribunal of the world' (p. 46). He calls for witnesses to all corrections and the keeping of a corrections record, open to review. Resembling the Bentham who is an advocate of wide-ranging cross-examination in his writings on legal procedure (*Rationale of Judicial Evidence*, vi. 24–5, 33–4), he says: 'I make [the inspector] examinable and cross-examinable *viva voce* upon oath at any time' (p. 48). The open committee of the tribunal of the world anticipates what Bentham calls in his *Constitutional Code* the Public Opinion Tribunal. Since he expects to see no end to the sway of self-interest among those who rule in any form of government, including representative democracy, he places reliance on public opinion for stemming government abuses as well as abetting government through popular support. 'To the pernicious exercise of the power of government [public opinion] is the only check, to the beneficial, an indispensable supplement. Able rulers lead it; prudent rulers lead or follow it; foolish rulers disregard it' (*Constitutional Code*, 36). The *Code* expressly prohibits legal restrictions and taxation that obstruct publication of political tracts, especially newspapers or other periodicals—short of challenging false defamation. Bentham says: 'the military functionary is paid for being shot at. The civil functionary is paid for being spoken and written at' (p. 40).

The press is able to exercise its oversight because of provisions for public access that Bentham also designs into the operations of a reformed political constitution and ministry and court systems. Philip Schofield describes his architectural designs for 'securing the publicity of public actions' in an assembly debating hall, ministerial audience chambers, and courtrooms, as well as the Panopticon.[12] Important to such public monitoring is what Bentham terms 'single-seatedness'. This means clear designation of authority for officials, without anonymity or committee-style power-sharing that provides a shield from scrutiny or challenge (*Constitutional Code*, 171–4).[13] In this sense Foucault is far from Bentham when he speaks of panoptical institutions as automatizing and deindividualizing power (p. 202). Foucault does not much dwell on the inspection of the inspector. He calls the panoptic idea democratic but hardly sustains such an understanding by his choice to characterize its workings as those of a prison (p. 222).[14]

When Bentham comes to a panoptical application for schools he casts his proposal in a quizzical light. His humour brings out the critical self-reflexivity that he, like Smith, sees as important in human mentality. Thus he waxes facetious on the likely eagerness of gentlemen to set up inspection schools for girls to ensure the virtue of their future wives and says he stops short of laying out uses for Turkish seraglios and savings in the article of eunuchs.

As Bentham points out the advantages to schoolboys (or schoolgirls) of more efficient learning, lesser liability to punishment, and more playtime thanks to closer supervision by their teachers, he contemplates costs as well as benefits and lays out scruples for consideration. The worry is the evident one, Foucault's concern: a social control so strong as to become despotic. Bentham asks whether advantages on the intellectual side might be outweighed by disadvantages on the moral side. And he gives weight to the question by calling the moral side the 'most important branch of instruction' (p. 64). He reviews what children learn from 'struggles of passion against passion, and reason against reason', free-form lessons 'administered by the children to one another and to themselves' (p. 64). With this in mind he asks:

whether the liberal spirit and energy of a free citizen would not be exchanged for the mechanical discipline of a soldier, or the austerity of a monk?—and whether the result of this high-wrought contrivance might not be constructing a set of *machines* under the similitude of *men*? (p. 64)

It is not the usual thing to notice any Benthamite turning back of questions on its own thinking.[15] The work of Javed Majeed stands out in this regard for acknowledging such a critical quality in Bentham's follower James Mill. But a self-questioning spirit is surely spawned by self-interest conceived as caring greatly about outside approval or disapproval. It is by this perspectival dynamic that Utilitarian political economy conceptualizes other selves as having self-interests which may or may not jibe with or serve our own. This feeds into the constant mental tallying of benefits and costs, relative advantages, temporal contingencies, and possible trade-offs in any position.

So Bentham gives a slyly side-stepping answer to his doubts: 'Would *happiness* be most likely to be increased or diminished by this discipline?—Call them soldiers, call them monks, call them machines: so they were but happy ones I should not care' (p. 64).[16] He sets out his idea as one to be tested to see if it will bear up to 'the shocks of discussion' and experience (p. 66). His rhetoric of address to a reader provides a reminder that the subject is not closed but open to further judgement, including possible alarmed doubts, on the part of another person.

One response of alarmed doubts is Frances Ferguson's. In her study theorizing pornography Ferguson draws a seemingly unlikely connection between Benthamite schemes for the 'panoptic classroom' and the Marquis de Sade's 'carceral' erotic philosophy (pp. 26–7). This becomes somewhat easier to comprehend in relation to an insight she offers. She agrees with Foucault on the carceral implications of institutions designed for panoptic sightlines (pp. 18–22). But while Foucault portrays a social discipline keyed largely to punishment, she portrays one keyed also to reward. Not in the 'Panopticon' essay but in his later detailed proposal for founding a day school, the *Chrestomathia*, Bentham adapts existing monitorial schemes (particularly that of Joseph Lancaster) by making provisions for the visible ranking of students so that all may recognize, esteem, and emulate those who do well in given lessons. Bentham banks on children's wish to gain respect in the eyes of others and to avoid the opposite—he banks on the moral sanction operating through spectatorship. For an example of such dynamics, Ferguson repeatedly gives us the spelling bee, which to my mind is a better fit than pornography. But her main point of reference for the visibility-heightening regime of the Benthamite classroom is that of de Sadean pornography. She compares the two for establishing pervasive, finely graded, continuously reshuffled rank-orderings. Competition comes into the picture here, high and low merit, winners and losers, social pressure, power differentials, and displacement of attention from intrinsic values to the artificially structured inducements of a gamelike system. Bentham does, in fact, speak of the conversion of lessons from a burden to a sort of 'pastime', on top of the ending of corporal punishment and 'the reign of juvenile terror' (*Chrestomathia*, 55–6, 35). These outcomes are expected to result from back-and-forth observation between student and student as well as from observation that is partly, if not so continuously, reciprocal along the line from teacher to student-monitor to student. Yes, there will be some suffering for those who fall behind. However, the expected learning curve is to be gentle, not steep, so everyone will advance. Also, everyone will be likely to do well in at least some lessons or class groupings and to discover where his or her strengths lie, a help for setting the direction of future pursuits in life (pp. 105–6, 110, 114, 25–6).

With his more fully developed pedagogical ideas in the *Chrestomathia* than in the 'Panopticon', Bentham seems to have assuaged his concern about loss of energy and liberal spirit in the classroom. Indeed he anticipates an invigorating effect. He surmises that some detractors, especially people of high class, may dislike the school for encouraging widespread 'uppishness', vanity, pride, or 'self-sufficiency' among its pupils, boys and girls 7–14 (up to apprenticeship age) of the humbler and middling classes. But for Bentham, an 'uppish' spirit is rather a good thing (pp. 111, 44, 46). So: maximized utility, meaning maximized learning, made more pleasant, lively, and painless, with greater work efficiency and lesser tuition costs—all to increase educational benefits in aid of class advance for those lower down. Bentham calls the plan experimental. He includes a ten-page section hypothesizing and answering objections and says that when the plan is put into operation, its advantages *and* disadvantages must be monitored (pp. 25, 37–47). Still, he expects pleasures to make a strong showing. Doubtless pornography offers pleasures, too, though to typify Utilitarian systems in schoolroom as carceral-de-Sadean world, as Ferguson does, is to emphasize tolls, deficits, pathologies, and pains.[17]

In the 'Panopticon' essay, Bentham says: 'Don't be frightened now, my dear *****.' 'Your candour will prevent you from condemning a great and new invented instrument of government, because some of the purposes to which it is possible to apply it may appear useless, or trifling, or mischievous, or ridiculous.' Bentham is aware that the power of mind exerted upon mind that he proposes can work evil as well as good. 'One thing only I will add, which is, that whoever sets up an inspection-school upon the tiptop of the principle, had need to be very sure of the master.' He acknowledges dangerous possibilities. In his image, 'knives, however sharp, are very useful things, and, for most purposes, the sharper the more useful'. He ends banteringly on the point that the panoptical idea may not give an equal relish to every palate (pp. 64, 66).

'DEFENCE OF USURY' AND 'SEXTUS'

Other works of Bentham's seem no more likely to please every palate, and if they please, it will be by provoking. 'Defence of Usury' and 'Sextus' speak on behalf of utility, the pleasure principle, even as it drives the most powerful but seemingly dubious desires. These writings have good words to say on behalf of money and sex. Both turn on arguments against the principle most fundamentally antithetical to Utilitarian political economy: that of asceticism, as this is taught by Christianity.

There is an evident spice of devil's advocacy in defending the oft-decried practice of usury. With all due respect to the master, Smith, Bentham goes beyond him to argue for a freedom in the money market to match other elements of laissez-faire. As in the 'Panopticon' piece, Bentham adopts a tone of bright spontaneity, writing in the form of a series of 'letters to a friend', the last one directly to Smith. He says, 'a fancy has taken me just now to trouble you with my reasons' for defending usury (p. 3). He leaves it to readers to determine whether his pages should be forwarded to the press or committed to the fire.

He argues that people are best left to follow their own assessments of self-interest in matters of borrowing or lending. Rates should not be subject to governmental regulation. Bentham notes that the folly of those who follow their own lights has often been expatiated on, 'but the folly of those who persist, without reason, in forcing their advice upon others, has been but little dwelt upon, though it is, perhaps, the more frequent, and the more flagrant of the two' (p. 8). He details the case against presuming to protect people from their own mistakes or to know better or care more than they do what risks are or are not justified in given individual circumstances.

The essay quickly comes to its core as an exposé of hypocrisy and prejudice regarding money. 'Now, to get money is what most men have a mind to do' (p. 16), says Bentham, as one speaking a home truth. This parallels Smith's dictum that most men look to increase of fortune to 'better their condition'—following a 'desire which ... comes with us from the womb, and never leaves us till we go into the grave' (i. 341). But such pecuniary self-interest is hardly ever neutrally designated and most often cast in dyslogistic terms, so that getting money for money is dubbed usury.

Bentham ascribes such denial of legitimacy to money motives to an ethos of self-denial at large in the culture, 'not ... self-denial for the sake of society, but ... self-denial for its own sake' (p. 16). He derives this ethos from Christian teaching. But he suggests that it finds a far from holy opportunity to confirm itself by condemning moneylending as a practice tantamount to 'acting like a Jew' (p. 16). Attributing bias against usury to anti-Semitism,[18] Bentham cites plenty of evidence that Christians like to profit well enough in other markets, while leaving Jews the taint of greed for making gold on gold. He identifies what is not so truly a despising as an envy and resentment of the usurer's wealth. 'The children who have eaten their cake, are the natural enemies of the children who have theirs' (p. 17).

He waxes warm and reminds his reader to recognize the spirit of provocation and polemic in what he says: 'I hope by this time you are worked up to a proper pitch of indignation' (p. 15). Throughout he emphasizes self-awareness concerning language and verbal style, for his defence of usury is a defence of the word 'usury' against its derogatory connotations. He mounts a kindred defence against derogatory connotations of the words 'prodigal' and 'projectors', such as figure even in Smith. Bentham makes a case that prodigals may have their reasons and do less harm than we might suppose, or do harm that is less preventable than we might wish. But ultimately 'Defence of Usury' might be retitled not 'Defence of Prodigals' but 'Defence of Projectors'.

Projectors are inventors and entrepreneurs, the very people to want access to risk-tolerant, high-priced capital. Bentham, himself projector of the Panopticon scheme designed to yield him a profit after a considerable start-up investment, lines up with Smith to laud the 'progress of mankind' from economic growth. In so doing he cleverly enters into debate with Smith on his own ground, taking the opportunity that Smith had missed to praise projectors—those who may need money at high rates in order to be builders of the wealth of nations. Projectors exhibit 'liberal spirit and energy'. They are best left to act as 'free citizens' according to their inner springs of action. Addressing Smith in a rhetorical question, Bentham asks, 'Sir, let me beg of you, whether whatever is now the *routine* of trade was not, at its commencement, *project*?—whether whatever is now *establishment* was not, at one time, innovation?' (p. 22).

'Defence of Usury' is daring enough. 'Sextus' shows Bentham at his most untrammelled and far from carceral or Gradgrindlike. In it he justifies indulgence of the senses and seems to indulge himself in being shocking, though he knows others will not like it. Asceticism is again the object of attack, with an even more pitched assault against its basis in Christian doctrine. My discussion concerns a work, only the first part of which saw publication, and that under a pseudonym. Prospective Parts II/III exist only in draft, along with a twenty-two-page manuscript account of the plan of the whole labelled 'Sextus'. This defends utility against asceticism in a manner that goes straight to basics, affront to religion be damned. Bentham anticipates that Parts II/III of the projected work will be even more 'obnoxious', guaranteeing 'nothing but unpopularity, and *that* to a degree beyond all powers of measurement' (box 161a, fo. 14). This is because he undertakes to critique the theological authority of St Paul in order to call into question the doctrine of self-denial introduced by Paul into the Christian tradition. Or, more strongly put, superimposed by him, foisted by him upon it. Bentham's intent is to expose Paul's moral teachings of abstemiousness—in eating and drinking and especially sex—as being at odds with Jesus' own teachings and to point out the blessings He gives to food, drink, and the pleasures of the bed. Indeed, there is a focus on 'eccentric' sexual practices that have fallen under Pauline condemnation in a way not justified by the sayings and actions of Jesus, as they are not justified by Utilitarianism.

The 'Sextus' manuscript takes the form of a proposal for a large work to be realized in cooperation with another author. While it anticipates unpopularity, it also contemplates the advantages of a title likely 'to attract attention, and excite sensation' (box 161a, fo. 14). (Might there be suggestive, not to say pornographic, possibilities?) Bentham pitches his proposal to the author of *Vathek* (William Beckford), the spicy Arabian tale. He speculates that the task of writing will offer some amusement and that scholarship from classical antiquity on 'pleasure in the shapes in question' will make 'no small addition . . . to the amusingness of the work' (fo. 14). The eccentric as well as more centric sexual pleasures are a main concern. These are the most denied, deplored, and socially, legally, and religiously punished ones: from 'the act, solitary', to fornication and adultery, to the 'Attic mode'. The Attic mode might be the most worth rescuing in regard to its extensiveness, its relative harmlessness to self or others, and the severity of sanctions that fall on it.

Bentham is true to the principle of utility in arguing that pleasures vary by individual and that a pleasure is a pleasure and thus a good, only offset by any attendant pains, though we lose sight of this through the tendency of language to insinuate judgements. While in his *Essay on the Principle of Population* Malthus is a spokesman for the strength and benefit of the passion between the sexes despite all the problems it brings, Bentham goes a step further in his vindication of eros.[19] He questions terms like 'natural' and 'unnatural', 'pure' and 'impure'. He raises questions about Malthus's word 'vice' for alternative sexual practices. They may, after all, cut back or delay marriages, and 'vice' may be a misnomer for pleasures that check population growth, if overpopulation is an evil (fos. 16–18).

Bentham certainly considers the evils that may attend good in sexual activities. He acknowledges evils risked, especially by women, in fornication, whatever its satisfactions. He weighs whether same-sex preference may diminish sympathy for the opposite sex, particularly that of men for women. But he concludes that history does not give evidence of this—for instance, not in the ancient cultures of Greece and Rome that gave legal protection to Attic love. He recognizes some dangers in seduction of pupils by preceptors in boys' schools but seems to regard youthful sexual overindulgence as the more pressing concern. This makes limitation of partners to a single preceptor look like something of a good thing compared to relations with a multitude of fellow-pupils.

Bentham recognizes as an evil the affront to others of witnessing aberrant acts but says this should be punished in a manner proportioned to the offence of the display, not to the supposed offence of the act itself. There might be 'slight penalties analogous to those attached to nonsense in the form of cussing and swearing' (fo. 17). Bentham unleashes a far from delicate irony in passages on drastic punishments, double standards, and absurdities. Concerning non-genital congress between the sexes he says that unless capital punishment is to apply to all and sundry cases where there is an effort to avoid pregnancy, the authorities should give 'proper warning, accompanied by a very particular and correct map of the human body in the female subject' (fo. 16).

Bentham comes across as more outrageous than brightly provocative in 'Sextus'. He refers to reasons to believe that Jesus himself may have been a participator in the Attic mode (fo. 19). His rough-draft notes give more detail on this. Besides instancing Jesus' lack of attention to Mosaic prohibitions against eccentric pleasures of the bed, and lack of condemnation of them in allusions to Sodom and Gomorrah, Bentham entertains the question whether He may have had sexual relations with the Apostle John. He shows sustained interest in Mark 14: 50–2 and the postulate that the last of Jesus' followers to forsake Him was a boy prostitute, wrapped only in a linen cloth, who, being laid hold of, fled naked (box 161b, fos. 476–7, 489, 491–4, 497). This material has made Bentham part of Louis Crompton's study *Byron and Greek Love* as an enemy to homophobia (pp. 251–83).[20]

Even in the not quite so 'obnoxious' Part I of the planned larger work described in its whole intent in 'Sextus'—the part safe enough to publish under a pseudonym anyway—Bentham advocates for Jesus over Paul on pleasures of the senses. The published book is called *Not Paul, but Jesus* (not coauthored by Beckford, as it turned out). It constitutes a kind of sustained prosecution against Paul, some 400 pages long, and calls into question his visions, his miracles, and his right to equal standing with the Apostles. Bentham examines the Acts and Epistles almost as if cross-examining testimony in court, looking for internal contradictions, insufficient evidence in support of claims, signs of dubious motivation, and charges against Paul in the biblical record that undermine his credibility. He mounts a particularly legalistic case in regard to Paul's facing of an inquiry into wrongful preaching held at Jerusalem at the house of the Apostle James with Elders of the church

(Acts 21: 18–36). Bentham develops a brief for the prosecution on grounds of either perjury or apostasy on Paul's part, and he calls for a verdict of guilty. Paul, who gave us his vision of the Anti-Christ, himself becomes the Anti-Christ for Bentham (p. xii).

The reason for this attack on Paul's authority is to justify an attack on his ascetic doctrine. Paul barely even tolerates marriage in 1 Corinthians 7: 1–2, 9, as Bentham remarks in 'Sextus'. *Not Paul, but Jesus* does not venture so far into the sexual arena for defence of the pleasures of the senses. It confines itself more to matters of eating and drinking:

Whoever the people were, whom [Paul] had to address himself to,—they had contracted, he found, a bad habit: it was that of *eating and drinking*, [being] seduced by, and enlisted in the service of [the] most dangerous enemy— *Appetite*.... Not so Jesus: no harm did he see in eating and drinking, unless with the pleasure it produced greater pain...no harm did he see in any thing that gives pleasure.

The passage concludes with a wicked wit:

What seems evident enough is—that, in whatever manner served up to them, *his* resurrection, whatever it was, was considerably more effectual in *making* people eat and drink, than in *weaning* them from it. (pp. 393–5)

And this is the *less* obnoxious Part I! It came out under the name Gamaliel Smith. Gamaliel was one of the Pharisees with whom Paul (at that point Saul) first worked in persecuting the Christians. But then Gamaliel spoke up to advise, 'let them alone' (Acts 5: 34–9). Though Paul went over to the Christian cause, he did not let it alone (or practise laissez-faire), according to Bentham, but hijacked it for a judgemental, meddling, and punitive asceticism.

'PEOPLE MUTHT BE AMUTHED'

In the tradition of Bentham, J. S. Mill defends 'doing as we like' ('On Liberty', 226), even in the case of the drinker, so long as he does minimal harm to others. No more than Bentham does Malthus look for or want the withering away of sexual desire as a means of solving the population problem. He contends against the views of William Godwin on this point:

Men in the decline of life have in all ages declaimed against a passion which they have ceased to feel, but with as little reason as success. Those who from coldness of constitutional temperament have never felt what love is, will surely be very incompetent judges with regard to the power of this passion to contribute to the sum of pleasurable sensations in life. (*Essay on the Principle of Population* (1798), 146)

By pleasurable sensations Malthus means those of the body as well as of emotion and mind.

Dickens paints a portrait in *Hard Times* of an exponent of Utilitarian philosophy and political economy (pp. 77, 46), Mr Gradgrind, who names his sons Adam Smith and Malthus. But though an affectionate father who wants his children to be happy and who is 'not unkind, all things considered' in his schemes for social improvement (pp. 14, 165, 26), Gradgrind is angular and hard like his house, Stone Lodge, or like his wholesale hardware business. He sponsors schooling in Facts not Fancy for his children and the children of industrial Coketown. He favours strictly practical, improving books for workers to read in the town library. His daughter Louisa languishes in ennui for never playing music or singing, never reading amusing books, never seeing amusing sights. Mr Gradgrind is far indeed from Bentham as a killjoy who does not teach doing as we like. This is wrong for a Utilitarian political economist, and Dickens shows it to be wrong.

As Bentham allows, happiness is a very pretty thing to feel but can be very dry to talk about. Gradgrind is hardened and dried out and concerns himself with the springs of human action only in the form of tabular statements or arid statistics. This is a problem, though Gradgrind is well-meaning, socially progressive, and personally gener-ous, bringing the circus-clown's daughter Sissy Jupe into his model school and then into his own household to give her a chance to gain education and better her condition.

For Gradgrind and most of the characters in *Hard Times* the problem is not so much the lack of inner springs of action, of inner spirit and energy, but their repression and distortion. Such inner springs are pointed to in the novel through references to Fancy, Heart, wonder, imagination, love, and the beauties, graces, and delights of life. They are often associated with childhood, while remaining no less important for adults. They are symbolically represented through images of fire— fire that burns in a low, smothered state in Louisa and that she watches for outside herself on the hearth and in the burning smokestacks of Coketown. Catherine Gallagher points to the usage that makes 'to fancy' mean 'to desire'.[21] Another word Dickens uses for the inner fire of desire is 'craving'. Speaking of the people of the town, Dickens says that, like the Gradgrind children, they never know what they want, but they have a 'craving [that] must and would be satisfied' (p. 24). They show their craving at a physical level—as craving for drink, for opium, for holiday from work, for singing, for dancing. Blocked in lives of factory and town monotony, their craving 'struggles on in convulsions' and 'must and would be satisfied aright, or must and would inevitably go wrong' (p. 24). In a main plotline, Louisa's craving manifests itself as sexual desire. Frustrated in an unromantic, mercenary marriage to Bounderby, she follows the flame of attraction to Mr Harthouse and almost 'falls'. Her brother Tom also pursues 'grovelling sensualities' (p. 101). Among the workpeople we see a plotline of sexual craving on the part of Stephen Blackpool for another woman besides his dissolute wife. There being no chance for divorce, his craving can be said to shift from that of love to that of hatred and antipathy. In perhaps the most powerful and sustained depiction of repression of desire in the novel, Dickens describes Stephen's vivid wish-fulfilment dream of wife-murder, which he casts off with horror at the conscious level.

Further examples are Mrs Sparsit's appetite for tea and muffin and Bitzer's desire to feed himself: 'I have only one to feed, and that's the person I most like to feed' (p. 91). Both have an interest in money as well, like Coketown's mill owners, bankers, and tradesmen. Bitzer cherishes the precept of buying in the cheapest market and selling in the dearest. He is the pupil who has learned the most basic principle of the Gradgrind philosophy and recites it back to his teacher: that 'the whole social system is a matter of self-interest' (p. 211).

Indeed, the philosophy is held up to question in the novel and seems to be answered by an opposite teaching from the philosopher of the circus, Mr Sleary. But what is his answer? It is that 'people mutht be amuthed' (pp. 36, 215). A number of critics have noted a peculiar inaptness of the circus to illustrate a pure opposite and alternative to the rest of Coketown, though this is what Leavis and the main line of criticism since his time insist it is. But as Alexander Welsh remarks, 'Dickens's novel is more puzzling than this ideological opposition by itself implies'. He speaks of some uneasiness in the novel's handling of its themes, of some distrust or caution that Dickens expresses about Fancy as a nostrum for curing the ills of Fact, since he embodies it in Mr Sleary and the circus.[22]

An influential essay treating ambiguities in the representation of Sleary's Horse-Riding is Joseph Butwin's 'The Paradox of the Clown in Dickens'. Indeed, Mr Sleary declares for love and 'not all Thelf-interetht' (p. 215), but in many ways he validates personal craving. With his rolling eye, slurred speech, and brandy he is always between drunk and sober. He runs a show offering pretty sexy family fun. Grahame Smith speaks of its atmosphere of sexual freedom and 'gin soaked moral laxity and rowdyism'.[23] Circus members of both sexes 'all assumed to be mighty rakish and knowing, they were not very tidy in their private dresses, they were not at all orderly in their domestic arrangements' (p. 32).

The 'Fairy Bithneth' is a business, and Cupid, or Master Kidderminster, wants only customers who pay their ochre. He presides over the exchequer with an 'extreme sharpness of his look out for base coin' (pp. 28, 205). Sleary has not been easy on bad job-performance by his clown (who, failing, beats his dog Merrylegs and decamps). The ringmaster says: 'I don't pretend to be of the angel breed mythelf, and I don't thay but what, when you mith't your tip, you'd find me cut up rough' (p. 34). Sleary encourages Sissy to take Gradgrind's offer and make her fortune by leaving the circus (p. 35). Early on he asks Gradgrind for good words by way of advertisement, or to give the Horse-Riding a 'Bethpeak'. At the end he doesn't take money himself for helping Tom to evade arrest for theft with the help of a trained dog and dancing horse, but he suggests that others in the troupe might like a little something like a £5 note. For him, a 'Bethpeak' would 'more than balanthe the account' (pp. 36, 213). He does not disavow his company's own interests as he offers to satisfy those of his paying public. He holds that 'people mutht be amuthed', and this is a philosophy of pleasure.

Further, he holds that 'You *mutht* have uth, Thquire... make the betht of uth; not the wortht! (pp. 215, 36). What Gradgrind must acknowledge is the craving, the fire of desire, the energy of personal interest at the springs of human action. Sleary's philosophy calls for acknowledgement of desires which may flatter people to admit or not, but which motivate them all the same. I interpret Sleary to mean that we should make the best of what might seem the worst in us. It appears throughout the novel that repression of craving does not produce edifying sublimation but often only deformation. Nor is low energy or lack of craving preferable—as in the case of Harthouse, who displays such lassitude in amusing himself with Louisa as to lack even an 'energetic wickedness' (p. 126), or in the case of Mrs Gradgrind, who is so devoid of self-interest as hardly to feel pains, any more than pleasures, in her life. She is unable to identify a pain 'somewhere in the room' as her own. In a variant on the novel's fire imagery, the light that had always been dim in her goes out, and this equates to loss of energy of self and death (pp. 149–50). Such images and themes invite discussion in Freudian terms, terms I sometimes use myself, and rampant in studies of Dickens. But the discourse of desire in this pre-Freudian novel may be less anachronistically cast as that of Benthamism. Indeed, one theory staked to the pleasure principle points forward to the other.

As Butwin has it, Dickens does not cast the circus as ideal antithesis and antidote to the industrial capitalism of Coketown but exposes it as a dubious double in the business of selling 'the shallowness of mere amusement' (p. 131). This departs from the Leavis line of interpretation. Still, not unlike Leavis, Butwin holds a view of industrial capitalism that makes the circus look the worse for operating at the margins of Coketown, not really outside it nor outside the values of Utilitarian political economy. The clown represents the 'ultimate capitalist' under the aspect of loser and grotesque, creation and victim of industrialism (p. 132). A step from this is to perceive, like John Holloway, some compromise with the philistine. Similarly, Patrick Brantlinger views Dickens as a would-be critic of Utilitarianism so weakly countering Fact in his representation of Fancy as to seem no more than 'the ultimate capitalist-with-heart-of-gold, or the ultimate good bourgeois liberal' (*Fictions of State*, 170). Gallagher believes Dickens gives 'unwitting' support to a 'dismal' Benthamite work ethic in portraying circus work itself as heavy labour (*Body Economic*, 66, 81).

I judge differently, being less disturbed by Sleary's philosophic link to the Gradgrind school. As I interpret the novel, Dickens gives a lesson in seeing the worst in ourselves as not so bad. That is why he makes Sleary and Co. profit-seeking and sometimes hard-driving (demanding good clown job-performance), non-angelic, low-life, and disreputable. Sleary vouches for amusements, even those that go by bad names, as if under the dyslogistic terms for pleasures in Bentham's 'Table of the Springs of Action'. The point is that we can think of our craving, our desire, our spirit and energy of self-interest, our strong wish to be amused in more neutral or even eulogistic terms.

Smith envisages amusements for the people as an adjunct to commercial society. He associates an austere system of morality, which he calls melancholy and gloomy, with religious teaching (one would think ascetic and Pauline). This contrasts to a 'liberal' morality that encourages 'the frequency and gaiety of publick diversions'. The latter would give 'entire liberty to all those who for their own interest would attempt, without scandal or indecency, to amuse and divert the people by painting, poetry, musick, dancing, by all sorts of dramatic representations and exhibitions' (*Wealth of Nations*, ii. 794, 796). Smith would stand up for Sleary.

Smith would also stand up for Gradgrind in a number of respects, the one I now have in mind being in support of educating the people—like Sissy and Bitzer at the model school. Smith argues that the liberal, laissez-faire state has enough interest here even to justify undertaking the expense. He points towards what would ultimately be establishment of state-mandated and funded compulsory universal public education some hundred years after the publication of *Wealth of Nations*. More directly than in his discussion of popular amusements, Smith makes popular education a corrective to the problems that are generated along with the progress of a market society. Smith's own thought displays the self-reflection and self-critique that are important aspects of mental functioning in the theory of mind of his school. He concedes that for all its wonderful productivity, division of labour confines working people, the mass of the population, to a narrow range of routinized activities. This puts them at risk of stultification, 'torpor...of mind', 'drowsy stupidity', and loss of habits of exertion (ii. 782–3). Smith's concern bears resemblance to Bentham's in the 'Panopticon' essay. Smith worries about the automatizing of the workman in an all too labour-divided, if efficient, factory regimen, as Bentham worries about the automatizing of the pupil in an all too panoptical, if efficient, school regimen, potentially compromising 'the liberal spirit and energy of a free citizen'. In fact, Smith offers schooling as an enlivener of minds—as does Bentham in *Chrestomathia*—thus counteracting industrial torpor. And beyond schooling, a choice of a variety of amusements should help

keep up a 'liberal' mentality in the people. So there is a fit to Smith and
Bentham if the school provides a corrective to the mill, and the circus to
both school and mill.

The affectionate father and social do-gooder Gradgrind, wanting to
see his children happy and the lives of the people of Coketown improved, has not known how to promote these things, but Sleary shows
him how. Sleary's principle of amusement is Benthamite in essence as a
principle of pleasure. *Hard Times* holds Utilitarian political economy to
the standard of its own first principle, and a Slearyite Gradgrind school
is not far from Dickensian: 'I often say to Mr. Gradgrind that there is
reason and good intentions in much that he does—in fact, in all that
he does—but that he overdoes it. Perhaps by dint of his going his way
and my going mine, we shall meet at last.'[24]

PUSH-PIN

An oddity of *Hard Times* is that it draws lessons from a tawdry circus, as
an oddity of Benthamism is that it upholds a frivolous game like push-
pin even against poetry. The latter oddity presents a particular affront to
critics and teachers of Victorian literature.[25] Mill honours Bentham as
one of the seminal thinkers of the age, but what sticks with us from his
essay seems to be the critical commentary accompanying the praise—
such as a charge of one-sidedness (something found in other moral
philosophers, not only Utilitarians, says Mill) in emphasizing moral
over aesthetic and sympathetic aspects of experience ('Bentham', 112).
Mill came to feel he had overstated his criticism and swung back to
express strong affiliation. He declares that he had erred in over-readiness
to touch on unfavourable points on Bentham, while overprivileging the
favourable side in his companion essay on Coleridge. He makes it clear
that there had been a rhetorical strategy in this, namely, to overcome the
likely resistance to Coleridge among a readership of Radicals and
Liberals, while these readers would not have needed Bentham to be
so tenderly treated (*Autobiography*, 227).[26] In any event, 'I had now
completely turned back from what there had been of excess in my
reaction against Benthamism' (p. 237).[27] Actually, in the Bentham
essay Mill explains that Bentham speaks by way of paradox in calling
poetry no better than push-pin if the pleasure given is equal. He declares

that Bentham would have said the same of any art that he himself particularly valued (p. 113). Indeed in Bentham's own statement, only partially paraphrased by Mill, he lines up not only poetry but music for comparison to push-pin, and, as we know, Bentham was a lover of music.

The discussion of push-pin appears in a section of 'The Rationale of Reward' on the arts and sciences (pp. 253–4). Bentham declines to sharply divide the two (unlike Gradgrind, who initially sets off 'ologies' against amusements). He calls what are usually termed the fine arts the arts and sciences of amusement (subdivided from the arts and sciences of curiosity, which are also pleasing if less intensely, like learning languages or hobbyist studies). The arts and sciences of amusement comprise music, poetry, painting, sculpture, architecture, ornamental gardening, etc., and 'there is nothing, the utility of which is more incontestable'. But favourites vary, and all carry value in proportion to pleasure rendered—a main point here.

It is an egalitarian, a levelling point. Bentham inveighs against judging for others and judging against others on the basis of their preferences. Thus 'prejudice apart, the game of push-pin is of equal value with the arts and sciences of music and poetry. If the game of push-pin furnish more pleasure, it is more valuable than either.' This applies at the level of each individual, but if many can share in the enjoyment, that counts for something, too. 'Everybody can play at push-pin: poetry and music are relished only by a few.' And push-pin is 'always innocent', that is, not prone to produce bad effects along with the good ones. 'It were well', says Bentham, 'could the same be always asserted of poetry.'

With this, poetry comes in for further discussion. That it does reflects Bentham's hypersensitivity to language and his close, persistent attention to it as a thinker and as a writer. The deepest soundings of his linguistic ideas are to be found in his essays on language, logic, and ontology.[28] These theorize the necessity of language to communication and to thought itself. They also theorize a fictionalizing operation indispensable to language, namely, the creation of words for abstractions, conceptions of the mind, that cannot be located anywhere as real, tangibly existent entities. In Bentham's terminology, these are 'fictitious entities'. And he sometimes refers to them as 'figurative' ('Essay on Language', 331). 'Utility' would be a 'fictitious entity' or figure in this sense. Language serves communication and thought, so it serves utility. And people enjoy language directly, as a utility. Under the term 'ornament' Bentham identifies uses of words that 'have the effect of producing... pleasure'. He speaks of ornament in both poetry and rhetoric. And he points to a prominent fictional element (pp. 307, 331). There is another element that he does not discuss under 'ornament' but that seems conceptually linked in having the effect of producing pleasure. This consists in uses of words to 'excite', to stir affections and passions (pp. 301–2), for, after all, affections and passions are the felt impulses of personal desires and social sympathies and antipathies at the experiential heart of utility. Capacity to excite is linked to 'impressiveness' or force of style in Bentham's discussion. Stylistic 'impressiveness' attends clarity, while it can mount up to communicate a collateral 'dignity' or sense in the reader or listener of the writer's or speaker's strength of mind and mastery of the subject and its arrangement in presentation. 'Impressiveness' so conceived operates on the understanding, and it can be exciting to the affections and passions as well (pp. 307–8, 310–11).

So far so good. But there is another side. The 'fictitious entities' of verbal naming or figuration may be too uncritically accepted as if really existent. They may be 'yielded to without a sufficiently attentive caution'. All too frequently this may result in 'error, misconception, obscurity, ambiguity, confusion, doubts, disagreement, angry passions, discord and hostility' ('Essay on Logic', 262, 'Language', 327–8). Thus, as noted in Chapter 1, Bentham brings a sceptical eye to many fictions of the law, and there are political fictions, like those of natural rights and an original social contract, that he is bent on exposing as mental constructs only, and misleading and unhelpful ones (*Rationale of Judicial Evidence*, vii. 284 and see Stone; 'Pannomial Fragments', 218–19; *Fragment on Government*, 51–2). Then too, the excitation of affections and passions all too frequently carries dangers, for, important as they are, affections and passions are 'in every part of the field, the everlasting enemy of reason... of sound judgment' ('Language', 301, also 310–11). So language can be deceiving, and it can be loaded or insinuating in rousing response and swaying judgement. Conceptions of the mind, all the more so when attended by felt value judgements, can lead to actions, bad as well as good. This being the case, language can be deliberately put to use for insincere, manipulative, and pernicious purposes ('Fragment on Ontology', 199).

In 'The Rationale of Reward' Bentham voices concern about poetry's basis in ornamental fictions, rather than truth in the sense of 'exactitude'. And he voices concern about the poet's business of 'stimulating our passions', tantamount, as he states it here, to 'exciting our prejudices' (p. 254). He goes on to qualify. He acknowledges 'noble spirits' who have contributed to both poetry and philosophy. And within a page comes a reminder that philosophy, not only poetry, faces problems with language. Here Bentham observes the difficulty of finding a 'nomenclature of morals' that consists of pure, simple designations, and ones that do not excite approbation or reprobation, that are not 'tinctured with . . . prejudices' (p. 255). Behind this we may read his own struggle as a moral philosopher to name the springs of human action, which are necessarily 'fictitious entities', but to name them in terms that are exact and neither eulogistic or dyslogistic but neutral, non-prejudicial, with regard to exciting responses, judgements, and actions. In this context we may better understand his characterization of poetry as a 'magic art', yet one that in presenting everything through 'coloured media' is capable of causing 'mischiefs'. It is not always as innocent as push-pin.[29]

I would have to say, though, that with his fascination and frustration with words, Bentham never purges his own writing of a certain colourful mischief. The push-pin passage itself illustrates the point (and indeed it has been a cause of mischief to Bentham's reputation among literary and cultural critics). Instead of exact, neutral exposition there is an 'ornamental' and 'impressive' rhetoric of vivid and clever paradox. Push-pin—what a figure! and what could sound sillier to praise? except to give the reader a push to set 'prejudice apart'. I say, think again about the passage, and enjoy it.

Bentham defends other popular, innocent amusements, though they are looked down on: 'acrostics, conundrums, pantomimes, puppet-shows, *bouts-rimés*, stanzas in the shape of eggs, of wings, burlesque poetry of every description' ('Rationale of Reward', 254). He perceives that some amusements are of comparatively simpler and more childish kinds and that people pass beyond childhood to seek more complex pleasures. But he might almost be Dickens as a cherisher of childish Fancy in asking, 'Is this a reason for pride? It may be so—when to be hard to please, and to have our happiness depend on what is costly and complicated, shall be found to be advantageous. The child who is building houses of cards is happier than was Louis XIV, when building

Versailles.' And contemplation of the often expensive, ruinous, far-from innocent games of princes, including their wars, 'may furnish us with strong reasons for regretting that princes should ever cease to love the *games of children*' (p. 255). Recall that Bentham himself enjoyed pleasures of the table, domestic economy, good company, amiable and pretty women, music, gardens, architectural design (such as for the Panopticon), word coinages, prose to 'alleviate the tedium of a dry discussion', memories from childhood, cats and mice. He might have liked Merrylegs and the dancing horse and stood up for the circus (if not for Sleary's drinking) as he does for pantomimes and puppet-shows along with push-pin.

'The Rationale of Reward' ends with ideas on how higher education might incorporate teaching of the arts and sciences. The focus is establishment of several colleges in London suited for the more numerous classes of those with moderate fortunes pursuing art, trade, or commerce. We may bring to mind University College London, founded by Henry Brougham, a liberal Reform Whig, working in association with Benthamites such as James Mill. (Brougham was also involved in plans for the Chrestomathic day school, which was never actually built.) Franklin Court points out that this college, when it began operations in 1828, featured the first Professorship in English Language and Literature in Britain.[30] We may gather a Benthamite openness to the teaching of literature, with an emphasis on its more popular forms and in the vernacular rather than the classic languages preferred by elite university standards.

Bentham does not want to deny pleasures where they can be taken for the greatest happiness of the greatest number. No Pauline ascetic against sex or eating or drinking, no Gradgrind except as taught by Sleary, Bentham is not among those 'modest judges of elegance and taste [who] consider themselves as benefactors to the human race, whilst they are really only the interrupters of their pleasures—a sort of importunate hosts, who place themselves at the table to diminish, by their pretended delicacy, the appetite of their guests' (p. 254).

Even the 'Panopticon' essay offers pleasures of Benthamism. Indeed Bentham sketches out plans to provide popular entertainments on the Panopticon grounds. Semple's study of his more fantastic brainstorming for his scheme shows that he envisages satellite institutions— Metasylum, Sotimion, Paedotrophium—set within pleasure gardens, with prize plants gathered from around the world. These would be for the enjoyment of the inspector, family, staff, ex-prisoners, unmarried mothers, fatherless children, and prisoners working as gardeners under an identification system providing security, and would help draw the public to the site for a pleasant airing out of the city as well as for curiosity to see the Panopticon, so that they might function as the great open committee of the world. One gets a most amazing picture of the Panopticon Tavern, where visitors would arrive by riverboat. It is to be full of coloured lights, fountains, perfumes, gilt, mirrors, and flowers, according to projections by which Bentham surely amuses himself (and any readers of these notes of his) as he describes amusements for residents and the visiting public.

NOTES

1. A major dictum. See Ricardo's insistence on Smith's very words (*Principles of Political Economy and Taxation*, 293). Ricardo derives a case for the limitless call for capital from the limitless scope of investment opportunities in supplying limitlessly demanded 'conveniences and ornaments' of life. He also acknowledges Jean Baptiste Say's law: 'there is no amount of capital which may not be employed in a country, because demand is only limited by production' (p. 290). While Malthus entertains possibilities of lagging demand (*Principles of Political Economy*, 359–67), Mill follows Ricardo (*Principles of Political Economy*, ii. 66–8). Gagnier associates insatiability of human wants with latter-day capitalist economics, the neoclassical school dating from the 1870s, identified with William Stanley Jevons, Carl Menger, and others. She considers it a substantially new theoretical development, underpinning a new day of consumerism (*Insatiability of Human Wants*, 4, 20, 26, 41, 45, 47, 50, 59–60). But Jevons, too, cites the passage from Smith (*Theory of Political Economy*, 149). Gagnier does acknowledge how much Jevons et al. look to the 'hedonics' of Bentham (*Insatiability*, 41 n. 32). And for the most part in his 'Manual of Political Economy' Bentham endorses Smith's precepts. Thus one finds an adaptation of Smith in Bentham's discussion of items of two types (leaving aside a third, items of defence) that a country may gain wealth by producing. These are 'articles of subsistence'—up to some limit—and 'instruments of *mere* enjoyment'—'without limit' (p. 37). Gallagher recognizes 'eudemonism' in classical theory, not considering this only or primarily a neoclassical feature. However, she thinks pain ultimately wins out over pleasure—in both schools. She speaks of the predominance of

pain over pleasure in a wealthy society and declares that 'the dismal science... spawned an equally dismal culture' (*Body Economic*, 60, 184). She especially dwells on work as pain, consumer satiety, and the sufferings and sacrifices of sexuality involved in motherhood. See also nn. 3, 19; Ch. 1; Ch. 5 n. 17.

2. See Rosen, *Jeremy Bentham and Representative Democracy*, 206–8.

3. I think David Levy is right to indicate the importance of desire to please for Smith (*How the Dismal Science Got its Name*, 244). In Smithian sympathy Herbert discerns anomie, evaporation of direct desire for carnal gratification and its replacement by a 'passionless' state, 'vicariousness', 'masochism', etc. (*Culture and Anomie*, 86–7). He provides an important counterview to notions of simple egotistic desire but to my mind overlays Smith with Freudian ideas of a repressive superego to the point of underestimating the actual quotient of pleasure in the approval of others or of the impartial spectator, according to Smith. Herbert resembles Gallagher in emphasis on pain; and see nn. 1, 19; Ch. 5.

4. Despite more background on Smith, Bentham, Malthus, Ricardo, and Mill than is usual for Victorianist literary critics, Josephine Guy still sums up their model of humanity as a 'crude abstraction' featuring 'principally... a selfish, profit-seeking agent, motivated only by a desire to increase his own wealth' (*Victorian Social-Problem Novel*, 128). A similar assessment appears in her introduction to *The Victorian Age: An Anthology of Sources and Documents* (pp. 16, 19–21). Amanda Anderson says Mill finds in Bentham only a 'narrow formulation of self-interest [that] failed to give this principle its proper scope and thereby prompted justifiable criticism that utilitarianism held a reductive and ultimately dishonorable view of human nature'. She dismisses any adequacy of 'love of reputation' to expand Bentham's 'more narrowly construed self-interest' (*Powers of Distance*, 18). She gives no comment on Smith. John Whale notes the notion of 'sympathetic imagination' in Smith but speaks of Bentham's 'myopia', 'narrowness', 'materialism', and 'want of imagination', thus his limitation to a concept of the 'isolated individual' (*Imagination under Pressure*, 182). He instances the stimulation to imagination and feeling that Mill drew from Romanticism. True, but neither imagination nor feeling should be underestimated within Benthamism. As regards imagination, Engelmann considers it central to economic rationality, which he equates with Benthamite rationality. He speaks 'Against the Usual Story' (ch. title), calling interest itself a product of imagination (*Imagining Interest in Political Thought*, 50, book title). His emphases are on imagination in conceiving commensurability for cost–benefit analysis and conceiving time present and future to gauge resources and structure expectations (p. 3). As regards

feeling, Frances Ferguson says Bentham 'admits an extraordinarily wide range of emotions into his catalogue of motives' ('Beliefs and Emotions', 232). Most notably she addresses the moral sanction as a generator of feeling (*Pornography*, 'Envy Rising'). The moral sanction operates through awareness of self vis-à-vis others; compare Engelmann's perception of critical self-consciousness in economic, Benthamite thinking (p. 8), also Herbert's perception of reflexivity in Smithian sympathy (*Culture and Anomie*, 83–7). And see below, n. 15.

5. See Long, *Bentham on Liberty*, 75, 220.

6. While more knowledgeable about political economy and more sympathetic to it than most scholars of Romanticism—or Victorianism—Connell generalizes about 'strict Benthamite universalism' and 'extreme, universalist tendencies' (*Romanticism, Economics*, 92, 294).

7. Blainey, *Immortal Boy*, 68. See Connell (*Romanticism, Economics*, 214–19) on convivial encounters—with some tensions—between Bentham's coterie and Hunt's literary circle.

8. Semple, *Bentham's Prison*, 6–7.

9. Ibid. 214.

10. Though he stands out for sympathetic insight into Bentham, Engelmann sometimes expresses a standard view, making Benthamite utility sound rather abstract. Directly experienced present pleasures lose emphasis as emphasis falls on mental processes such as expectation, which projects happiness to future time. Consider this de-concretizing treatment: 'It should be clear from my analysis that I do not believe that Bentham's government by and for expected happiness was really about happiness; it was instead about government' (*Imagining Interest*, 149).

11. Williford, 'Bentham on the Rights of Women', 172–3; Semple, *Bentham's Prison*, 175, 177–87, 288–95.

12. Schofield, *Utility and Democracy*, 253–9.

13. And see Halévy, *Growth of Philosophic Radicalism*, 397–9; Rosen, *Jeremy Bentham and Representative Democracy*, 136; Schofield, *Utility and Democracy*, 296.

14. I agree with Semple (*Bentham's Prison*, 321, 314) in thinking Foucault treats the Panopticon unjustly in *Discipline and Punish*. He gives too grim a picture of what should be seen, in the context of the brutality of prisons of the time, as a humanitarian reformist scheme. He also presents the Panopticon as if it were paradigmatic for government generally. While Utilitarian principles are at work in the plan, they operate in service of a specific limited penal function. Foucault later qualifies some of his views on panopticism, suggesting that 'perhaps I've insisted too much on the technology of domination and power', and he seems to give more credit

to self-discipline—when 'an individual acts upon himself'—as constituting authentic action, not only a being acted upon within a nexus of power (*Technologies of the Self*, 19). Semple reviews negative judgements of Bentham and his prison by intellectual, social, and institutional historians and biographers on the grounds of authoritarian repressiveness (besides Foucault—Halévy, Himmelfarb, Long, Manning, Ignatieff), or, alternatively, among those more positive on Bentham, a downplaying of the importance of the Panopticon in his thought (Harrison). She notes revisionist studies of prisons and madhouses that give some credit to the Panopticon (DeLacy, Porter). Still, Haslam and Wright's essay collection on prisoners' writings illustrates continued reliance on the Foucauldian carceral paradigm. See also Engelmann, who faults Foucault's account of the Panopticon for contributing to a 'dominant illiberal image of Bentham' in political science (*Imagining Interest*, 9).

15. Like Anderson in *Powers of Distance*, David Wayne Thomas is interested in Victorian liberal thinking involving critical distance and self-reflexivity. Though less harsh in language, Thomas dissociates Mill's 'many-sidedness' from Utilitarianism, at any rate as a feature of an individual mind (*Cultivating Victorians*, 6, 28–9). He concedes that representative government, backed by Utilitarians, provides for many-sidedness across the body of representatives. Neither Anderson nor Thomas brings Smith into consideration of critical thinking, or relevant aspects of Bentham. See also n. 4 above.

16. A passage to raise the hair on the neck of Victorianist scholars harking back to such work as Herbert Sussman's *Victorians and the Machine*, which characterizes Victorian literature as generally opposed to 'mechanistic thought' (p. 11). This view persists, again articulated by Sussman in *A Companion to Victorian Literature and Culture* (pp. 253–4). In an interesting twist re *Hard Times*, Tamara Ketabgian ('"Melancholy Mad Elephants"') discerns a critique of a Benthamite ethos of the machine according to which the mind itself is mechanical; here, however, mind-as-machine does not exhibit the bad traits usually attributed to it, rationality and lack of emotion, but other bad traits, irrationality and brutishness.

17. Frances Ferguson more than once acknowledges advantages Bentham looks for in the panoptic classroom (*Pornography, the Theory*, 23–5, 55, 155). But for her a major sticking point lies in the question, 'what can be done for those who are last?' She further questions whether individuals are free to choose the panoptic systems in which they are evaluated and whether such systems are themselves subject to independent outside scrutiny (pp. 23, 22). Indeed there is an element of compulsion in the education of children that is hardly to be done away with. As for external

monitoring of a panoptic school, I would actually have expected Bentham to pay more attention to that. Still he calls the scheme experimental, requiring assessment over time, and, in effect, opens it up for outside examination by means of his detailed prospectus addressed to potential financial backers and parents of potential students. There are clearly enumerated listings of advantages and objections answered, plus panoptic tables offering an overview at a glance.

18. See Boralevi's chapter on Bentham's anti-anti-Semitism in *Bentham and the Oppressed*.

19. With Gallagher, I would underscore Malthus's insistence that sexual relations are ineradicable and essential to happiness, while I disagree with her overall portrayal of the culture responding to the Malthusian condition as 'dismal', like the 'dismal science' (*Body Economic*, 10, 184). With Laqueur ('Sexual Desire and the Market Economy'), I see market economics as conceptually tied to the validation of eros. Though I do not see the special tie between Benthamism and pornography that Frances Ferguson does, I certainly consider Bentham no prude. And see above, nn. 1 and 3.

20. Referenced by Crimmins, *Secular Unitarianism*, ch. 9; see also Boralevi, *Bentham and the Oppressed*, ch. 3. Crimmins argues that Christianity itself is Bentham's target, not only its Pauline ascetic strain (p. 257). See Engelmann: Bentham 'is profoundly liberal toward even the most widely condemned desires' (*Imagining Interest*, 75).

21. Gallagher, *Industrial Reformation*, 164.

22. *Dickens Redressed*, 187, 205. Cf. Williams (*Culture and Society*, 108, 107); Webb (*From Custom to Capital*, 90–1); Eagleton ('Critical Commentary' on *Hard Times*, 296); Patricia Johnson ('*Hard Times* and the Structure of Industrialism', 135); Josephine Guy (*Victorian Social-Problem Novel*, 123, 135–6); Brantlinger (*Fictions of State*, 169–70); Gallagher (*Body Economic*, 62–6, 80–4).

23. 'Comic Subversion', 155, 151.

24. To Henry Cole, 17 June 1854 (repr. *Hard Times*, Norton edn., 274). Cf. Dickens's letter to Charles Knight, 30 Jan. 1855, declaring the object of his satire to be men who, by overdoing figures and averages, 'damage the real useful truths of political economy' (ibid. 275). Cf. his 'A Nightly Scene in London', *Household Words*, 26 Jan. 1856 (*Dickens' Journalism*, 351), where he makes reference to those who push arithmetic and political economy beyond the bounds of sense and humanity and goes on to remark: 'Without disparaging those indispensable sciences in their sanity, I utterly renounce and abominate them in their insanity.' His complaint is against 'the unreasonable disciples of a reasonable school'. On occasion Martha Nussbaum articulates a position I would share, characterizing

Hard Times as Dickens's internal critique, not total repudiation, of Utilitarian political economy (*Poetic Justice*, 33). She recognizes individualism and reform intentions as values common to Dickens and Benthamites. But in this essay she also draws strong contrasts, and in 'The Literary Imagination in Public Life' she declares that literature is the enemy of economic thought (in the cruder forms she takes to be defining) and calls the very act of reading *Hard Times* an act of rebellion against political economy (pp. 879–81).

25. A 'notorious example', says Newsome (*Victorian World Picture*, 52), a 'celebrated comparison' and resisted by Dickens in *Hard Times*, says Kieran Dolin (*Fiction and the Law*, 76), an 'infamous declaration' and a basis for Bentham's philistine reputation, says Whale (*Imagination under Pressure*, 100). Nussbaum, in 'The Literary Imagination', speaks for the standard view that a literary mentality stands in antithetical relation to a Utilitarian economic mentality (pp. 879–81). Beyond literary studies, Hinderer says that, for many in philosophy, 'poetry is no better than push-pin' is a tag-line that creates the impression of Benthamite hostility to the arts ('Bentham on Poetry', 57). He seeks to counter this impression, pointing to Bentham's critique of snobbery and defence of popular taste. See also Linda Dowling's *The Vulgarization of Art*. Dowling argues that John Ruskin, William Morris, Walter Pater, and Oscar Wilde declare an interest in 'aesthetic democracy' but never really let go of an aristocratic standard of sensibility. See also nn. 29–30 below. I also discuss aesthetic levelling, vulgarization, or democratization at the end of Ch. 4, in Ch. 6 and n. 32, and in Ch. 7.

26. On Coleridge: 'I might be thought to have erred by giving undue prominence to the favourable side, as I had done in the case of Bentham to the unfavourable. In both cases, the impetus... may have carried me, though in appearance rather than in reality, too far on the contrary side.' Re the Coleridge essay, 'my defence is, that I was writing for Radicals and Liberals, and it was my business to dwell most on that in writers of a different school, from the knowledge of which they might derive most improvement' (p. 227). See also next note, and Chs. 5 and 7.

27. David Wayne Thomas speaks of the 'so-called two-Mills problem' (*Cultivating Victorians*, 29). This involves some mix of considerations of Mill's Benthamite education under his father's demanding tutelage, his 'mental crisis' at the outset of his 20s when he had completed his education and undertook to reflect for himself on his feelings, convictions, and plans, and his 'Bentham' and 'Coleridge' essays, conceived as defining alternative strands of thought between which he would choose or which he would synthesize for a new point of departure. Stillinger's account of

Mill's education ('John Mill's Education') sums up a common view of it as a sort of indoctrination, along with his own counterview of an education, however demanding, that taught independent thinking. Stillinger thinks Mill's schooling included companionable moments with his father and did not rule out a happy childhood. Schumpeter speaks for the widely held view that Mill drew apart from and significantly 'rose above' and at least in part 'shook off the shackles' of Bentham and James Mill (*History of Economic Analysis*, 430, cited in Hollander, *The Economics of John Stuart Mill*, ii. 604). Along similar lines see Peter Berkowitz, Nicholas Capaldi, Richard Ashcraft, and Eldon Eisenach in the Eisenach collection on Mill (pp. 18–20, 27, 50, 94–5, 170, 201); Capaldi (*John Stuart Mill*, 58–60, 65, 72); Wendy Donner ('Mill's Utilitarianism' 255); Zastoupil (*John Stuart Mill and India*, 30–47 and 'India, J. S. Mill, and "Western" Culture', 111–14); Anderson (*Powers of Distance*, 17–19). Klaver speaks of Mill's move beyond 'the narrow confines of utilitarianism' and 'conversion' to Romanticism (*A/Moral Economics*, 136). Goodlad speaks of Mill's 'drift from the Benthamite stance of his father' and ultimate synthesizing of 'a too-deterministic Benthamite materialism and a too-metaphysical "Germano-Coleridgean" tradition' (*Victorian Literature*, 29, 201). Bernard Semmel and Eisenach in the Eisenach collection illustrate a familiar playing off of the Bentham and Coleridge essays to indicate Mill's leaning towards the Coleridge side (pp. 61–2, 195–6). Likewise Capaldi juxtaposes the essays and argues that Mill rejected the radical version of the enlightenment project exemplified by Bentham and James Mill and sought to synthesize Radical and Conservative thought, with the Coleridge essay providing that synthesis (*John Stuart Mill*, 140–6, 99–100). Anderson describes Mill as so harshly critical of Bentham that he must appear, by comparison, a warm sympathizer with Coleridge (*Powers of Distance*, 17–19). But I would ask, what about the way Mill closes the Coleridge essay?: 'Lord, enlighten thou our enemies.' For Mill, Conservatives are enemies who are many and powerful, and Liberals cannot expect simply to convert them. Therefore Liberals should be glad to find someone like Coleridge in the enemy camp who can lead Conservatives 'to adopt one liberal opinion after another, as a part of Conservatism itself' (p. 163). More positive than many on Bentham, Pitts blames Mill for disservice to him in some of his characterizations (*Turn to Empire*, 133–5). I take her point but believe there are many evidences of Mill's strong, on-going affiliation. Similarly, Hollander believes Mill made a strong return to Bentham (*Economics of John Stuart Mill*, ii. 605). Henry West says Mill 'revised and perhaps broadened and softened Benthamism, but he never deserted it' (*Introduction to Mill's Utilitarian Ethics*, 5). He

titles an essay collection he edited *Mill's Utilitarianism*. See also n. 26
above, and Chs. 5 and 7.

28. A useful source is C. K. Ogden's *Bentham's Theory of Fictions*, an arrangement of various writings of Bentham's on language, with an important
introductory essay. Also useful is Schofield's chapter on 'Real and Fictitious Entities' in Bentham in *Utility and Democracy*. Neither is particularly directed towards poetry, literature, or the stylistic aspects of
language.

29. For kinder words on the fictions of the poet, see 'Fragment on Ontology',
199. Bentham distinguishes the fictions of the logician and of general
human discourse from those of the poet and from those of the lawyer and
priest. Thus 'in the mind of all, fiction, in the logical sense, has been the
coin of necessity;—in that of poets of amusement—in that of the priest
and the lawyer of mischievous immorality in the shape of mischievous
ambition'. He states that poetic fictions are 'pure of insincerity'. His main
emphasis here is to draw a contrast and to charge the fictions of lawyers
and priests with frequent insincerity—for purposes of deceiving in order
to govern in a way favourable to these groups. At the same time, Bentham
glancingly raises the possibility that an object and effect of poetic fictions
may not be to amuse only, but 'in some cases to excite to action ... for this
or that particular purpose'. The 'exciting' aspect of literature comes into
view, and a hint of wariness seems to return. Still, given developments in
literary criticism and theory in the last few decades, should we be shocked
by a certain hermeneutics of suspicion on Bentham's part as regards
literary and other uses of language?

30. In *Institutionalizing English Literature* Court notes a co-founder, the poet
Thomas Campbell, who soon dropped away. He discusses Brougham's
role in appointing Thomas Dale as Professor of English Language and
Literature, with James Mill convening the committee that made the
recommendation. He also looks back to Adam Smith's lectures on English
rhetoric and literature. According to Court, 'it is drastically shortsighted
to assume, as so many critics have over the years, that the rise of capitalism
in the eighteenth century and of utilitarian doctrines in the nineteenth
were naturally antithetical to the interests of literary study'. 'Brougham
has not always been treated fairly by literary historians. In recent years he
has been depicted as the enemy of imaginative literature, a political
Gradgrind promoting tracts on hydraulics and metallurgy, another "tech-
nologico-Benthamite" straw man. ... He was not an enemy of imaginative literature. That's a certainty. The record for his support of literature
and other artistic pursuits disproves the charge' (pp. 29, 51). Also note
further markers of Brougham's leadership in promoting popular

education, e.g. his support for the Lancastrian monitorial system, attempted legislation for government extension of primary education (failed) (1820), his contribution to establishment of Mechanics' Institutes (1825), his attempted legislation for the establishment of a central board of education (postponed) (1837), his support for another education bill (withdrawn) (1843) (Smelser, *Social Paralysis*, 70, 73, 75, 87, 94). See also n. 25 above, and Ch. 1 n. 21; Ch. 7 and n. 18.

3

Pains—'Work while it is called Today'

Utility, Political Economy, Carlyle, and Trollope

Inseparable from the principle of pleasure is that of pain, as pain enters into the reckoning of the greatest happiness. After the focus on pleasures in Chapter 2, Chapters 3 and 4 focus on pains, starting with the pain of work. The work ethic of capitalist culture has often been remarked, as have themes of work in nineteenth-century British literature. Bowring brings Bentham's *Memoirs* to a conclusion underscoring the lifelong habits of industry that attended Bentham's lifelong pursuit of amusement, as he wrote day in and day out by a strict routine till breaking to enjoy a walk in the garden, then dinner and conversation with friends. In these remarks on Bentham, Bowring alludes to the passage in John 9: 4 that also gives Carlyle the formula for his Gospel of Work in *Sartor Resartus*: 'Work while it is called Today; for the Night cometh, wherein no man can work' (p. 197).

Carlyle is a critic of Utilitarian political economy who is also its collaborator in forging the Victorian work ethic. He draws on Utilitarian-economic as well as German Romantic-Goethean[1] strains of thought, though the former has received far less attention than the latter. Such a broadly conceived work ethic stands behind reform politics in the period, such as those we shall look at in Anthony Trollope's *The Warden*.

Political economists extol work, though it counts as a pain on a Benthamite balance sheet of pleasure and pain, and work-as-pain may seem a dismal idea of the 'dismal science'. That is how Catherine Gallagher sees it (*Body Economic*, 72, 81). Carlyle, too, extols work, and work that is not easy but arduous. Some sharing between work ethics is evident, but also some difference. In fact, of the two work ideas, Carlyle's may seem the more dismal, or downright ascetic. He has recourse to Romanticism, celebrates Renunciation, and chides Benthamism for being at base a philosophy of pleasure. Yet in the various accounts of work that I analyse in this chapter I find testimonials to considerable satisfaction. There is devotion to pleasure and to labour in Bentham and political economy. There is devotion to play and to vocation and down-to-earth work in Romantic philosophy and literature. Oddly but aptly, Carlyle preaches his stern Gospel of Work in a humorous *jeu d'esprit* of a text, and Trollope offers charming entertainment in a novel on the reform cause of making idle clergymen work harder.

THE LABOUR THEORY OF VALUE

Bentham lists labour as a pain in the 'Table of the Springs of Action'. The pleasure that is its opposite number is the Interest of the Pillow. Labour is an instrumental pain, undertaken to obtain pleasures that exceed it and are its recompense. These utilities take the form of value-in-use or value-in-exchange. There are use values obtainable without work, but not exchange values, for political economy theorizes that utilities only enter into exchange—take on value in a market—if they do not come freely to hand (like air to breathe or the beautiful sun in the sky) but require work to obtain or make. As Adam Smith says,

> The real price of every thing, what every thing really costs to the man who wants to acquire it, is the toil and trouble of acquiring it. What every thing is really worth to the man who has acquired it, and who wants to dispose of it or exchange it for something else, is the toil and trouble which it can save to himself, and which it can impose upon other people. (*Wealth of Nations*, i. 47)

Both *The Wealth of Nations* and Mill's *Principles of Political Economy* begin with labour and its productive power. Mill follows Smith, while fleshing out his predecessor's dictum that goods find their 'natural price' in a free market in close proportion to their quotient of human labour. He takes account of supply and demand as well as monopoly and naturally occurring scarcity for their effect on price. He also identifies a portion of price that pays profit to the capitalist for his abstinence and risk. At the same time, Mill characterizes capital as 'a stock, previously accumulated, of the products of former labour' (ii. 55). Labour is 'fixed and embodied' in products capable of being saved as capital (ii. 48). This renders a good deal of the return on capital that is part of a product's price as a return on the labour of the past. Thus the price gives return on past as well as present labour. In the large role of labour past and present in setting exchange value we see the labour theory of value.

Marx hews to the line of classical economics to a great extent before diverging.[2] Many passages in *Capital* enforce the idea of labour as 'the universal value-creating element' (p. 313) and highlight the human vitality of labour embodied in products. Marx speaks graphically of this embodiment, which makes for storability over time. If not quickly consumed as utilities, products become commodities for exchange and are further abstracted from the labour that made them when they are represented by gold, paper money, or credit, and when (as commodities, money, or credit) they are accumulated and redeployed as capital. Marx speaks of the embodiment of labour in these forms as its fixing, materialization, congelation, crystallization, impersonation, fetishization— its preservation as 'dead labour'. Dead labour in this sense sustains present life like the blood sucked by a vampire, though we forget the live human source (*Capital*, 109, 86, 140, 117, 129, 32, 143).[3]

Labour is certainly pain, according to Marx. He devotes a good deal of *Capital* to deploring overlong workdays. Mill, however, believes that socialists, too, commonly underestimate the pain of work. They underestimate people's pleasure in indolence (Bentham's Pillow). They count too much on workers' industriousness—and efficiency and productivity—if the incentive of gain from working hard is removed (iii. 795). Of course, Marx decries modern industrial labour and cites the passage in Smith I discussed in Chapter 2 concerning the toll on workers of factory division of labour. Marx also decries what he considers to be exploitation in the form of surplus labour, by which he means extra hours of work in the day beyond what is needed to provide sufficient return to the labourer for present work. For political economy, on the other hand, these hours pay a return to the capitalist on past work embodied, saved, and invested, or capital. I will say more about capital in the next chapter.

Mill too hates the idea of wealth gained without relation to labour. His complaint is directed against landlords rather than capitalists. Landlords accrue gains by means of rent, and rent is conceived as lacking any basis in labour, whether of the present or the past. Landlords 'grow richer, as it were in their sleep' (iii. 819).

Still, though work is not pleasant or easy but a pain in the theory, political economists express an attitude towards it that hints, or more than hints, at enthusiasm. This can hardly be missed in Smith's description of the pin factory (*Wealth of Nations*, i. 14–15). He uses a 'trifling manufacture' to convey the idea of a manufacturing power that is far from trifling. Workers who might not have been able to produce a pin a day on their own produce 4,800 pins a day by means of division of labour. The production of ten persons is upwards of 48,000. So many pins! Such productive coordination of efforts!

Smith and Mill express a kind of wonder at the output of a long and complex chain of labour. Smith exclaims over the woollen coat that covers the common day labourer, which, however coarse and rough, is a testament to 'the joint labour of a great multitude of workmen'. He uses a rhetoric of fast-paced, running enumeration to describe a seemingly almost endless 'multiplication of the productions of all the different arts'. Long sentences interspersed with exclamation points list the work of the shepherd, sorter of wool, wool-comber, dyer, scribbler, spinner, weaver, fuller, and dresser. The passage goes on to detail various kinds of work in commerce and transport that are necessary to delivering not only the coat but the supplies and tools to those who make the coat or make what is needed to make it. Smith then proceeds to the work of provisioning all the workers along this chain with linen shirts, shoes, etc., coals, bread, beer, etc., kitchen grates, knives and forks, beds, etc. The passage grows bright describing window glass for workmen's houses. Window glass lets in light and keeps out cold and wind—so utilitarian in the usual sense and so Utilitarian in the philosophical sense, so pleasing, so 'beautiful and happy [an] invention'. Smith concludes by glorifying the productivity made possible by division and interlinking of labour on such a scale. Such productivity creates many utilities. It creates the wealth of nations and brings 'opulence' even to those of the lowest rank. He declares that despite differences in accommodation between peasant and prince in modern European countries, a European peasant enjoys comforts that surpass those of an African king in a 'savage', less efficiently productive society (i. 21–4).

Mill writes comparable passages. He uses the multiplier effect of lengthy enumeration to suggest the awesome productivity of work along a chain of subdivisions (ii. 31–2). Much as he credits capital, the saved and invested accumulation of past work, he gives most credit to what people do and make in the present. This explains why countries recover as fast as they do from floods, war, and other devastations. As he roundly declares, 'the greater part, in value, of the wealth now existing in England has been produced by human hands in the last twelve months' (ii. 73). This strikes even the preacher of the Gospel of Work, Carlyle, as coming on strong, according to annotations on his gift copy of Mill's *Political Economy*. But more on those annotations later.

Marx too salutes productive power amplified by the division of labour, which, to him is 'cooperation' (p. 195). He salutes the genius of James Watt, inventor of the steam engine, which powered the Industrial Revolution (p. 224). Friedrich Engels, in *The Condition of the Working Class in England*, marvels at the greatness of England as he contemplates the London of the 1840s, commercial capital of the world (p. 30). Viewing thousands of ships—many of them steamships—in crowded shipping lanes and at the docks, Engels says onlookers must be lost in admiration before he goes on to launch his communist indictment.

An inclination to admire work shows up even in passages in Mill that indicate difficulty in defining exactly what work is and what makes it admirable. One of the more perplexing aspects of political economists' thinking concerns a differentiation between productive and unproductive labour. In Mill's account, productive labour is that which fixes itself in forms of some temporal durability, thus being capable of carrying value-in-exchange in a market and being saved as capital to provide means of future production. The work of ploughman or cotton-spinner is directly productive, that of gaining a trade skill indirectly so. By contrast, the work of a musical performer or showman (Mr Sleary?) is unproductive. It makes what is immediately consumed and cannot be fixed into a form for exchange or for accumulation as capital for investment. Mill complicates the theory by proceeding to discuss productive and unproductive consumption. The implication emerges that making a serviceable coat for a worker is more productive than making a fine coat for pure display for a man who produces nothing (ii. 45–54).

Comparative terms in this discussion of productive versus unproductive labour give expression to a sense of worth in work. Productive work gains a eulogistic connotation set off against the unproductive alternative that is likely to be quite 'dyslogistically' understood. At the same time, Mill insists on the neutrality of his usages. He reminds us that utility, value-in-use, or pleasure is the ultimate object of all labour. From this point of view a fine coat justifies itself in consumption, whether or not it helps a worker work, and the same would go for a musical performance or show. Recall Bentham and Smith (and Sleary) on amusements for the people. Mill contends that a rich and productive society can well afford to sustain much unproductive labour—meaning labour undertaken at some pain while creating close to immediate net gain in pleasure. For both Mill and Marx, in the best society there would be a good deal of such clear, direct positive return of pleasure upon pain, with less delay and displacement of gratification. There would be closer alliance of work and enjoyment and closer merging of worker and consumer for a more even distribution of the pains of work and the pleasures of enjoying its products. Put at the extreme—no leisure class or slaves for Mill or Marx. Marx decries de-energized, alienated labour on the factory floor; so does political economy in citations from Smith I have given before.

Nevertheless, Marx does not envisage a labour so unalienated as to constitute in itself a pleasure. This shows his participation in the Utilitarian logic of political economy. He does not describe pre-industrial labour as intrinsically satisfying. For the industrial labourer he wants nothing so much as the shaving off of hours of surplus labour. But even after subtraction of surplus hours, the day's toil would still be toil. In a delicately poised position, Utilitarian political economy denies that labour has ultimate worth because it is not pleasurable in itself, and admires it for producing many things that satisfy many desires. Indeed labour's cost in forgone leisure should not be forgotten, nor its cost, often enough, in too-long deferred or insufficient compensation. It is basic to the discourse to place work on the side of pain in the pleasure–pain binary. But there are expressions of enthusiasm in describing work's utility-producing power that convey appreciation, a certain sense of satisfaction.

'WORK WHILE IT IS CALLED TODAY'

Carlyle records in his *Reminiscences* that *The Wealth of Nations* was an important book to his father, out of the way as such reading was for a humble Scottish mason. At one time Carlyle was considered for the chair in philosophy at the Benthamite University College London. He was not found to be suitable, but he writes in a letter of 'the clear Scotch head on my shoulders', which should have offset any doubts about his more mystical side.[4] Mill and Carlyle became friends after meeting in 1831, and there was talk of Carlyle's contributing to or even editing a Radical-Liberal journal, *The London Review*, to carry on from the Benthamite *Westminster Review*. The terrible episode is well known of Carlyle's lending Mill the manuscript of the first volume of *The French Revolution* and Mill's responsibility for its accidental burning by a parlour maid. Carlyle records repair of the friendship and money reparations. Mill sent him 200 pounds, of which Carlyle spent 100 on house rent while rewriting. He always wished to repay the other 100, but Mill would not take it. Carlyle's Scotch economy is evident in this desire to pay off the debt. Similar attitudes appear in remarks on his father's hard work, thrift, and success in bettering his condition and making his way to wealth, as he accounted wealth. Likewise Carlyle praises his wife's, Jane Carlyle's, practicality as a housekeeper and her ever-ingenious economizing. He speaks disapprovingly of the household management of Leigh Hunt (original of Skimpole): 'Huggermugger was the type of his economics, in all respects, financial and other' (p. 407; see also p. 435).

Carlyle's and Mill's relationship fell off, and their views could hardly seem more divergent, say, by the time of Carlyle's near-defence of slavery in 'The Nigger Question' of 1849 and Mill's sharp riposte in 'The Negro Question' of the following year. Thereafter the two parted ways over supporting, or not supporting, Governor Eyre and his bloody quelling of the 1865 colonial uprising in Jamaica. And Carlyle was far less hopeful than Mill about the further extension of suffrage in the Liberal-driven (Tory-passed) 1867 Reform Bill.

Still, there being no doubt that a divide opened up between these friends and widened over the years, the reminder is needed that they remained for a good while within hailing distance. Louis Cazamian's interpretation remains pretty typical if not always so violently asserted—that Carlyle held nothing but scorn for Utilitarians and economists as 'arid, abject, pedants' with an altogether 'miserable concatenation of ideas'. Carlyle 'rent their system to pieces, and liked nothing better than to toss its wretched fragments to the winds'.[5] It might come as a surprise to note that even in 1848 (not long before the duelling essays on the Negro question) Carlyle was reading and annotating his gift copy of Mill's *Principles of Political Economy.* I agree with Murray Baumgarten in perceiving a seriousness of engagement with this text that belies the standard view that economics was no more to Carlyle than the 'dismal science' (a phrase from the outré, perhaps even ironically ranting and excessive 'Nigger Question').[6]

The standard view emphasizes a double influence upon Carlyle of Scottish Puritan-Calvinist and German Romantic-Goethean world views.[7] There are several books on Romantic-era influence on Carlyle from Germany (Harrold, Ashton, Vida, Mellor). Ralph Jessop's *Carlyle and Scottish Thought* promises to provide greater balance on the other side. This study considers the influence of the Scottish Common-Sense philosophy of Thomas Reid and Sir William Hamilton within Carlyle's circle in Edinburgh. The philosophic issues involved are largely ontological and epistemological, while ideas on economics, society, and politics do not much figure. With Jessop, I believe Scottish influences on Carlyle are worth considering, but I would also place among these the influence of Smith, important to Carlyle's father, and of Smith's followers such as Mill, trained in the tradition by his own Scottish Benthamite-economist father, and Carlyle's friend.

In fact, with Baumgarten, I see Carlyle as a believer in the labour theory of value in its broadest terms (p. 119). He preaches a significantly economics-laden Gospel with the 'Produce! Produce!' of *Sartor Resartus,* or, 'Work while it is called Today; for the Night cometh, wherein no man can work' (p. 197). Some of Carlyle's annotations of *Political Economy* illustrate his stand with Mill on quite particular technical points. For instance, he responds favourably to Mill's Ricardo-based criticism of landlords and their reaping of the reward of rent without doing any work. He goes so far as to call the radical corrective of land redistribution a 'grand reform!' He salutes it again, saying 'very good' ('In the Margins', 83 re *Political Economy,* ii. 227, 231).[8] In these notes Carlyle applauds a position that he also speaks for in *Past and Present.*

In that book he challenges the Corn Laws that enlarge rent and challenges the very right of the Unworking Aristocracy to their land on the basis that property in land must rightfully flow from work (pp. 180, 176).

SARTOR RESARTUS

On its first pages *Sartor Resartus* places the Philosophy of Clothes side by side with other philosophic offerings of the age such as the Theory of Value and the Doctrine of Rent. According to the Clothes Philosopher Diogenes Teufelsdröckh, Clothes are the creations or productions of spirit. 'For Matter, were it never so despicable, is Spirit, the manifestation of Spirit. . . . The thing Visible, nay the thing Imagined, the thing in any way conceived as Visible, what is it but a Garment, a Clothing of the higher, celestial Invisible?' (pp. 66–7). Divine spirit is active in God, in the Erdgeist weaving Nature, and in man, the 'Tool-using Animal' (p. 41), using his tools to make Clothes. Carlyle gives this human activity less the cast of pure spontaneity or organic growth than of effortful making through his reference to the use of tools and his figure of Clothes for what is made. Clothes are in no way self-generating but require work to make.

Let me call attention to the initial purpose of Clothes, according to the philosophy. It has puzzled me to understand Teufelsdröckh's postulate that 'the first purpose of Clothes . . . was not warmth or decency, but ornament'. He states again that 'for Decoration [primitive mankind] must have Clothes' (p. 39). After all, there is a great deal in *Sartor Resartus* that seems sternly ascetic—stressing the pain of hunger that drives us to labour and the pain we undergo in its performance. There is a call for Renunciation and Worship of Sorrow. Teufelsdröckh's philosophy does not come easily to him. He has to go through Byronic/Wertherian sufferings and a three-stage crisis, moving through the Everlasting No and the Centre of Indifference to the Everlasting Yea before he can begin to write. Once begun, his pages are deep-thinking, historical-speculative, ethereal-saturnine, transcendental-descendental, allusive and poetic in language, ironic and labyrinthine in form. He could not pen his grand opus without making an effort. Indeed it takes hard work to keep the study where he writes from deteriorating into a chaos of books, papers, shreds, and litter. Old Lieschen, Teufelsdröckh's housekeeper, is one of the hard workers of *Sartor Resartus*, with her 'look of helpful intelligence' (p. 25). Another hard worker is Teufelsdröckh's English Editor. He has to toil mightily to convey to his sensibly minded English readers the dense yet nebulous Clothes Philosophy of a perhaps even wilfully semi-intelligible and possibly wrongheaded and intellectually and politically dangerous German. The Editor frequently exclaims at his difficulties, frustration, and fatigue as he strives to piece together the Philosopher's life and thoughts from miscellaneous research materials contained in six paper bags, each marked with a sign of the zodiac. He observes that readers must also take upon themselves the 'self-activity' demanded by the best reading (p. 28), and he frequently opines that reading this book will be no light or always pleasant task. On the last page he bids farewell to 'one and all of you, O irritated readers'. Tailoring and re-tailoring are toil.

And, with such seeming stress on asceticism, the text repeatedly challenges Utilitarian political economy for its basis in a pleasure principle. It criticizes a Profit-and-Loss Philosophy that makes Soul synonymous with Stomach and grinds out Virtue from the husks of Pleasure, that is preoccupied by Desire and Fear and calls Happiness the ultimate human aim. In a satire of Bentham-like calculation applied to human desires, Teufelsdröckh proposes a new arithmetic. Set one's claims for satisfaction at zero for division into the large number of one's wishes so as to come out with infinity. But this is, in fact, a formula that yields a lot, not a little. A lot of what? *Sartor Resartus* does not call it happiness or pleasure.

Yet *Sartor Resartus* is a text about Clothes that traces their first purpose to ornament, to decoration. Clothes-as-Ornament, Clothes-as-Decoration suggest beauty and personal display. And yes, happiness or pleasure. Further, a proper understanding of Clothes leads not only to a Gospel of Work but to a Gospel of Wonder. Wonder is full of joy and teaches by charming (p. 97). One feels Wonder when beholding the world at large, for instance, Teufelsdröckh's town of Weissnichtwo. Laboriously erected over centuries, Weissnichtwo is as wonderful to see as Thebes, raised artfully in an instant by Orpheus' or Amphion's mythic lyre. One feels Wonder when beholding the world in small of oneself. This self-world appears reflected in one's works as if in a mirror (p. 162). 'I too could now say to myself: Be no longer a Chaos, but a

World, or even Worldkin. Produce! Produce!' (p. 197). The Everlasting
Yea overcomes the suffering first confronted in the Everlasting No,
which is to feel oneself a 'feeble unit' (p. 163), isolated, weak, lacking
in energy, anxious and stymied, overpowered by things outside. Teufelsdröckh does not resolve the problem by dissolving the unit of feeling,
the self, but by advancing its feelings along a line from defiance to
indifference to affirmation. These become feelings of personal energy,
free agency, and power—feelings of Freedom and Voluntary Force
(p. 183). The Everlasting Yea links exuberant Wonder with the drive
to work. A strong element of self remains, and a strong element of
satisfaction. As one regards oneself in the mirror of one's works, there is
even *self*-satisfaction.

What strikes me is retention of a principle of pleasure in a discourse
that overtly repudiates that principle as theorized by Utilitarian political
economy. On the pleasure principle the two philosophies appear to be
very much at odds, while they are close together in the high worth
they place on hard work. But examination reveals that, for Carlyle,
Work never loses its character of pain, yet produces Clothes that are
at some deep level ornamental and pleasing and affirm the self and
gratify it with Wonder. This makes for a surprising affinity between his
thinking and that of Utilitarian political economy, according to which
work is pain, yet when recognized for its power to supply demand and
serve 'selfish' pleasure, yields a wondering appreciation.

Concerning pleasure or happiness as an aim in life, Carlyle, in an
essay on Friedrich von Schiller, concedes that he could go along with the
idea if cast in alternative terms to imply more than 'agreeable sensations'. He says the word 'welfare' would do ('Schiller', 191–2). He cites
a passage from Schiller's *On the Aesthetic Education of Man* (p. 116) that
chides Happiness-Systems for undue stress on appetite and animalism.
But after complaining of '*Utility*... the great idol of the age' (p. 26),
Schiller hardly throws out Happiness-Systems. Rather, he expounds
a Happiness-System of his own.[9] His letters on aesthetic education
present an apologia for the play-impulse, by which Schiller means
aesthetic self-delightingness. In an oft-cited passage: 'To declare it
once and for all, Man plays only when he is in the full sense of
the word a man, and *he is only wholly Man when he is playing*' (p. 80).
No, this is not quite the Philosophy of Push-pin or the Circus! Art is
Schiller's ultimate play.[10] It is known by beauty and enjoyment. It offers

delight in pure appearance, embellishment, display, and ornament (pp. 128, 132–3, 125). In Schiller's conception, delight involves action, more particularly, the mind's self-awareness of its action as a maker. Aesthetic awareness consists in perception of things around us as not made by ourselves but at the same time available for us to play with; in this way they render it possible for us to be makers of things on our own account. The play aesthetic 'only attains the absolute by means of limitations, only works and fashions insofar as it receives material' (p. 93). So 'to shew himself spirit Man does not need to eschew matter' (p. 123). For Schiller, active making or creation, whether in thinking and imagining or more material shaping, is self-delighting play. Cast in these terms, Carlyle's work ethic looks less insistently self-denying, more oriented towards realization of personal welfare. It looks more akin to the labour theory of Utilitarian political economy.

Schiller theorizes play. Another favourite German author of Carlyle's puts theory into practice. This is Jean Paul Richter, an essay subject for Carlyle and named in *Sartor Resartus*. When Teufelsdröckh laughs his great laugh, we hear it is Jean Paul's doing. Jean Paul is a humorist from his inmost soul, 'a Titan in his sport as in his earnestness'. He is the great practitioner of irony ('Jean Paul Friedrich Richter', xxvi. 13–14). There is a dash of the ridiculous in Jean Paul's favourite characters ('Jean Paul Friedrich Richter', xxii. 123), which certainly also holds for Carlyle's struggling English Editor and his Philosopher of Clothes and Professor of Things-in-General from Wahnstrasse, Weissnichtwo (Nonsense Street, I Don't Know Where), who emits wisdom like water from a fountain at the coffee house Zur Grünen Gans (at the sign of the Green Goose), holding his tumbler of Gukguk and maintaining the same assiduous look whether any wisdom is flowing or not. Jean Paul revels in a flamboyantly outrageous verbal style:

Not that he [Jean Paul] is ignorant of grammar, or disdains the sciences of spelling and parsing; but he exercises both in a certain latitudinarian spirit; deals with astonishing liberality in parentheses, dashes, and subsidiary clauses; invents hundreds of new words, alters old ones, or by hyphen chains and pairs and packs them together into most jarring combination;...He introduces figures without limit; indeed the whole is one tissue of metaphors, and similes, and allusions...interlaced with epigrammatic breaks, vehement bursts, or sardonic turns, interjections, quips, puns, and even oaths! ('Jean Paul Friedrich Richter', xxvi. 12)

This is very much like Teufelsdröckh's style: 'Of his sentences perhaps not more than nine-tenths stand straight on their legs' (p. 31).

Thus *Sartor Resartus* is a flaunting and funny book that has inspired critics to speak of its joco-seriousness and transcendental buffoonery of Romantic irony; dandyism; grotesque conceits; and inverse sublimity of humorous deconstruction and mock apocalypse (Mellor; Adams; Barlow; Dale). With its sportive verbal style, it also features dialogic interplay in overall construction. The Editor constantly comments on and questions the Philosopher and addresses the English reader as a fellow-toiler amidst German profundities and farragos. These formal features foreground the activity of making and cast making as delightful and difficult, play and hard work.

Carlyle has been understood to draw on Kant and especially the post-Kantian Johann Gottlieb Fichte, though he imbibes their ideas in good measure from Schiller and Jean Paul, also from Novalis, and he makes repeated disclaimers as to his technical grasp and reserves judgement on philosophic conclusions. I find Elizabeth Vida's tracing of affinities between *Sartor Resartus* and Fichte's *The Vocation of Man* persuasive (though there is no external proof that Carlyle read it). One may take Carlyle's terminology of the ME and the NOT-ME to be a spin on Fichte's Ich and Nicht-Ich. The exchanges between Editor and Philosopher resemble those between an I speaker and a Spirit in *The Vocation of Man*. There is dramatic sequencing by crisis and resolution in Carlyle's and Fichte's texts. Carlyle's call to work resembles Fichte's call to vocation.

In Fichte's exposition, the speaking I confronts personally wrenching dilemmas of epistemology and 'practical reason' in Kant's sense of morality for guiding worldly acts. The first crisis is precipitated by a too-materialist conception of the determination of self by external realities through the impress of sensation. This induces an anxious feeling of paralysis and lack of freedom and agency. With help from the Spirit, this crisis is resolved through a Kantian theory of the mind as itself an active force. Operating by its own internal categories, the mind creates the realities it knows, or phenomena. But this resolution spawns another crisis. The problem is no longer materialist determinism but idealist solipsism. This induces an anxious feeling that all we know is merely of our own making. Reality is dematerialized, including the reality of our own selfhood. The mind becomes a site of phantasmagoric projections of 'pictures without anything which is pictured in them'.

Worse, 'I myself am one of those pictures' (p. 80). What would be the reality, freedom, or agency of such a picture-self? *The Vocation of Man* finds resolution of this crisis through rematerialization of external reality, which also brings the self back from phantasm to actuality and to free action. Carlyle's dictum could be Fichte's—that not only to know but to act is the human vocation. Indeed, Carlyle says, 'Doubt of any sort cannot be removed except by Action' (p. 196).

I want to emphasize the rematerializing process in *The Vocation of Man*. It begins when we attribute reality to other people by an act of faith. At the heart here is a sense that other people are self-existent beings who exact such a conception of themselves by their expectation of being treated as such, that is, treated with consideration and respect. This calls forth such treatment on our part. In the process we confirm a world of real people and real things, which constitutes the sphere of our action, and we confirm our own reality as actors who bring about real consequences, just as we also bear the real consequences of others' acts. Such action is that of 'practical reason'. In understanding this to mean moral action, we should recall the connotation of the word 'practical' (in German as in English). Action in the world is indicated, impacting other people and everyday realities.

Fichte speaks in philosophical terms of vocation as material, practical action in the world. Johann Wolfgang von Goethe makes material, practical vocation more concretely recognizable as work. Advice to 'Close thy *Byron*; open thy *Goethe*' in *Sartor Resartus* (p. 192) might be restated as advice to close thy Goethe of the *Sorrows of Young Werther* and open thy Goethe of *Wilhelm Meister*. Werther despairs and leaves the world, a suicide; Wilhelm Meister finds his way towards personal *Bildung* via work in the world. Carlyle draws on *Wilhelm Meister's Travels* for the injunction to undertake tasks in 'this poor, miserable, hampered, despicable Actual', in this way discovering that 'America is here or nowhere' (*Sartor*, 196–7), in oneself and one's labours. This teaching out of *Wilhelm Meister* points forward to the teaching at the conclusion of *Faust* in its final version. Faust dies having identified a moment that could satisfy him. This would be the moment of achievement in his work as a drainage engineer reclaiming marshland. Faust's project is material and practical in the most down-to-earth sense, while it is material and practical in a philosophical sense as well, denoting moral action in the world, for opened-up farmland will benefit people now and to come. The moment of work-achievement would be the one to which Faust would say 'Tarry yet, thou art so fair!' Indeed in a foretaste of this future happiness Faust enjoys his highest happiness in the present—and without losing his soul to Mephistopheles, as their contract would seem to demand, but achieving salvation (*Faust* II. Act V, ll. 11581–6).[11] All this is worth noting (though Carlyle only refers to earlier published portions of *Faust*, not the ending, which came out after he had written *Sartor*)[12] because, more even than *Wilhelm Meister*, the culmination of *Faust* makes manifest Goethe's affirmation of material, practical work and the satisfaction it gives. Such work produces, in its very contemplation, the fairest of moments, the utmost enjoyment, a soul-saving happiness.

Carlyle cites remarks of Novalis's identifying a 'prosaic, mechanical, economical, coldhearted, altogether Utilitarian character' in *Wilhelm Meister*. Novalis even calls Goethe's Bildungsroman 'as we should say, a Benthamite work!' ('Goethe', 231). Carlyle says of Goethe that 'the dullest plodder has not a more practical understanding... than this most aërial and imaginative of poets' ('Goethe's Helena', 197). He exclaims that Goethe, a writer who seems almost a Benthamite to Novalis, seems a mystic to the English—'so difficult is it to please all parties!' ('Goethe', 231). Carlyle also shuttles between parties. His thinking is informed by Schiller's play aesthetic, which locates delight in material as well as imaginative making. It is informed by Fichte's idea of vocation, which locates confirmation of self in material, practical action, and by Goethe's representation of material, practical, prosaic, even plodding work that nevertheless consorts with aerial imagination, and—if we look ahead to the end of *Faust*—consorts with the soul's highest happiness. Carlyle's thinking is informed by Mill's Utilitarian labour theory, which lays stress on the prosaically, ploddingly material and practical, the mechanical and economical, yet, while placing work on the side of pain, points to some element of satisfaction in recognizing all work does for pleasure.

My object now is to note the workaday productions that count as creations to be joyfully wondered at in the Clothes Philosophy. We would be wrong to reach a one-sided conclusion from certain Carlylean diatribes against excessive materialism in Profit-and-Loss Philosophy. Yes, there are passages that express longing to apprehend a world not materialized as phenomena in Time and Space, a world out of Clothes.

One such passage describes a longing to lay aside outward physical wrappings and step forth naked and unencumbered like, say, the horse. But in the Philosophy of Clothes the value of undressing lies mainly in the opportunity to dress again in new-made Clothes. Carlyle could hardly give more importance to human making of material things for ornamental and practical purposes than by choosing Clothes as his figure and theorizing a 'Society founded upon Cloth' (p. 51).

A well-known passage leading up to the Everlasting No gives Teufels-dröckh's nightmare vision of the universe as 'one huge, dead, immeasurable Steam-engine, rolling on, in its dead indifference, to grind me limb from limb' (p. 164). This can prompt a notion of recoil from steam engines, machines, and work in the form of modern industry and commerce. Not so, when the Philosopher is in a better state of mind. Elsewhere he salutes Iron Force and Coal Force in a breath with the force of Man (p. 71). He salutes magic in Watt's invention of the steam engine:

the grand thaumaturgic art of Thought ... [in] the Scottish Brassmith's IDEA. ... [C]annot the dullest hear Steam-engines clanking around him? ... [Are these not] travelling on fire-wings round the Cape, and across two Oceans; and stronger than any other Enchanter's Familiar ... not only weaving Cloth; but rapidly enough overturning the whole old system of Society; and ... preparing ... Industrialism and the Government of the Wisest? (p. 118)

In the passage that defines Clothes as the manifestation of spirit in matter, he gives the example of Richard Arkwright's spinning frame (patented 1769). He syntactically equates what is 'woven in Arkwright looms, or by the silent Arachnes that weave unrestingly in our imagination' (p. 67).

Liverpool Steam-carriages are a case in point in the chapter explaining that Clothes are made by the Tool-using Animal and are themselves tools but nevertheless take their rise from the love of ornament and decoration, from the play of mind. Clothes are laborious material, practical productions; they are joyful, wonderful imaginative creations.

Teufelsdröckh observes with joy and Wonder the weaving action of economics—the transport and commerce represented by stagecoach traffic through his native Entepfuhl and by its annual cattle-fair. Entepfuhl is connected by markets to the larger world, as the little Kuhbach is connected to the ocean. Here Teufelsdröckh hails interconnection through economic exchange, and interconnection is an important opposite to the isolation that was one of the miseries precipitating the Everlasting No. But then, too, he elsewhere expresses fear of loss of social connection in competitive laissez-faire (p. 232). One of Carlyle's annotations in response to Mill's *Political Economy* gives further insight into his viewpoint. The context is Mill's remarks on the mutual reliance involved in labour-capital and business-to-business contracts. He says, 'the advantage to mankind of being able to trust one another, penetrates into every crevice and cranny of human life: the economical is perhaps the smallest part of it, yet even this is incalculable' (ii. 110). Carlyle's response is to bracket 'the smallest' ('In the Margins', 76). He scales back recognition of mutuality in economic relations but does not deny its role there.

When Teufelsdröckh moves from the Everlasting No to the Centre of Indifference (advancing towards the Everlasting Yea), he actually expresses a certain respect for standing on one's own and standing up for one's own interests as against those of others. In Arctic latitudes, in solitary contemplation of the abyss, Teufelsdröckh is confronted by a monster or a man, perhaps a Russian smuggler. In one of *Sartor's* funnier passages the Philosopher reports how 'with courteous brevity, I signify my indifference to contraband trade, my humane intentions, yet strong wish to be private'. The means of securing his privacy turns out to be a Birmingham Horse-pistol. This would be the product of the great industrial town known for engineering, machine tools, and gunsmithing. The incident spurs a disquisition on gunpowder to illustrate the theme that 'Animalism is nothing, inventive Spiritualism is all'. Spiritualism gives rise to real-world manufactures and to ideas with real-world consequences, here to guns and to a notion of equalized if sometimes competitive social relations, for guns make 'all men alike tall' (p. 180).

Annotating a section of the *Political Economy* where Mill promises to provide proof at a later point 'of the ultimate benefit of mechanical inventions to the human race', Carlyle writes, 'no 'proof' needed!' (ii. 98; 'In the Margins', 76). It is true, Carlyle does not want to fetishize made objects highly tangible to the senses so as to make them seem to be the only proper products of labour. A passage of Mill's on productive and unproductive labour prompts a question from Carlyle. Mill differentiates the work of a tailor from that of an actor. The one performs productive labour with output of a durable item for exchange and potential service to future labour, while the other does not because his performance produces a utility that does not last. But is it right to say the latter leaves 'no article of wealth for the spectator's indemnification'? Carlyle brackets 'no' and poses the question 'none visible: but *none* absolutely?' (ii. 51; 'In the Margins', 70).

Still, cloth is a visible, a material product. It is a product of Watt's steam engines powering Arkwright's frames. Teufelsdröckh's figure of Cloth highlights the relevance of his Gospel of Work to the industrialism of the times. After all, textiles was the lead industry of the Industrial Revolution.[13] I will return to the textile industry in Chapter 6.

With regard to social and political issues connected with industrialism, Teufelsdröckh leans towards the radical side. He is a Sansculottist; he favours democracy, though he expects no panacea from the ballotbox. The Editor reports that he has been lost sight of in Weissnichtwo and that he may be in Paris or London—on the scene of Jacobinical revolution (July Revolution of 1830) or epochal democratic reform (First Reform Bill of 1832). Teufelsdröckh envisions the 'monster UTILITARIA' as an insurgent power destroying the *ancien régime* of Church and aristocratic rule. He says UTILITARIA needs restraints and moderation (by nose-rings, halters, foot-shackles, ropes) but not stopping (p. 236). In *Sartor Resartus* Carlyle scorns the Dandy aristocracy. He mocks its idea of honour that would make the number of partridges shot the proudest inscription for a tombstone. He commiserates with working-class Drudges, and—jumping texts here to *Past and Present*— looks to find leaders in Captains of Industry, once tempered by his philosophy. Let us not forget that while *Past and Present* critiques the Cash Nexus, it also repeatedly backs Repeal of the Corn Laws, or freetrade laissez-faire, and in no uncertain terms (pp. 166, 178, 180, 183).[14] Corn Law Repeal was the touchstone issue of Utilitarian political economy of the time. Furthermore, as I observed earlier, Carlyle's *Past and Present* and his notes on Mill's *Political Economy* show engagement with the economic doctrine of rent in expressing animus against gentry landlords who do not work. Unworking landlords offend against the labour theory of value as they do against the Gospel of Work. Challenge to rent would ultimately carry more liberal, indeed radical, implications than Corn Law Repeal. It would mean advocating a levelling land redistribution through tax revenue reforms. But these are later developments, which I will take up again in my last chapter.

To return to the 1830s and *Sartor Resartus*, Carlyle declares the Gospel of Work—attended by the Gospel of Wonder—to be his ultimate Political Evangel. It calls for the career open to talents—'The Tools to him that can handle them' (pp. 178–9). One of the early actions of the reformed Parliament was to establish a commission to investigate an offender against the Carlylean/Benthamite-economic/Romantic-Goethean work ethic, namely, the non-work/non-talent-based career system of the Church of England. Beginning in 1835, the Ecclesiastical Commission probed salaries, patronage, and sinecures in the Church. Carlyle shows an interest in this. He makes reference in *Past and Present* to scandals concerning clerical overcompensation for scant labour (p. 187). Also in 1835, a Select Committee on Public Charities called for stepped-up inquiry into charitable endowments—many of them Church endowments—and the work they funded. There was mounting pressure in this area, while Parliament's establishment of a Charity Commission came only in 1853. Mill addresses abuses in Church employment and Church work under endowments in essays from 'Corporation and Church Property' of 1833 to 'Endowments' of 1869. Such scandals and abuses gave Trollope the subject matter for his first Barchester novel, *The Warden*,[15] and he says Yea to a Victorian work Gospel and labour theory. If it seems odd, it makes sense that Trollope, like Carlyle, affirms hard work in a most playful manner. This is my point of emphasis in rounding out the chapter with *The Warden*.

THE WARDEN

Reforms of Church work and its funding took various shapes and were instituted piecemeal, while serving a policy of 'appropriation' that was a rallying point for the Liberal party[16] and that we gain a good idea of from Mill's essays. With the country's growing and shifting population, there were growing and shifting needs in areas where the Church had long held responsibility, such as in charity and education. With new work to do, there were also increased resources to fund it in prosperous old Church endowments. The aim would be to empower public bodies like Parliament to intervene in the administration of funds in such old endowments, reinterpret best current uses, redistribute money accordingly, and maximize results by hiring for talent and willingness to work and setting compensation in relation to the job done. As Mill puts it, the aim would *not* be to ensure that 'some men then living, and an indefinite series of successors appointing one another in a direct line, might be comfortably fed and clothed' ('Corporation and Church Property', 202).

In Trollope's novel, Mr Bold, a bourgeois surgeon, son of a London physician, with new money from urban real estate, and an elected town councillor, is the lead critic of Church abuses in Barchester along lines resembling Mill's. Turning like a good Benthamite to the press as agent for the Public Opinion Tribunal, he finds backing from Tom Towers, editor at the London newspaper the *Jupiter*, a powerhouse for investigative reporting and reformist editorializing. The novel presents Carlyle, and also Dickens, as polemicists on the liberal reform side. This comes in caricatures of Dr Pessimist Anticant and Mr Popular Sentiment, whose writings are touted by Tom Towers at the *Jupiter*.

Dr Pessimist Anticant, the Carlylean Scottish sage steeped in German thought, puts forth an all-around reprobation in the quaintest language. We are told that his later writings have degenerated from his earlier ones (think of the playful *Sartor*), so that he is a gloomy Jeremiah, and possibilities of reform, however desirable, seem swamped by all there is to censure. Dr Anticant doubts what partridge-shooting aristocrats or political economists, what political parties or the government can do, only ranting that something must be done. Mr Popular Sentiment, Trollope's comic figure for Dickens, makes corrective action seem more imminent, and the stronger the better. The Drone Philosophy comes in for a drubbing. Mr Popular Sentiment's novel *The Almshouse* is an exposé of 'hotbeds of peculation' (p. 131) like Barchester. The demonic practices of the warden of a charity hospital are laid bare. With cruel bloodshot eyes and a red carbuncle on his nose, bespeaking the port he enjoys along with every other luxury, the warden lives at ease off funds that should rightfully be spent helping poor suffering pauper pensioners. This cries out for 'radical reform' (p. 137). Trollope satirizes such critiques as simple-minded and crude. His novel presents itself, by contrast, as more suave, more agreeable in tone, eschewing polemic, and making us smile at both sides of the matter.

On balance, *The Warden* has been held to lean to the conservative side due to its affectionate treatment of Mr Harding, the remarkably inoffensive offending warden, a truly gentle gentleman.[17] The novel has been seen as poking rougher fun at Mr Bold, who ultimately lets down his side to win the girl. In addition, it has not been thought to take the grievances of the pensioners very seriously. They are pretty comfortable but on the lookout for anything that might be coming their way. Still, I think it is right to say, with Coral Lansbury, that Trollope never denies the need for reform (*Reasonable Man*, 139).

Bold and Towers are opportunistic, and Anticant and Sentiment indulge in indiscriminate finger-pointing. But not so pure either are recipients of 'snug clerical sinecures attached to our church', who are granted patronage in the form of livings that are 'bishop's gifts' or 'in the gift' of dean and chapter, plus pluralities, or multiple livings, some or all held in absentia (pp. 4, 23, 2, 115, 82). One gentleman-cleric who makes out very well is Dr Vesey Stanhope. He fills the prebendal stall of Goosegorge in Barchester Cathedral Chapter along with holding the living of Crabtree Canonicorum and the united rectory of Eiderdown and Stogpingum, while living in a villa at Lake Como and collecting butterflies. Archdeacon Grantly is the great defender of Church privileges in the novel. He presumably owes his own position to being the son of the bishop, and he comes all the more zealously to Mr Harding's defence for Mr Harding's being his, the archdeacon's, father-in-law. Archdeacon Grantly is satirically pictured as the representative of a well-to-do establishment: with 'one hand ensconced within his pocket [he] evinced the practical hold which our mother Church keeps on her temporal possessions'. The archdeacon holds his other hand free as if ready to fight to keep these possessions (p. 42). Mr Harding is milder and lives with less display of rich household trappings and comestibles—the tea, coffee, cream, breads, eggs, fishes, kidneys, ham, and sirloin that load the breakfast board at the Grantly's plum of a residence at Plumstead Episcopi.

But the description we get of Mr Harding's garden at Hiram's Hospital is very lush. The garden is a symbol of the amenities in his life. So are his violoncello and his music, and here Trollope slips in sly details as to how many guineas it has cost to have *Harding's Church Music* so beautifully bound in vellum and edged with gilt. He also lets it be known how freely—in a manner financially all unawares—Mr Harding has spent beyond his generous income to fund this musical extravagance. In fact, he has gone into debt to his son-in-law Grantly. So the unworldly and generous Mr Harding—he likes sharing his garden and music with his wards—is worldly enough in his way.

In the course of the narrative the rights and wrongs of Mr Harding's wardenship are gradually brought home to him, and the novel surely supports him in his judgement that he should resign from his position. Besides being provided the lovely house and garden, he has been paid a great deal—£800 a year, plus £80 a year for his precentorship at the cathedral, while he also holds the right to another small living at Crabtree Parva. This is not because of talents and not because he earns his income by services rendered. Rather he holds the wardenship by the bishop's 'gift'. And he receives as much as he does because the Hiram's Hospital endowment has grown richer over the years from rising rents on pasture and residential land. These have gained greatly in value since the bequest back in the fifteenth century of John Hiram, a wool-stapler. Gain of this sort is what economists would predict, given rising population (Malthus) and therefore rising demand for land and rising rent to landlords (Ricardo). Here the landlord is a Church endowment. Over hundreds of years the number of pensioners has not grown beyond the original twelve. Expenditure on each has remained at roughly what was first stipulated, amounting presently to 1s. 4d. a day and lodging, plus a 2d. extra 'gift' from Mr Harding since board is no longer provided. The old men are actually there by something of a gift, too, a gift to bishop, dean, and warden who need a place to send superannuated 'hangers-on of their own' (p. 2). It is old servants of the clergy, not old wool-carders as intended by Hiram, who now receive the charity. The increased trust income does not increase the bedesmen's alms or the number of them receiving it. It goes almost entirely into the increased stipend of the warden.

Mr Harding fulfils his role with goodwill and is kind to his wards, but his work is very easy for the money. More work—care of more old men—is not contemplated. He might have to appear in Ecclesiastical Court, which he does *not* want. Even though, due to technicalities in the case, it seems unlikely he would ever actually be brought to trial, he doesn't care for being viewed as blameworthy by the *Jupiter* and the likes of Dr Anticant and Mr Sentiment and appearing in this light before public opinion generally. Agonizing over the harsh judgement he faces in these quarters, he comes to wonder whether he not only *seems* to be but *is* in the wrong. Ultimately, he decides to leave the wardenship based on his own conscience (pp. 24, 112).

Bentham would approve of the operation of the Public Opinion Tribunal (functioning panoptically in the liberal sense) in spurring Mr Harding's reflections, and he would approve of his deciding for himself. Further, he would approve of his doing so in his own interest, for Mr Harding fervently desires to avoid the pain of a bad reputation and longs for a life in which he may be poorer and have to work harder but will not be reviled. As Bentham himself might have said, 'no one knows where the shoe pinches but the wearer' (p. 142). Mr Harding does not blame but justifies the bedesmen for considering their own interests, even if these might be narrowly or only partially understood (p. 178).

Instead of receiving 'Eight hundred pounds a year!—eight hundred and eighty with the house—with nothing to do' (p. 161), Mr Harding gives up Hiram's Hospital and takes on more work for less pay to support himself and his daughter. He still performs the work he loves and does best, chanting the litany in Barchester Cathedral. He still plays the violoncello. In addition, he provides parish services in a small living in the city, which he prefers to going out to Crabtree, a parish too far away to make performance of his duties there compatible with performance of his duties at the cathedral. He also refuses a richer living at Puddingdale. To take it would savour of simony (p. 173). Mr Harding is not quite sure how the monies of the Hospital should actually be appropriated and administered. But he no longer feels justified in his position, based on a new-found work ethic.

And Mr Harding's fate is not so sad. What is interesting is that living by the labour theory and Gospel brings some pleasures along with some pains. The image of the warden's garden is so attractive in the novel that this might make us respond to its loss with sadness—too much sadness. This garden stands by the London road. Mr Harding takes leave of it and symbolically takes leave of his Church privileges by travelling to London. He travels there to escape from Archdeacon Grantly and to seek out independent advice from Sir Abraham Haphazard. Grantly wants him to stand and fight for the wardenship, whereas the warden is in the process of fortifying his own determination to give it up. The scenes in London have been said to illustrate the physical and moral ugliness of the modern city, standing in contrast to lovely, old Barchester and Mr Harding's garden home.[18] True, Mr Harding is at first rather at a loss in London, an up-to-date world, urban, technological, and ungenteel. He has consulted Bradshaw's and travelled by train, and, anticipating how Grantly might follow him on the night mail or send a message by electric telegraph, he stays on the move to make himself hard to catch up with. Gentlemanly Mr Harding rides in a crowded, clattering omnibus and, unable to remain too long in the refuge of Westminster Abbey, takes again to the streets. Getting through the hours until his meeting with Sir Abraham, he is a city sightseer. He notices people, like the damp old woman on the bus who reappears at the abbey. Trollope says eating alone in a London eating-house can be melancholy, but the place turns out to be lively, too. The warden gets the hang of ordering his chop and potatoes. The chapter on this long day in London builds up to the warden's adventure at a 'cigar divan', where he learns he can take a ticket for coffee, or sherbet. 'Sherbet!' 'Why, this divan was a paradise!' Mr Harding grows comfortable enough in this unfamiliar and somewhat tawdry but peculiarly pleasing setting to read a magazine, put his feet up, dream of his violoncello, and fall asleep. 'He was absolutely enjoying himself' (pp. 148–9).

Modern-day vulgar London is not so terrible an opposite to lovely, clerical, aristocratic old Barchester and the garden. It is novel and invigorating and ultimately puts Mr Harding at his ease. It is fun. It is also a place of escape from Grantly and provides a source of other advice, while in the end Mr Harding decides for himself what to do. Announcing to Sir Abraham that he will resign his position, he stands erect as if with the help of his instrument; in a manner that is comical but full of spirit, he sweeps his right hand before him in gestures of playing. The face-off with the archdeacon is deliciously funny. It takes place over dry bits of bacon and dry toast at the London inn, a breakfast most unlike the one at Plumstead Episcopi so richly described before. Mild and meek, the warden has his way. His mastery of Bradshaw's allows him to control the situation, to escape the scene of conflict by declaring he has a train to catch. But he has really settled his business, leaving his letter of resignation to be read after his departure. Out of range of the archdeacon's harangue, he achieves a 'triumph' (p. 167).

In this novel Trollope portrays the pains of life as limited and bearable and very considerably compensated by the pleasures. He makes light of any ideal of tragic self-sacrifice, ringing changes on this theme in the comic secondary storyline of Mr Harding's daughter Eleanor. Eleanor, like her father, faces losses from the reform campaign. This is especially the case because she is in love with the leader of the cause, Mr Bold. In the wittily allusive chapter entitled 'Iphigenia' Eleanor searches for the high ground of asceticism and sacrifice of self. She resolves to give up Bold to stand by her father. In the course of her reflections she realizes that Bold may offer to withdraw charges against Mr Harding to secure his daughter's heart. This prompts a worry in Eleanor—that she may lose her chance to live up to her grand 'wish to save her father at any cost to herself' (p. 94). Trollope has a good time throughout the chapter describing her efforts to keep up the cost to herself as she seeks to direct her interchange with Bold to an Iphigenian outcome. But, poor Iphigenia, the only sacrifice she manages to make is sacrifice of her aspiration to give up all on a classical scale. As it turns out, Bold does compromise on his reform agenda to satisfy his interest in winning Eleanor, and this is in Eleanor's interest, too; it satisfies her heart. The chapter ends with a love scene and Trollope's smilingly wry last words, 'And so the altar on the shore of the modern Aulis reeked with no sacrifice' (p. 101).[19]

The warden's tale could be called one of sacrificing the easy life for a harder regime of work. And yet in the main storyline, as in the secondary love story, Trollope offers a very pleasing narrative. He bathes it in charm and humour. He is a master of comic pleasure, a confirmed anti-puritan.[20] He purveys 'pleasure . . . in the immediacy of the reading' and, in book after book, the pleasurable 'quality of quantity'.[21] It is well known that this novelist is a master-worker as well. He describes his industrious habits of writing in his *Autobiography* and how he produced his allotted pages per day, enough to amount to forty pages a week (250 words per page), before going off to his job at the post office. He maintained the routine even when travelling, for instance, noting the rigours of producing his pages when interrupted by the need to be sick while on a sea voyage. He tots up the books he wrote—forty-five and sundries—and the money he made from them—£68,939. 17*s*. 5*d*. He compares the work of a novelist to that of a common labourer. But he says it can be done well without the writer's being a slave to work. He himself did not give up 'the amusements I have loved'. By the same token he says that the writer of fiction must please and charm the reader, all the while that he preaches his sermons out of his system of ethics (pp. 302–4, 185).

Trollope's ethics do not minimize desire and its satisfactions. He speaks of the human bent to fill one's belly, put clothes on one's back, and make money. 'All material progress has come from man's desire to do the best he can for himself and those about him', and such progress has not been limited to the material realm but has made possible the progress of civilization and religion (pp. 88–9). On the ethics involved in reform of Church endowments, salaries, patronage, and sinecures, the *Autobiography* delivers a judgement against the 'evil' of 'egregious malversation' of endowed charity funds for the support of 'idle Church dignitaries', while also pointing to the evil that may arise of over-harsh and personal newspaper exposures (pp. 78–9). Himself a post office civil servant, Trollope had doubts about new proposals for choosing the best talents for the career by means of competitive exams. Yet he upholds a standard of fitness for doing the work at hand as a criterion for employment and attests that, if methods for selecting the best workers can be found, the demise of patronage will make things 'cleaner' (pp. 32–3).

Most telling to me is Trollope's preaching of a work ethic not sharply dissociated from pleasure. Here he resembles Carlyle, with his meshing of Benthamite economic labour theory and Romantic-Goethean discourses of play, vocation, and work. In economic theory, work is pain but is sometimes described with lively appreciation. Romantic play is imaginative while sometimes also material making, and full of delight. Romantic vocation emphasizes material, practical action that confirms self. And material practicality comes across in concrete terms in Goethean work. This encompasses the plodding and prosaic, the mechanical and economical, without ruling out the aerial and imaginative. The direction of Goethe's thought is to locate life's most satisfying and 'saving' moments in contemplation of its most down-to-earth work.

Stylistically, Carlyle and Trollope offer texts that are highly worked and highly entertaining. Thematically, they confirm the worth of labour, which is painful but yields satisfactions. By book's end, Mr Harding has discovered new London enjoyments and experienced a triumph in giving up his post to undertake more rightful work. He is remunerated with closer proportioning of pay to job performed, an arrangement no longer deserving of public scorn but of respect, and he feels good about it. His provision of day-to-day parish services might be called productive labour, while his chanting in the cathedral and, even more so, his performance on the violoncello might be called unproductive labour, where, indeed, work comes closer to play. The greatest value is still confirmed in value-in-use.

NOTES

1. Linking Goethe with Schiller, Richter, Fichte, and Novalis puts some strain on the Romantic label. See Vida, *Romantic Affinities*, 5–6 on both critical and accommodating remarks by Goethe on Romanticism. Scholars call phases of Goethe's work Sturm und Drang, Romanticism, and Weimar Classicism. Stuart Atkins says: 'Though not in any narrow sense a German Romantic drama, *Faust* is a drama from the Age of Romanticism'; he reads the completed *Faust* as employing Romantic form to mount a Classical critique of Romanticism (*Goethe's Faust*, 2; *Essays on Goethe*, 321). John Williams calls *Faust* I in many ways a Romantic work, though not a product of German Romanticism as such, and *Faust* II a work with Classical but also many Romantic features (*Goethe's Faust*, 25). Carlyle compares the Goethe of *Wilhelm Meister* to authors of Greece and Rome, while he notes that *Wilhelm Meister's Travels* is called a Romance ('Goethe's Works', 431; 'Goethe', 233). He observes that the 'Helena' material (ultimately part of *Faust* II) unites Classical and Romantic styles ('Goethe's Helena', 196). He dubs Goethe the Reconciler ('Goethe's Works', 434).
2. Gagnier links Marx with classical economics on labour (*Insatiability of Human Wants*, 129). Jean Baudrillard considers Marx the ally rather than critic of political economy re the labour theory of value ('Mirror of Production', 104).
3. See Gallagher re Dickens's *Our Mutual Friend* on symbolism of suspended life in commodities and money and sometimes drawing a connection to capital (*Body Economic*, 90, 97, 104, 61). However, her focus is on 'waste' that can feed new life, whereas capital, as I understand it, is something saved through abstinence rather than wasted or thrown out as without value. See Ch. 4.
4. Neff (*Carlyle and Mill*, 6); quoted in Ashton, *German Idea*, 75, citing a letter to Mrs Montegu of 17 Aug. 1828.
5. Cazamian, *Carlyle*, 275.
6. David Levy echoes others in dismissing the notion of Carlyle's knowing much about economic theory (*How the Dismal Science Got its Name*, 111). Vanden Bossche (*Carlyle and the Search for Authority*, 178 n. 6) as well as Baumgarten (in Carlyle, 'In the Margins', 109–10) and I say otherwise. Levy also dismisses the notion of reading an element of parody into 'The Nigger Question' (p. 99), although he catches Dickens's humour and himself sports a tone of humorous exaggeration. See also Ch. 1 n. 40.

7. Cazamian, *Carlyle*, chs. 1–2; Harrold intro. to *Sartor Resartus*, pp. xxxiii–xl.
8. Baumgarten finds some sarcasm in this exclamation on 'grand reform' (p. 114). I do not see why.
9. I disagree with Baudrillard ('Mirror of Production', 109) that Schiller's play aesthetic takes us to a realm beyond political economy. This misses the importance political economy places on utility, value-in-use.
10. But the play aesthetic can fulfil itself in other things; e.g., far afield from what would generally be called an artistic experience, the aesthetic can be experienced in observation of a man's fine character. Above all, the sign of the aesthetic is to be *pleased* (p. 99 n. 1).
11. Zum Augenblicke dürft ich sagen:
    'Verweile doch, du bist so schön! . . . '
    Im Vorgefühl von solchem hohen Glück
    geniess ich jetzt den höchsten Augenblick.
    Perhaps the reverberation between an anticipated moment of supreme happiness and a present such moment in that anticipation keeps us from conceiving of a single, absolute satisfaction that would put an end to striving. For striving, according to angelic pronouncement at the drama's close, is key to Faust's salvation, along with love from above (Act V, ll. 11934–41).
12. *Faust* II appeared posthumously in 1832 in vol. 41 of *Ausgabe letzter Hand*, after Carlyle had finished writing *Sartor* in 1831. Carlyle had seen the earlier published 'Helena' portion of *Faust* II and published 'Goethe's Helena' in 1828. He published 'Goethe's Works' in 1832 but here treats vol. 40 of *Ausgabe letzter Hand* as the culmination of Goethe's collected works, not addressing vol. 41 and the completed *Faust* II.
13. Chris Vanden Bossche observes what is generally overlooked, the aptness of Clothes to represent the era of the Industrial Revolution, considering that a chief product of industrialism was textiles. To my mind, he returns to more familiar interpretative ground when he links Clothes to organicism, de-links them from amoral mechanism (steam engines, Utilitarianism, laissez-faire, James Mill), and positions Carlyle in *Sartor* and elsewhere with Burke and Coleridge as an overall critic of political economy (*Carlyle*, 42–4, 10, and see 172–4). Lee Erickson observes the tie-in between industrialization of cloth and book production, since, till the mid-century, paper was made of rags, which had become newly cheap and abundant. He further observes Carlyle's interest in the cloth–paper tie-in. As he sees it, Carlyle worried about literature's cheapening through overproduction for a mass readership, often in periodical formats for fast turnover. According to *Sartor*'s Editor, one may read Teufelsdröckh's words on Clothes-as-Paper (in a passage Erickson cites in part) with 'a very mixed feeling'. But I think

such a feeling should include a sense of something 'wonderful enough', too (Erickson, *Economy of Literary Form*, 6–7, 104, 106–7; Carlyle, *Sartor*, 44–5).

14. Also see Carlyle's positive review of 'Corn-Law Rhymes' by a Sheffield metalworker (pp. 136–66).

15. On the Ecclesiastical Commission see Parry, *Rise and Fall*, 136–7; on the Select Committee and Charity Commission see Owen, *English Philanthropy*, 190–202. On cases from the 1840s and 1850s alluded to in the novel see Gilmour's introduction to *The Warden* (pp. xiv–xvi).

16. Parry, *Rise and Fall of Liberal Government*, 108–9.

17. Gilmour calls him the novel's moral touchstone and characterizes his morality as gentlemanly disinterestedness (*Idea of the Gentleman*, 163, 183–4). Nardin characterizes it as a 'common morality' that aims to wrong no man but is less intent on doing active good and does not demand great feats of benevolence. For Nardin, the novel's morality is Stoic–Hebrew–Christian (*Trollope and Victorian Moral Philosophy*, 5, 9, 16, 10). Kucich thinks *The Warden* expresses more sympathy for Mr Harding as a victim of social change than for victims of the established regime (*Power of Lies*, 78). While Durey finds Trollope to be generally quite critical of Church patronage, she thinks *The Warden* tips the scales to favour the Church and the warden's claim to his position by making Mr Harding a kindly old man missed by his wards when he's gone (*Trollope and the Church of England*, 43, 48, 79, 166). Blumberg positions Trollope ethically apart from both self-sacrificing evangelical Christianity and egoistic, individualist consumer capitalism ('"Unnatural Self-Sacrifice"', 507, 512–14), in that he especially values mutuality of enjoyment. From this perspective *The Warden* critiques the warden's sacrifice of his position, ending pleasures he and his wards had shared. Blumberg does not take up issues re Church reform, where conflicts of interest would not be so easily resolved and mutuality would be rather hard to come by. McDermott goes against the prevailing trend, locating the novel's values in the warden's 'radicalized conscience', which prompts him to resign in service to modernization of social institutions, peace, and justice. McDermott's focus is a feminine aspect of heroism in the warden's empathy for the bedesmen, i.e., not wanting to treat them unfairly ('New Womanly Man', 79, 85, 87).

18. Polhemus, *Changing World of Anthony Trollope*, 30.

19. See Blumberg, '"Unnatural Self-Sacrifice"', 531 for more on the satirical treatment of Eleanor's yen for self-sacrifice.

20. Herbert, *Trollope and Comic Pleasure*; Polhemus, *Changing World*, 246.

21. Crosby, '"A Taste for More"', 301, 294.

4

Pains—Capital versus the Gift
in *The Mill on the Floss*

There is another pain to reckon with besides the pain of work in Utilitarian political economy. That is the pain of capital savings for investment. Max Weber has familiarized us with the idea of a puritanical spirit in capitalism. He speaks of the capitalist's avoidance of spontaneous enjoyment and lack of any hedonist admixture (*Protestant Ethic*, 53). (We might think once again of the 'dismal science'.) Weber points not so much to a capitalist commitment to hard work—while that is there—but to a drive to accumulate what is produced. His words suggest a judgement against the life purpose of the capitalist 'to sink into the grave weighted down with a great material load of money and goods' (p. 72). I think Weber misses a great deal in overlooking the fundamental pleasure principle of Utilitarian political economy, but he is not wrong to observe the importance of pain in the theory.

The starting point for my reading of *The Mill on the Floss* is an audit of Mr Tulliver's accounts, with an eye to his discrepant accounting between loans and gifts. Loans are governed by an economics of capital that George Eliot sets in contrast to a pre-capitalist economics of the gift. Pain functions in both cases, but in very different relations to pleasure.

The novel's action takes place in the latter 1820s–30s, when capitalism was actively layering onto a still persistent older system. But a demarcation clear in theory may easily be lost sight of, and characters in *The Mill on the Floss* sometimes operate according to the older, sometimes the newer economics, without heeding the difference. Indeed, Mr Tulliver's confusion over money signals troubles to follow. The storyline, as it moves across two generations, may seem loose or disjointed, and the ending has struck many readers as problematic. But attention to economic transactions not usually looked at reveals a compelling narrative logic. This links the fatal financial ruin of Tulliver Sr to the fate of his children, which seems so different—the sister's leaving her lover, cleaving to her brother, and dying with him seeking to save him from a flood.[1]

Before proceeding to Mr Tulliver's accounts and their implications for his children, I will outline fundamentals of capital and its investment, as in loans, and fundamentals of gift-exchange. I will distinguish principles of pain relative to pleasure that operate in the two systems and generate their characteristic social structures, noting matters of class and gender also important in *The Mill on the Floss*.

CAPITAL VERSUS THE GIFT

Within capitalist theory, capital is a stock of the products of former labour. It is labour fixed and embodied in forms capable of being stored or accumulated. So says Mill in *The Principles of Political Economy* (ii. 55), and in *Capital* Marx gives graphic imagery for the 'embodiment' of labour as capital that can be stored or accumulated (pp. 109, 86, 140, 117, 129, 32, 143, 145, and see Mill, ii. 48). Whether in products, money, credit, or literally embodied human capital of productive power in reserve (Mill, ii. 49), accumulation derives from saving. Capital is the result of saving, says Mill (ii. 68). It is increased by parsimony, says Smith in *The Wealth of Nations* (i. 337). To save is to give up, to go without. It involves the pain of forgone pleasures of consumption.

Here I will instance a corollary in Malthus's *Essay on the Principle of Population* applying economic theory to sexual relations. Malthus presses the idea of 'moral restraint', meaning sexual giving up or going without (1803 edn., 207–16). However, painful privation is not justified in itself but only as it serves ultimate gain in a theory that, above all, validates self-interest, value-in-use, utility. Thus Malthus acknowledges the pleasures of passion (1798 edn., 146–7), and by his lights consummation is not to be indefinitely forgone. This means delay of marriage to limit family size for reasons allied to those for saving, but there is to be ultimate advantage reaped in more prosperous, happier married life.

Just so, mere painful restraint in the form of hoarding is not enough for the capitalist. There must be investment for capital to function as capital (Mill ii. 73–4). An investment such as lending capital, just like saving it, involves giving up or going without; present pleasures of consumption are still forgone. However, lending is a giving up or going without to get more back, to procure pleasures ultimately in excess of pains incurred. Capital, past labour power embodied, stored up, joins with the present power of labour for new production. With investment, consumption resumes. In the short term workers consume the capital that pays them to work; in the longer term the capitalist enjoys profitable return for present giving up or going without. The capitalist receives this return because he or she invests in productive labour, distinguished in the theory from unproductive labour. Goods produced must be of utility to consumers for these goods to sell and keep the worker on the payroll and the capitalist in profit. By this capitalist rationale, consumers are to be gainers, too.

In the whole scheme each self is theorized to have its interests, these being as important for any one person as for any other. In this sense the theory supports equality of persons. It follows that clear contracts and accounting are called for in capital exchanges. Each party is to be able to recognize its self-interest at any given moment and to secure the terms for tracking and realizing it over time. This is very much to the point for interest-bearing loans.

The economics of gift-exchange is decidedly pre-capitalist, indeed archaic, as set forth by Marcel Mauss in his classic study *The Gift*. At the same time Mauss and other theorists such as Pierre Bourdieu acknowledge some continuity of formerly widespread gift-economies only partially overlaid by newer capitalism. As Mauss makes clear in discussing aboriginal tribes and their practices of potlatch, such regimes are characteristically aristocratic—hierarchical in social structure (p. 63). By the same token, they are characteristically male-dominated. Mauss tells us that women, as well as children, wealth, feasts, rituals, entertainments, and courtesies frequently *are* the gifts (pp. 3–4). This is in contrast to the theoretical equality of persons in capitalism.

Like capital, the gift depends on accumulation, accomplished by giving up, going without—by saving. But the accumulation is not to be invested—loaned. It is to be given away. The giving up and going without of saving leads to a next step of painful sacrifice in the rendered-up gift.

The gift is to display disinterested generosity rather than calculated self-interest in expectation of a later, larger return, like return on a loan.

However, Mauss, Bourdieu, and others stress that interest is, in fact, at work in this display of disinterestedness. Lavish giving attaches prestige, rank, and credit to the giver, creating an obligation in the receiver to give back gifts of even greater worth at a later point and to remain under obligation during the interim. During that interim the gift-receiver remains in a subordinate position in a hierarchy, perhaps never to rise above that level if unable to return the gift in full measure and good time. While self-interest is crucially involved in the system, it is also crucial that the gift-giver cannot contract to secure and set a date for receiving a return on the gift because that return itself, to release the receiver from humbling obligation, must allow for a display of unselfish giving that answers and exceeds the one that prompted it.

In one of Bourdieu's examples, clansmen, recipients of largess from their family head and patron, are retained in a not sharply delimited obligation to perform services at a later time. Particularly important is their obligation to provide labour at harvest time. Meanwhile they 'give back' by ritual 'visiting the fields'. This is unproductive labour from a capitalist perspective. While the system has its material economic rationale, the rationalization is not maximal, for it does not distinguish unproductive from productive labour nor maximize the latter for the benefit of consumption all around ('Symbolic Capital', 116–19).

Besides exemplifying an element of material economic self-interest in gift-giving that on the face of it seems self-denying in its generosity towards others, Bourdieu's example illustrates an element of inefficiency, waste, or failure to maximize utility through the sponsoring of unproductive labour. The example also illustrates what Mauss calls 'formal pretense and social deception' (p. 1) and Bourdieu calls 'misrecognition' in a gift economy (p. 118). That is, the system masks the economic by casting the initial patronage as freely and selflessly given and the payback likewise, especially as it largely takes the form of ritual performance rather than harvest work of evident material benefit.

Thus an economics of the gift eschews sharply distinguishing between free giving and giving that creates obligation, but that of capital investment aims to do so, by strict accounting.[2] But economic like other social relations evolve with overlays of practices and mentalities. Bourdieu is very apt at illustrating uneasy moments when different economic systems are revealed and what was misrecognized in terms of one comes into recognition in terms of another. He gives the example of a mid-twentieth-century North African mason who has learned new ways in Europe and scandalizes his traditional employers back home by requesting cash added to his wages in lieu of the gift of a free lunch.

In *The Mill on the Floss* there are such uneasy moments that reveal usually unheeded distinctions between economic systems. The novel points to a considerable persistence of gift-exchange in cross-class transactions and a still greater persistence in transactions between the sexes.[3] It makes evident the resemblance yet deep difference in the functioning of pain and pleasure in gift-giving compared to capital transfers like lending, though this difference tends to escape notice—a cause of confusion that may lead to tragedy.

MR TULLIVER'S TRAGEDY: MISRECOGNIZING LOANS AND GIFTS

Eliot says an insignificant miller may be a tragic figure, just as she casts Maggie's problems, even when she is a little girl, in terms of tragedy. Eliot alludes to *Hamlet* to make the wry point that her young protagonists might not have done so badly, as Hamlet might not, if their respective fathers had lived to a good old age (p. 353). This draws us to consider Mr Tulliver's tragedy as one leading to Maggie's and Tom's. And Mr Tulliver's ruin is financial. So . . . let us get to an audit.

What we find is that Mr Tulliver does not keep his accounts very well, for in some sense he does not know how much money he has. Tom, like others in the town of St Ogg's, has believed Mr Tulliver to be a man with funds in reserve, owner of farmland and a mill for flour and malt, able to afford an expensive education for his son, to hire lawyers to protect his mill's water rights, and to live well. Mr Tulliver, however, may be said to suffer from economic misrecognition. This takes the form of discrepant accounting between loans and gifts, as becomes very evident in the confusion left behind after his death about whether the £300 he provided to help his sister, Mrs Moss, was lent or given.

This confusion is a consequence of prior confusions. Mr Tulliver has inherited 'his own mill' and land and lived at a rate of outlay proportioned to 'his' capital, leaving out of account the £1,000 dowry owing to his sister at the time of her marriage. To pay this he has taken out a £2,000 mortgage. The small hold this has on his attention shows in his almost forgetting about it between the half-yearly calls for payment. Mr Tulliver operates according to a gender-based presumption of economic advantage, rather like young Tom's when he says to Maggie, 'I've got a great deal more money than you, because I'm a boy' (p. 31). True, Mr Tulliver's equity in the property must be worth more than the £1,000 apportioned to his sister. But he acts as if her receipt of capital does not exactly subtract from his. Rather, the demand on him is for kind-heartedness and willingness to give her help, at his discretion (she having married an unsuccessful farmer, while the pair have eight children). Help means a loan to Mr Moss on Mrs Moss's behalf. When financially pressed himself, Mr Tulliver decides to call in his money. But he does not end up doing so because he discovers that in his mind, if not on paper, the loan is more properly a gift. This actually remains vague to him, for the loan only gets definitely recognized as a gift after Mr Tulliver's death, when his family figures out what he must have intended and destroys the promissory note.

With regard to a sister, Mr Tulliver retains a notion of gift-giving, of taking care of her, because he is thinking of his own daughter Maggie and wants his son Tom, in turn, to take care of *his* sister. Such reflections bring a moment of recognition to Mr Tulliver, economically speaking. But Eliot shows the usual subconsciousness or intermittency of his thinking on the matter. By his peculiar reckoning, he both has and does not have the £300 of the loan/gift. I would say the same for his having and not having the £1,000 from the all-but-forgotten mortgage that funded his sister's dowry. Mr Tulliver customarily feels better off than he is. He is not very parsimonious, not a careful saver or investor. He sends Tom to Mr Stelling's school at a cost of some £100 and threatens to go to law against Dix over water and does go to law against Pivart, braving the formidable legal adversary Wakem. He stands surety for a £250 loan to Mr Riley, putting up personal household property that his wife brought into the marriage. He owes £50 that the hired man Luke put into his business. There is the £2,000 mortgage. Plus a £500 loan from his sister-in-law Mrs Glegg.

Mr Tulliver particularly resents criticism of his money management from Mrs Glegg. He rebels against feeling beholden to her. Money from his sister-in-law to him is not like money from him to his sister. There is discussion at the family dinner table of its status as a loan, not a gift, for it bears interest. This shows the likeness yet difference between forms of money transfer. But Mr Tulliver again blurs the distinction, especially where gender is involved. The money feels to him too much like a favour. Such a favour bothers him more than the mortgage, which does not put him under obligation to a sister-in-law. As gift theory tells us, gift or favour in its very generosity implies hierarchy and subordinates the receiver so long as he has not made return, or cannot, or not soon or generously enough. It is harder to delimit the time-frame and scale of obligation for a gift than a loan and harder to liquidate the obligation. Mr Tulliver baulks at feeling beholden not only to Mrs Glegg but to a whole Dodson family of sisters, 'a whole litter of women' (p. 66). He wants to feel he takes 'no gift or favour' (p. 172) from that quarter. It is precisely this episode that occasions Eliot's passage on the tragedy that may befall an ordinary miller.

Vis-à-vis sisters Mr Tulliver is especially prone to operate on the basis of gift-exchange. He compromises his solvency by misrecognizing gift as loan to his sister and loan as gift from his sister-in-law. He pays in Mrs Glegg's money, gets a less flexible creditor, and ultimately, when he loses his court case and must pay costs,[4] faces claims for more than £500, over and above loss of the mill and land and the personal property put up as security. He falls under heavy debt to many creditors.

His greatest desire is to be able to pay off these creditors. He commits himself and his family to endure painful privations in order to save. This shows him shifting to a capitalist stance. But he is ensnared in an economics of the gift. He is least able to clear the account precisely where he receives most favour. The favour is from Wakem, the new owner of the mill, who allows Mr Tulliver to remain living there. Here we see gift-giving between men in a relation of advantage and disadvantage, rather than between the sexes, not the only time Eliot associates the two sorts of gift-exchange. In this example she lays bare a dynamics in the giving and receiving of charity that is troubling when directly recognized, ill-adapted and destructive in a capitalist context. Wakem's explicit intention is to exercise charity as a means to humiliate a man who has been loud-mouthed against him. This is not lost on Mr Tulliver. Though with Tom's earnings, painstakingly saved, he has begun to look forward to a day when he might settle his debts like a good capitalist, he can conceive of no such settlement with the lawyer, his overbearing patron. He dies of his resentment. He suffers his fatal stroke attacking Wakem. Eliot ends Mr Tulliver's tragedy with overt violence over gift patronage between men in a social hierarchy, but the tragedy's source and its repercussions trace to relations of gift and favour involving women.

LENDING AND BORROWING: MRS GLEGG, BOB, AND TOM

In the matter of the loan, Mrs Glegg keeps her eye on self-interest and interest payable and hardly thinks like a sister. She thinks like her husband, who holds 'no opinion of transactions where folks do things for nothing' (p. 277). She does not like to 'give' anything but advice (a witticism of Mr Tulliver's; p. 63). She does not fancy her husband's giving away her money either, as she charges him with doing in an interchange concerning financing for Tom's schemes to restore the family fortunes. Mrs Glegg came by her money by bequest from her father and certainly likes to think of it as her own. She has carefully saved and invested it as capital to accumulate more capital. Her sisters, on the other hand, only express satisfaction in personal ownership when it comes to the china and linens they brought with them when they married. They have no capitalist visions of building up more from what they have. Legally speaking, Mrs Tulliver has no actual grasp on such possessions, as we see when her husband disposes of them as he sees fit in his own financial dealings. By the same token, Mrs Glegg's capital is only hers through the generosity of her husband, given the period of the novel—years before the 1882 Married Women's Property Act that empowered wives to possess property and enter into contracts, thus to save, invest, borrow, lend, profit. That is why Mrs Glegg resents the idea of her husband's 'letting' her keep her money and reminds him how mean it would look to take back a gift, should he decide on an outlay of funds he only 'pretended to leave at my own disposal' (p. 187).

Mrs Glegg goes against the gender norm in her society. For all their sparring, the Gleggs actually get on very well because they mostly see eye to eye economically. Mr Glegg enjoys a comfortable retirement from his prosperous business as a wool-stapler, cultivates his garden, and considers his wife a paragon, though she can be sharp-tongued in defending her own interest. As her sister says, Mrs Glegg sees into men's business. She is a far more consistent capitalist than her brother-in-law.

She saves. Indeed, she hoards when she sequesters valuable silk gowns in the clothes-chest, from which they emerge later in order of antiquity to be worn spotted with mould. This shows self-denying parsimony but is not in the full sense a capitalist practice. The accumulation only loses value over time rather than increasing in value by going forth to be consumed by labourers who create new goods by productive labour, to the benefit of themselves, the investor, and the consumer. Mrs Glegg does better with her capital when she loans it out at interest. She likes to get her 5 per cent, even from her problem brother-in-law; so she does not call her money in even after the dinner-table spat. She is pleased to earn a high rate of 6–7 per cent on an unsecured loan to Tom when he begins to invest in Laceham textile goods to be peddled by Bob Jakin.

Critics seldom talk about the chapters on business featuring Mrs Glegg.[5] These chapters also frequently feature Bob, a rustic lad who is bettering his condition by saving and investing in pack-goods with the 10 sovereign capital first received as reward for dousing a mill fire. Later he is a householder renting out lodgings. And these chapters feature Tom, who shows himself to be a true nephew of Mrs Glegg by parsimoniously saving his earnings from his warehouse job with Guest and Co. after his father's bankruptcy, and borrowing more from his aunt to invest in marketing textiles via Bob. He prefers to advance in his work for the Guest firm not by gaining a higher salary but a share, or capital holding. His object is to pay off his father's debts and finally to buy back the mill, and in the course of the novel he makes considerable progress towards this end. The novel places Tom among other characters who are bettering their conditions. Mr Deane rises to become the best off of Tom and Maggie's uncles, a substantial holder in Guest and Co. The Guest family's successful mill-owning, ship-owning, and commercial activities prepare the son, Stephen Guest, to aspire to election to Parliament.

But, of course, success eludes Tom, as it does his sister, and the second generation, like the first, comes to grief. Mr Tulliver came to grief between an economics of capital and of the gift. His children seek recovery according to economic mentalities and practices that initially seem not so entirely different but ultimately stand in conflict. Tom, as capitalist, has a strong appetite for pleasure and looks forward to living well some day, but meanwhile exercises abstinence and self-denial to save and invest (pp. 272, 427). Saving and investing mean giving up, going without. In this he compares to Maggie, who has a 'hunger of the heart' (p. 34) for many things but exercises abstinence and self-denial. She too gives up, goes without. But not like any capitalist.

PHILIP

For purposes of further commentary on Maggie and Tom, it is worth turning attention to their friend Philip Wakem. In the symbolism of the novel Eliot employs an elaborate figural doubling, and Philip often serves as a stand-in for one sibling or the other. Eliot brings sister and brother into near likeness to set a mark for measuring how far they also diverge from each other.

Philip doubles Maggie through the lameness that gives him psychological experience of disadvantage, so that he is repeatedly called 'like a girl' (pp. 152, 375). Also, as a cripple he has not been raised to business, again being 'like a girl' (p. 370). But in a different manner he doubles Tom. During schooldays he is the surrogate brother who cares for Maggie when her actual brother does not. Through a yet more complex configuration, the doubling with the sister allows for another sort of doubling with the brother. At least in the short term Tom is brought together with Maggie by being brought together with Philip in disadvantage. While with Mr Stelling, the hearty Tom suffers an injury to his foot that makes him share Philip's experience of lameness. The two are quite close during this period. And this disability symbolizes Tom's more general experience of disadvantage at school, where his poor performance as a student undermines his usual boyish self-assurance so that he feels more than ever before in his life 'like a girl' (pp. 124, 125). This makes him rather generous. He even 'sacrifices' a treasure of some percussion-caps in a gift to the schoolmaster's little girl to amuse her and make her his playfellow, as he misses Maggie. But Tom, when he is grown, does not remain close to a feminine position and mentality. Thus to face his hard times Tom makes painful 'sacrifices' according to a capitalist economics of saving—tied to lending, borrowing, paying off debt—but not, like a girl, according to gift-exchange.

GIFT-GIVING: ST OGG, PHILIP, TOM, AND MAGGIE

Symbolically in the novel, the legend of St Ogg is of great significance, and Philip figures here again, along with Tom and Maggie. St Ogg, namesake for the town, is the saintly boatman who ventures onto the water even in flood time, and multiple allusions to his legend foreshadow the flood that ends *The Mill on the Floss*. In my perspective St Ogg's is a legend about giving.

St Ogg meets needs whatever they are. He gives one what one wants not as due or desert but as kindly favour, charity, or gift. The legend tells how St Ogg satisfies a woman's craving to be rowed with her child across the river though the wind and water are very high (pp. 102–3). This is unwise; in fact, men say it is a 'foolish' desire. St Ogg does not deny the folly but overlooks it to satisfy 'the heart's need'. In the legend this produces a miracle of salvation and a vision of the woman with her child as the Blessed Virgin to serve as an image of hope in future times of flood. Eliot emphasizes the pure gift in St Ogg's action by making the claim for receiving it so weak and doubtful. The saint gives the woman more than she should ask for according to the judgement of ordinary discretion. He bestows a lavish favour.

St Ogg makes an important appearance in a dream of Maggie's which also features Philip and Tom (pp. 412–13). The dream pictures St Ogg in a boat with the Virgin on the wide water. The images change, and Maggie sees Philip and Lucy as boatman and Virgin; then Philip's image as St Ogg turns into Tom's image as St Ogg. From a boat carrying herself and her lover Stephen, Maggie calls out and stretches out her hands to Tom/Ogg, who rows past without looking. The meaning I take is that Philip/Ogg can only offer Maggie so much of what she ultimately wants from her brother/Ogg. What she wants is very much—it is like the gift of the saint. Tom does not have that much to give. And Maggie's own wanting sinks her. In the dream it is her movement to reach out to Tom/Ogg that overturns her boat. She feels herself going down.

The dream foreshadows the novel's ending in which Maggie reaches out to her beloved, estranged brother. Wanting to be given very much, one must also give very much. At the risk of her life she rows out to Tom on the flooded Floss. Now she is the saint, she is the gift-giver. This is at the same time that she is the woman with 'heart's need'—for gifts of admiration and love—with what Eliot calls a 'peremptory' and one might more unflatteringly (or dyslogistically) call an unwise or 'foolishly' peremptory 'hunger of the heart'. Hers is a 'hungry nature' with 'illimitable wants'. She wants 'too much'. She longs for 'indulgence' from people like those she has read of in books who would be 'delighted to do things that made one happy' (pp. 338, 286, 269, 205).

At one point Eliot casts a sceptical light on Maggie's relation to the saint through Philip's jibe about her 'selling her soul to that ghostly boatman' (p. 403). She and Tom do have a final moment when their childish bond is reaffirmed, but Maggie does not survive the flood nor rescue her brother. Their drowning suggests not salvation but a heavy cost and perhaps a judgement on a devil's bargain in looking for gifts from St Ogg.

GIFT-GIVING: MR TULLIVER, MAGGIE, TOM, AND BOB

Maggie is positioned in large part by her sex to be a receiver and giver of gifts. When she was a little girl her father 'took her part' (p. 60) no matter what, covering all and sundry misdemeanours, from letting Tom's rabbits die and cutting off her hair to pushing cousin Lucy into the mud and running away from home. Mr Tulliver's attitude reflects his half-recognized special conception of economic relations with girl or woman. He is to take care of Maggie, just as he is to take care of his sister through the loan that is more truly a gift, and (as Mr Tulliver would have it) just as Tom is to take care of *his* sister.

Maggie as a girl is positioned to give gifts as well as receive them and to make sure that Tom as a boy gets more than his share in return. Take, for example, the great jam-puff exchange. Maggie is described as full of enjoyment of her part of the puff. Tom has to watch her finish eating it after his part is already devoured. (We may think of Bentham's precept that the children who have eaten their cake are the natural enemies of those who have theirs.) Tom shifts in his mind from one economics of equal and fair division with no gift or favour to another based on the presumption that he should be rewarded for a fairness that has been, in fact, a generous gift on his part—he should be given the jammier portion because he did not demand it. Thus he considers Maggie greedy for not being generous. Eliot remarks that by this reasoning Maggie falls short in 'sacrifice'. Maggie laments, too late, that she would have been glad for Tom to have what he wanted, if this would have made him pleased with her and won his favour. She, too, shifts in her mind to the economics of gift-exchange.

This episode is directly followed by another like it. The two illustrate how class difference works something like gender difference in positioning people economically. Eliot describes a boyhood tussle over money and a gift between Tom and Bob. Tom declares himself winner of a coin toss based on a charge that Bob has cheated, and he uses physical force to back up his status as 'master' and to claim the halfpenny. He will not just take the coin but makes Bob give it to him. Then when Bob angrily throws it down, Tom does not pick it up but lets it lie. It becomes a tribute spurned, leaving him in mastery. This is especially the case because Bob has been shown up as failing in generosity—he did not help Tom be the winner he thinks he should be. Tom, on the other hand, has previously demonstrated generosity by giving Bob a knife. Bob tries to give the knife back, but Tom will not take it. Again Tom prevails as the giver of a gift that has not yet been matched or exceeded in return. Bob does not have the fortitude to actually give up the knife and go without it. After throwing it away he returns to retrieve it. He fails in the self-sacrifice that links to generosity in the economics of gift-exchange. The power dynamics of social hierarchy are brilliantly displayed here. Bob is not quits as he would be upon a capitalist basis. He is not quits as Mr Tulliver and Tom seek to be with their creditors after the bankruptcy, by paying off loans with due interest. He is not quits as Mr Tulliver is not in suffering under a sense of 'generous' patronage from Wakem that he cannot pay off.

At other points Bob is a gift-giver, as he has been a receiver. In the early days of Maggie's and Tom's poverty he presents Maggie with books and offers Tom money. Characteristically, the sister accepts, the brother does not. Tom says, 'I don't want to take anything from anybody, but to work my own way' (p. 211). In the course of the novel master and man shift largely from gift to capitalist relations whereby Tom and Bob are partners in selling Laceham goods. Bob remains ready to offer special help, but Tom, like the Gleggs, fends off any imputation of being in receipt of favour. They will not let Bob sacrifice himself for them. They insist on his having his percentage. Tom moves relations with Bob onto the same ground as he prefers for his relations with his aunts and uncles. Whereas Maggie thinks the family should be generous in their financial aid, Tom does not want to be beholden to them. These examples show that the gift economics that persists to an extent in class relations is more likely to do so in gender relations.

THE ECONOMY OF HUMAN LIFE VERSUS THE IMITATION OF CHRIST

Maggie receives instruction in gift-exchange, beyond what she learned in the jam-puff episode, from her gift-book from Bob, St Thomas à Kempis's *The Imitation of Christ*. à Kempis's little book is quite different from another of Bob's gift-books and marks once again a difference in economic systems. The gift-book Maggie does *not* prefer is entitled *The Economy of Human Life*.

The Economy of Human Life is a once-popular advice book cast as a letter dated 1749 from Pekin and purporting to offer a translation of an ancient Indian manuscript.[6] Pre-Smith in provenance, it is in no direct sense a tract of Utilitarian political economy. But its short, bland homilies on Emulation, Prudence, Contentment, Temperance, Hope and Fear, Desire and Love, Joy and Grief, Rich and Poor, Masters and Servants, Woman, Father, Husband, Brother promote self-confident pursuit of worldly success, cost–benefit analysis, frugality and prudence in saving and investment, reasonable profit in selling, payment of debts. From these one may expect personal, marital, and family prosperity and happiness, along with social improvement, all testifying to virtue and godliness. The god who is referenced is non-Christian, and the principles of *The Economy of Human Life* belong in a general way with those in the tradition of Bentham and Smith. There is parsimony, saving: 'Use not today what tomorrow may want.' Also: 'Let not thy recreations be expensive, lest the pain of purchasing them exceed the pleasure thou hast in their enjoyment.' All wishes will not be met, 'yet for all reasonable desires, for all honest endeavours, [the Eternal's] benevolence hath established, in the nature of things, a probability of success.' But 'if thou despairest of success, thou shalt not succeed'. Undue melancholy and gloom should be avoided, as well as jollity and riotous mirth. 'The improvement of arts is [the wise man's] delight, and their utility to the public crowneth him with honour' (pp. 30–1, 34, 43, 47, 74). These teachings are oriented towards men, for instance designating the child of the Father as the son. Under Woman, as well as under Masters and Servants, we hear of submission, obedience, and gratitude. Still, the Husband is told to share pleasures as well as cares with the Wife and told that she too has inclinations to satisfy (p. 64). There is not much here for Maggie, though Mrs Glegg, Bob, or Tom might well approve of *The Economy of Human Life*.

à Kempis's *Imitation of Christ* is Maggie's preference. This too is an advice book, of course better known and greater as a text, while easily enough made to yield simple maxims. There is appeal to the feminine in such Christian doctrine, though *The Imitation of Christ* speaks in as masculine a language as *The Economy of Human Life*, for instance calling upon the faithful 'manfully' to bear the cross (p. 87). Maggie learns of pain and suffering, sorrow, humility, resignation of self-love, renunciation, and self-mortification. Happiness is to be found nowhere in this world without turning to God, so that worldly desires and ambitions, the needs of the body, riches, and material things and pleasures are to be given up. 'Despise . . . every temptation to please others or yourself' (pp. 137–8). Even human love is of scant importance. Affections are to be mortified, and one should be ready to 'forego all human companionship' (p. 148). à Kempis's programme for monastic self-discipline suggests chastity, or erotic self-denial, along with every other kind.

à Kempis cites many biblical texts, and among them St Paul looms large. The monk's teachings would, in Bentham's perspective, provide a perfect illustration of the takeover of Christian morality by Pauline asceticism. While Weber associates capitalism with a puritanical Protestant spirit, Bentham would disagree. He dissociates capitalist Utilitarianism and political economy from Paul, if not Jesus. Eliot calls the capitalist saving, investing, profit-making, and prosperity-enjoying philosophy of the town of St Ogg's—as seen in the Gleggs—almost semi-pagan. Though it might be referred to as Protestant, she suggests that it is hardly Christian at all. It teaches some painful giving up for purposes of ultimate utility but hardly, like à Kempis, teaches imitation of the man on the cross.

à Kempis's principles belong with those of gift-exchange, for all things, even love, even life, are to be forgone, given up, given away, given back, in return for Christ's sacrifice, which is His gift of grace and gives salvation. The magnitude of His giving demands return without limit: 'you must give all for All' (p. 130).

MAGGIE'S TRAGEDY: GIVING ALL FOR ALL

Based on a Christian and feminine economics of the gift Maggie chooses first erotic sacrifice, then sacrifice of life itself. Eliot's description of Maggie's and Stephen's physical desire struck readers in the period as highly charged.[7] Stephen cannot take his eyes off Maggie's voluptuous bare arm. Maggie experiences heightened bodily awareness of Stephen's proximity: 'no distinct thought—only the sense of a presence like that of a closely-hovering broad-winged bird in the darkness' (p. 356). Through Philip's jealous point of view the reader perceives the sexual current. Meeting in a waterborne tryst, the lovers are literally carried away.

Yet, of course, Maggie reverses course, and Eliot shows how close to unwise or 'foolish' this is, for all the fervour and courage of her choice to give up her lover and return home. Here Maggie compares to the woman who craved to be ferried by St Ogg on high water though men advised against it. Eliot subjects such action to very mixed judgement.

There would be some betrayal of Lucy had Maggie chosen to stay with Stephen, given the prior courtship between her cousin and her lover. But their understanding is described as having been rather conventional and shallow, it was never formally declared, and Lucy proves capable of forgiveness. Stephen insists that the true love is between himself and Maggie and that their happiness is just as important as other people's. By the same token he insists that their unhappiness is just as important. With Maggie's return, unhappiness is assured all around. With regard to Maggie's sense of duty to return for Philip's sake, many details indicate that no real passion or strong obligation binds her here to make disappointing Philip a betrayal. He ultimately says so himself. Maggie actually agrees with Tom that marriage would be 'out of the question' (p. 340) to the son of the family enemy Wakem. She has been half relieved, in fact, to have this family opposition to a relationship that she herself does not desire at a sexual level (p. 306). To please

Tom and to be loved by him is her deepest wish, for him, like their father, to take her part, to be indulgent, to be her St Ogg and give her what her heart craves. Her oldest memory is of the two of them together on the banks of the Floss.

There is irony in Maggie's leaving Stephen to return to St Ogg's for Philip's sake since Tom objects to Philip for at least partly compelling reasons, making loyalty to Philip disloyalty to Tom. But there is another irony that makes a return to Philip a return to Tom. After all, since schooldays Philip has functioned in one of his figurations as surrogate brother. Strengthening this symbolism is Philip as St Ogg shape-changing to become Tom as St Ogg in Maggie's dream. This dream is the immediate spur for Maggie's resolution to go back home. There she becomes a would-be St Ogg herself, rowing out on flood waters on a charitable mission to her brother.

Bear in mind the complicated symbolism that makes Philip double Maggie, double Tom, and double St Ogg. Philip is like Maggie in being like a girl. He is like Tom in being like a brother. He is like Tom when Tom is like Maggie in being like a girl. He is like Tom when Tom is like St Ogg. He is like Maggie when she is like Tom and she, too, is like St Ogg. And in one more doubling, he is like Tom and Maggie in *not* being like St Ogg, *not* a bestower of kind gifts, *not* a saviour.

Philip is not so very saintly and generous. He is an important proponent in the novel of self-interest and seeking the pleasures one can. That is why he actively, rather aggressively, insinuatingly, and unscrupulously pursues Maggie. He involves her in clandestine meetings that she is not sure are right and encourages a sense of obligation to him beyond what is justified by her childish promises. He has a hunger to 'snatch an offered joy'. Eliot does not condemn this but expresses rueful understanding. 'Do not think too hardly of Philip' (pp. 290–1). She takes an ironic tone about the common expectation that disadvantaged people will have unusual virtues and forgo wanting what may be hard for them to get. She denies that privations are necessarily good for people. They remain privations and may well result in distortions rather than transcendence of self-interest.

Philip is the one who teases Maggie about something devilish rather than saintly in a pact with St Ogg. Just so, as anti-St Ogg, he is the great critic of lessons Maggie draws from St Thomas à Kempis. He calls her self-sacrifice cowardly negation, induced stupefaction.

He decries 'narrow asceticism' as a perversion, a mutilation, a 'long suicide' (pp. 288–9, 363, 269).

Another, more minor character interprets Maggie's case in a similar manner. This is Dr Kenn, a voice of mature, calm, if cool, benevolence. He is not one of the 'men of maxims', exponents of merely conventional thinking. Yet would he stand so far apart from all who distinguish folly from wisdom in the legend of St Ogg? He admires Maggie's efforts to do what's best by coming home. But he pretty much judges that she has done the opposite. The most satisfactory resolution for her—or, in a Bentham/Smith-style calculation the least unsatisfactory—would not be to stay in St Ogg's but to go away, take a job, and in due course fulfil her passion and marry Stephen (pp. 436–8). These actions would involve some privation, for Maggie dislikes being a teacher and doesn't want to leave her birthplace and feel she has been a cause of trouble to the people of her past. Yet she would be making a living by her pains and might find her way in the end to happiness and prosperity in marriage back in town.

Eliot makes it clear that the world and the world's wife would come around to accept a marriage between Maggie and Stephen, whatever moral lapses preceded it. Then too, Mrs Glegg doesn't reject Maggie, but backs her. She launches a campaign to combat tales against her niece's reputation. She has resources and makes a point of keeping Maggie in her will to maintain her 'life-long regard to equity in money matters' (p. 439). Surely Stephen as a husband would be far less likely to pain Tom than Philip would. Neither Lucy nor Philip holds out in condemning Maggie. But none of these indicators of accommodation catches Maggie's imagination. She does not choose some measure of unhappiness to gain some greater measure of happiness.

She knows how much people want because she knows how much she wants, and, wanting so much, she cannot bear to think of anyone's getting less than all. She cannot bear to think that her pleasure should come at the cost of others' pain, nor that her pleasure must be less than complete because of this. She refuses to tally up costs with benefits to work out net utility, to recognize that giving one man his dinner may mean taking away another man's breakfast (p. 192). This is a saying of Mr Glegg's apropos of clarifying the debt situation left so confused by Mr Tulliver. There is a similarity between Maggie's thinking and her father's even though he engages in money matters that seem remote from her concern. But I believe we observe the similarity in observing that the daughter, like the father—though in his case only sometimes—does not think like a Utilitarian political economist.

Mr Tulliver's and Maggie's—and Tom's—tragedies interrelate. Mr Tulliver is confused about how much savings he has at his disposal when it comes to the imperative to give to a sister and not to receive from a sister-in-law. He treats the loan/gift to Mrs Moss as if it were off the account, involving neither a subtraction somewhere else, nor a cost to anyone, and, accordingly, spurns making up the difference by taking anything that seems to him like a gift/loan from Mrs Glegg. He gives generously to his daughter, taking her part no matter what, and wants his son, too, to take care of his sister by gift. By his discrepant accounting he loses his capital and leaves his daughter no gift or bequest at all. Or rather, he leaves her only her acculturation to an economics of the gift. This is even though for himself at the end of his life he would like nothing better than to shift back to capitalist economics by parsimoniously saving in order to pay off loans, and he dies lashing out against humbling patronage. One who looks to receive 'heart's need' however unwise because she needs it, to receive full satisfaction of the 'hunger of the heart', to receive All, must 'give all for All'. She must return the gift unstintingly, without recognition of cost, at whatever painful sacrifice. This is what Maggie does.

She has fully learned the lesson of sacrifice only half-learned in jam-puff days. In the final pages of *The Mill on the Floss* comes the flood foreshadowed by the legend of St Ogg, augmented in meaning by ongoing symbolism of St Ogg/Philip/Tom/Maggie, and by another allusion to St Thomas à Kempis—Maggie murmurs words from à Kempis that merge with the sounds of the wind and rain. There is a repeated suggestion that she is passing into a 'transition of death' as she rows out on the water to find Tom (p. 455). Eliot uses economic terms to describe Maggie's undertaking, and she does so to describe it as one that will prove fatal, which it does for both sister and brother. 'More and more strongly [her] energies seemed to come and put themselves forth, as if her life were a stored-up force that was being spent in this hour, unneeded for any future' (p. 456). This casts Maggie's energy or life-force as a saved or stored-up accumulation. Indeed, political economy conceives of capital as a saved or stored-up energy, a force of human labour, which is then expended—invested—to sustain and augment present labour, to the benefit of labourer, capitalist, and consumer.

So Maggie rows with almost superhuman effort. But for Maggie, as not for the capitalist, all is to be spent till all is gone, dispensing with expectation that labour be productive and promise profitable return on investment.

BETWEEN ECONOMIC SYSTEMS

My commentary joins the critical debate concerning themes of egoism and sympathy, self and self-sacrifice, in George Eliot, especially in their bearing for women. And it joins the critical debate concerning the drastic, perhaps overstrained tragic ending of the novel.[8] There are classic feminist outcries by Elaine Showalter and Sandra Gilbert and Susan Gubar against what they judge to be the exaltation of Maggie's self-sacrificial end. Equally classic readings are by Elizabeth Ermarth, who believes that Eliot does not endorse but exposes the pathology in Maggie's 'long suicide', and by Nina Auerbach, who suggests that there is a residually egoistic, not-so-sympathetic/sacrificial aspect to Maggie's destruction of others—notably Tom—along with herself.

More recent critics incorporate attention to socio-economic conditions and class into feminist approaches. Susan Fraiman and Judith Lowder Newton consider Tom's story as well as Maggie's and identify it with a narrative of rising in the world representative of advancing capitalism. Fraiman believes Eliot presents this capitalist story to its discredit in Tom as a story that is generically male and at odds with a female story of development, thereby producing a kind of collision of storylines at novel's end. Newton believes Eliot presents the capitalist rise of Tom and other male characters as one that 'spells trouble for women'. She believes it is the capitalist order driving Maggie to a bad end and that the novel offers a 'criticism of bourgeois society'.[9] Margaret Homans likewise finds new economic developments and the rise of the middle class to be forces dangerous to women in Eliot's representation. This is not because women are left out of bourgeois economics but because they help advance it. She sees something deplorable in Maggie's enjoyment of the luxuries of the prosperous Deane household and her falling in love with the upwardly mobile son of Guest and Co. In this reading Maggie demonstrates the role of women to contribute as consumers to the rising wealth of the nation and the rising power of the middle class as they lend cover to bourgeois class self-interest by their apparent removal from economic motives.[10] Newton and Homans lay blame for Maggie's and Tom's deaths on capitalist industrial development as symbolized by the machinery adrift in the flood that bears down on their boat.[11]

Among socio-economic critics without a particular feminist focus, Joshua Esty considers the flooding river a symbol of capitalist modernity that sweeps away a pre-modern—what he calls a yeoman-class—mentality that is embodied not only in Maggie but also in Tom, Mr Tulliver, and the whole town of St Ogg's.[12] Deanna Kreisel sees the floating machinery as a capitalist force but one that eliminates Maggie not as a pre-capitalist, pre-modern figure but as an embodiment of a tendency within capitalism itself.[13] I agree with Kreisel that Maggie is self-denying and that self-denial is integral to capital savings and (I would add) investment. But unlike Kreisel, I think the novel places Maggie in the end across a major divide from an economics of capital that accepts pain—never eliminating its role—but accepts it only insofar as it serves greater pleasure, with keeping of close accounts. Particularly clearly through its Christian symbolism, the novel places Maggie on the side of an unbounded, non-account-keeping asceticism, an economics of the gift antithetical to capitalism. And unlike Esty, I do not think Eliot lumps Maggie in with everyone else in St Ogg's or characterizes the lot of them as holdovers from an era that is 'irreducibly different', so that 'modernization generates absolute losses' for what went before.[14] This suggests too absolute, too clear-cut a distinction and too preordained, too generalized a catastrophe. By contrast, I see characters in Eliot's novel moving back and forth between newer capitalist and older gift-exchange economics, often half aware, and putting themselves in particular peril in particular ways.

Indeed *The Mill on the Floss* depicts a society in process of rapid economic change. St Ogg's is an old market town with growing current business. It exports wool and cheeses and imports fir, probably Baltic, and Russian flaxseed. Before retiring, Mr Glegg dealt in presumably English wool, and Mr Tulliver mills presumably English wheat and malt, while the town has profitable oil-mills milling foreign flaxseed for linseed oil. No doubt this, like the timber, serves shipbuilding and port and warehouse construction in support of commerce. There is coal on the ships, and Tom is sent by Guest and Co. on business to smoky Newcastle. Steam comes to St Ogg's. Tom shares with Mr Deane the idea of bringing steam power to Dorlcote Mill, and Maggie and Stephen board a steamboat. According to Mr Deane, the population is expanding, boosting prospects for trade and investment. Such expansion helps explain why upriver farmers are engineering new dams to irrigate more farmland, producing the problems for Mr Tulliver's mill that he is so ill able to meet. Smart up-to-date shops, some with plate-glass windows, compete with old-fashioned peddling like Bob's. Bob is not actually so behind the times, as he sells Laceham goods, including machine-made cotton net.[15] He also begins merchandizing to profitable foreign markets. Along with the Deanes and the Guests, he illustrates a notable rise in fortune. And he prospers partnering with his former 'master', Tom, and former betters, the Gleggs, in a revised, less hierarchical class relation based on an economics of capital rather than the gift.

I call to mind George Eliot's remark concerning possibilities for 'railways, steamships, and electric telegraphs, which are demonstrating the interdependence of all human interests'. She does not repudiate but salutes a dynamic 'making self-interest a duct for sympathy'.[16] I call to mind Ruskin's description of *The Mill on the Floss* as the work of a 'common railroad-station novelist', oriented to modernity and written for readers 'behind the counter' and inhabiting new brick suburbs of manufacturing towns.[17] In *The Mill on the Floss* Eliot shows that pain functions in capitalist economics as it does in gift-exchange, but with far greater dedication to net utility, and to net utility more levelly distributed. She also shows the liabilities involved in transition between economic systems. The older economics of gift and favour still operates in cross-class transactions and to a greater extent in transactions between the sexes. Half-heeded as it often is, it operates at odds with developing capitalism, producing misrecognitions, discrepant accountings, and tragic consequences for Mr Tulliver and his daughter and son. But I do not think that the novel expresses a preference for lapsing pre-capitalist economics.[18] Nor that it disavows Tom and his efforts to save, invest, and pay off the mill, nor Mrs Glegg and her head for business, nor Bob and his bettering of condition.[19]

NOTES

1. U. C. Knoepfelmacher's 1968 commentary on Mr Tulliver (*George Eliot's Early Novels*, 193–220) still stands out in the limited field of discussions of Tulliver Sr. As I do, Knoepfelmacher sees Mr Tulliver as a tragic figure and seeks to link his tragedy to that of his children. His finding is that Tulliver's story actually carries fuller tragic meaning than Maggie's and Tom's. Since Knoepfelmacher sees an inadequately realized tragedy in the second generation, he does not ultimately establish the linkage of tragedies he had sought. Barbara Hardy perceives psychological interest in Mr Tulliver (*Particularities*, 72) but does not linger long on him. Jerome Thale links Maggie's story to her father's as well as her brother's, calling them all backward-looking in wanting to hang onto the past and the mill (*Novels of George Eliot*, 79). Thale and Knoepfelmacher bring in some economic considerations, observing that Tulliver has old-fashioned views compared to a foremost figure of new capitalist commerce, Mr Deane. But they quickly redirect attention from socio-economics to general character traits—Mr Tulliver's warmth, passion, lack of control, heedlessness of consequences (Thale); his pride, impetuousness, neurosis, inaptness for struggle, evasion of reality (Knoepfelmacher). Felicia Bonaparte speaks of a family-line transfer of traits between Mr Tulliver and Maggie (*Will and Destiny*, 64–5). More recently, Josephine McDonaugh speaks of Maggie's inheritance of traits from her father—here innovativeness, wilfulness, cleverness—and says, 'in the end the novel appears to dramatize an emotional conflict . . . rather than . . . broader social questions' ('The Early Novels', 54). Thus connections between the stories of two generations, when more than passingly considered, have mainly been explained by commonalties of character between father and daughter. The novel has not been known for clear narrative connections in any event. Many critics have questioned the intelligibility of its ending, going back to contemporary reviews, e.g. *The Guardian*, 25 Apr. 1860 (cited by Carroll (ed.), *George Eliot*, 129); Henry James ('Novels of George Eliot', 464–5); Leslie Stephen (*George Eliot*, 103); F. R. Leavis (*Great Tradition*, 45–6); George Levine ('Intelligence as Deception', 402); Knoepfelmacher (208–9). On this problem ending see also Nancy K. Miller, 'Emphasis Added'; Nancy Jacobus, 'Question of Language'; and Susan Fraiman, '*The Mill on the Floss*'. In the last section of this chapter I address criticism of the past several decades that has increased attention to socio-economics, though still giving limited attention to Mr Tulliver's finances and other economic specifics.

2. I do not mean to attribute complete certainty to capital transactions. Eventualities are not fully known in advance. Revealed over time, they

may, in fact, appear like the work of an 'invisible hand'. Jack Amariglio observes that uncertainty exists in all exchanges, and he conceives of the gift as a reminder or 'ghost' of the uncertainty that still remains in market transactions ('Give the Ghost a Chance!', 269–72). Still, I would stress that capital investment significantly differs from gift-exchange in its concerted effort to limit uncertainty through accounting clarity.

3. There is a tally with Margot Finn's history of a slow, uneven mid-18th-c. to early 20th-c. shift in Britain from instruments and legalities of credit and debt based on social ties, to such instruments and legalities based on contract between independent parties. In this shift, most lag is seen in cases involving social dependants, notably women. There is also a tally with David Cheal's sociological study of gift-exchange still found in predominantly capitalist—here latter 20th-c. Canadian—culture, with the marked prominence of women as receivers and givers of gifts.

4. Tulliver seems to have been outsmarted rather than clearly wrong at law. Riparian rights were under contestation in the 1820s–30s. Cases show decisions going Tulliver's way regarding a right not to be injured by upstream developments and a right based on longtime use (Wisdom, *Law of Rivers*, 93–5, 101, 104).

5. I disagree with José Angél Landa, who considers Mrs Glegg a figure of 'ideological immobility' re property and money ('Chains of Semiosis', 79). I see her as adapting to newer-style capitalism. Deanna Kreisel attends much more than most to Mrs Glegg's and other Dodsons' and Tullivers' capitalist financial habits. She notes the tension between hoarding and capital savings and thinks on balance Mrs Glegg and many in St Ogg's prefer the latter ('Superfluity and Suction', 69, 83–9). Nancy Henry references Mrs Glegg among other women characters in Victorian fiction who are investors. She is notably accepting in tone ('"Ladies do it?"', 124).

6. This curious compilation attributed to the Earl of Chesterfield and brought out by Robert Dodsley exists in many editions throughout the 19th c.

7. See reviews from *Saturday Review* and *Dublin University Magazine* and comments by Charles Algernon Swinburne from *A Note on Charlotte Brontë* (Carroll (ed.), *George Eliot*, 118–19, 150, 165) and a review from *National Review*, plus a summary of other coverage (Lerner and Holstrom (eds.), *George Eliot*, 37–8, 46).

8. See my 'George Eliot: The Critical Heritage' (205, 216–19, 223–4, 209–10, 217–18).

9. *Women, Power, and Subversion*, 141, 157. Newton sees some wavering on Eliot's part between censuring Maggie's response of suicidal self-sacrifice and acquiescing to standards that call this forth (pp. 153, 137).

10. For additional feminist socio-economic criticism, see Suzanne Graver, *George Eliot and Community*, concerning egoistic interest vs. sympathy in Eliot's writings re conflict between organic community and modern society; and Nancy Paxton, *George Eliot and Herbert Spencer*, concerning egoistic interest vs. sympathy re Eliot's responses to Herbert Spencer's socio-economic/evolutionist ideas.

11. Newton, *Women, Power, and Subversion*, 156–7; Homans, 'Dinah's Blush', 172.

12. According to Esty, Tulliver's loss of the mill undoes him as a man of the pre-modern yeoman class, and Tom's efforts to reclaim the mill likewise undo him as he throws in his lot with this doomed class ('Nationhood, Adulthood', 102–3, 111–12). Cf. Eric Levy, who links the machinery with property and commercial enterprise and suggests 'the disastrous effects of the property morality' ('Property Morality', 184–5). Cf. Barbara Weiss, who describes Tulliver's bankruptcy as destabilizing to his children's sense of economic status and identity, and, without closely examining Tulliver's hand in causing the failure, presents it as a grim example of the apocalyptic change brought by a new industrial age (*Hell of the English*, 94, 20–2).

13. Kreisel identifies Maggie's excessive self-sacrifice with excessive self-denial in the form of capital savings within capitalism. Her reading involves a debate between Ricardo and Malthus. Ricardo accepts Smith's, also Bentham's, belief in demand without limit or certain boundary and Say's law that capital savings and investment will not outrun demand for what is produced. But Malthus entertains the possibility of deficiency in demand, causing capital savings to be in excess of profitable investment opportunities. For me, Maggie's self-denying attitude hardly evokes this technical Malthusian point, especially considering its association with the Christian symbolism of St Ogg and St Thomas à Kempis. See also Ch. 2 n. 1; Ch. 5 n. 17.

14. Esty, 'Nationhood, Adulthood', 105.

15. West Surrey College of Arts & Design, *Five Centuries*, 68.

16. 'Influence of Rationalism', 404. Thanks to Laura Otis for highlighting this passage from Eliot's 1865 review of William Lecky's *History of the Rise and Influence of the Spirit of Rationalism in Europe*.

17. Carroll (ed.), *George Eliot*, 167. I take Ruskin's words from his 1881 article in *Nineteenth Century* (which became part of *Fiction, Fair and Foul*) out of his own context of disparagement. Note that in *Theophrastus Such* Eliot laughs at the presumptuousness of setting a norm of selflessness for other people. Even her poor underachieving Theophrastus hangs onto his ego though 'fitful signs of a lingering belief in my own importance

were generally felt to be abnormal' (p. 11). And note that the self-interested cotton-trader Spike finds his efforts to enlarge the market for himself also enlarge it for others, so that 'the nature of things transmuted his active egoism into a demand for public benefit' (p. 66). Here Eliot appears to hail the invisible hand of Smith! See Henry's editorial note suggesting that Eliot plays off Smith in the *Theophrastus Such* chapter (*Theophrastus Such*, 175 n. 1). See Imraan Coovadia, 'George Eliot's Realism', tracing similarity between Smith and Eliot (especially in *Middlemarch* and *Felix Holt*) in the way they envisage social formation as spontaneous web-like self-generation at multiple intersections. See Gallagher (*Body Economic*) on *Daniel Deronda* as an exploration of problems of market satiety in relation to the author's concerns about demand for her books; and on *Scenes of Clerical Life* as an affirmation of maternal sacrifice and suffering, which for Gallagher constitutes a Malthusian stance, in that Malthus anticipates achievement of ethical and cultural benefits from dealing with the difficult population problem. Gallagher says Eliot links 'art to sacrifice and sacrifice to sexual passion' (p. 179). Satiety, suffering, and sacrifice are prominent in these readings. See Mary Poovey ('Writing about Finance') for commentary oriented to narrative/genre analysis. For her, *Mill on the Floss* illustrates a formal element characteristic of Victorian novels—inclusion of a financial storyline that is subordinated to other storylines and remains 'imperfectly visible' (p. 37). She places this in parallel with formal elements characteristic of Victorian financial writing, which, in her view, promise disclosure, in the manner of accounting, while still communicating incomprehensibility. There is an important insight here into the limits of visibility in economic transactions and their representation. However, I would stress that capitalism, as compared to gift-exchange, strives to achieve a far higher degree of visibility. Not the former but the latter would be more typified by economic invisibility, incomprehension, or misrecognition. Perhaps compatible with Poovey's broad narrative/genre analysis and my own particular interpretation of *Mill on the Floss* would be to say that the increased standard of economic visibility in capitalism makes want of visibility more anomalous, disturbing, and disruptive within a capitalist society. Also see n. 2.

18. Esty does remark that the pre-modern situation is not very attractive for women. But neither is the modern in his characterization ('Nationhood, Adulthood', 110). Unlike Esty, I do not think capitalism is cast as a monolithic, inevitable, all-round destroyer in *Mill on the Floss*. Unlike Newton, Fraiman, and Homans, I do not think it falls under heavy blame in the novel, nor that, on close critical scrutiny, it deserves more blame

than the author herself expresses. I am more inclined to share the perspective of other critics with feminist and socio-economic concerns. This is speaking in broad terms and about studies not focused on *Mill on the Floss*. Elizabeth Langland, in *Nobody's Angels*, complicates simple binaries of approval or blame and acknowledges powers opened up for middle-class women as managers of cultural capital in developing capitalist culture, even if their activities were largely confined to the domestic sphere and implicated in exercise of class power. Susan Zlotnick, in *Women, Writing, and the Industrial Revolution*, argues that 19th-c. women writers are more apt than their male counterparts to bring out positive possibilities in industrialization, especially for women. Nancy Henry suggests that portrayals of women investors by Eliot and other women authors show them to be 'more tempered [than male authors] in their critiques of capitalism' ('"Ladies do it?"', 121). Margueritte Murphy, in 'Ethics of the Gift', points to ambivalence about gift-giving to women in *Daniel Deronda*, referencing gift theory, though without comparing that to capitalist theory or paying the same attention she pays to gift transactions to market transactions in the novel.

19. Homans, 'Dinah's Blush', thinks *Mill on the Floss* is hard on Tom for being straightforward about his middle-class aspirations. In her review in the 1861 *Macmillan's Magazine*, Dinah Mulock also thinks the novel is unsympathetic towards Tom. However, Mulock is far more inclined than Homans to approve of Tom's get-ahead ways. Indeed she says that, on reflection, she finds him the finer character of the two siblings. Her sense that this judgement goes against the author's intention roused a response from Eliot, who comments to John Blackwood in a letter of 4 Apr. 1861 that a reader could hardly regard Tom with respect if she had not painted him with respect. She says it was the 'very soul of my intention' to show right on both sides for brother and sister. In a letter of 27 May 1860, responding to *The Times* review, she tells William Blackwood that she wrote with as much love and pity for Tom as for Maggie and insists that she is very far from hating the Dodsons (Carroll (ed.), *George Eliot*, 157, 159, 162, 138). See n. 5 re Mrs Glegg.

5

'On Liberty' and Laissez-faire

Self-interest in pursuit of pleasure, balanced against the pain of work and the pain of capital savings and investment, sometimes bound up with the pain of sexual restraint: these are fundamental principles of Utilitarian political economy and important in the culture that brought it to its heyday. I will turn now to another deep-level principle, that of liberty. Tag phrases like free trade and laissez-faire identify the doctrine with liberty, and the word liberty provides the label of liberalism that attaches to Utilitarian political economy. Yet it is striking how often laissez-faire liberalism has been associated with the *opposite* of liberty, with Gradgrindian repression or prison-like social discipline.

In 'On Liberty' Mill seems to fence off certain aspects of liberty from consideration. He says he does not treat 'the so-called Liberty of the Will' as opposed to 'Philosophical Necessity', but restricts himself to 'Civil, or Social Liberty'. He also says he does not employ the grounds of argument for free trade. Here, however, he draws a nuanced, or I would say superfine, distinction in calling those grounds 'different from, though equally solid with, the principle of individual liberty asserted in this Essay' (pp. 217, 293). Free trade is the banner application of laissez-faire, and Mill elsewhere does not separate laissez-faire from related conceptions of liberty. *The Principles of Political Economy* concludes with a chapter titled 'Of the Grounds and Limits of the *Laisser-Faire* or Non-Interference Principle'. The chapter makes laissez-faire into a general principle in the light of which specific departures must be strenuously justified. It provides a summation for the whole of Mill's economics. His arguments for competition, against monopoly, for free trade, against usury laws, for freedom of association in trade unions, against slavery, etc.—all fall under the auspices of laissez-faire. And so does the principle of individual liberty in its non-economic aspect:

There is a part of the life of every person who has come to years of discretion, within which the individuality of that person ought to reign uncontrolled either by any other individual or by the public collectively. That there is, or ought to be, some space in human existence thus entrenched around, and sacred from authoritative intrusion, no one who professes the smallest regard to human freedom or dignity will call in question: the point to be determined is, where the limit should be placed; how large a province of human life this reserved territory should include. I apprehend that it ought to include all that part which concerns only the life, whether inward or outward, of the individual, and does not affect the interests of others, or affects them only through the moral influence of example. (iii. 938)

We expect such a defence of liberty from Mill, though we have often been taught not to expect it from his tradition. That is perhaps evident enough from Leavisite and Foucauldian commentaries I have cited before, but to call the prevalent viewpoint to mind for purposes of this chapter, I will give a few further, pointed examples. I will then indicate some broad lines of revisionist response before moving to close examination of 'On Liberty'. In his essay Mill salutes defences of press freedom that have been 'triumphantly enforced by preceding writers' (p. 228). One such would be his Benthamite economist father's—James Mill's—'Liberty of the Press'. J. S. Mill surely achieves a 'triumph', too. My reading demonstrates Mill's overall adherence to a Smithian–Benthamite conceptual frame, with the introduction of an important innovation. It also demonstrates how Mill's form of expression serves to 'enforce' his ideas. The chapter closes examining elements that are perhaps less 'triumphantly enforced', yet powerful in their way in exhibiting the critical dimension in Mill's thought and writing. Here, too, he is true to his tradition.

'THE LIBERAL SPIRIT AND ENERGY OF A FREE CITIZEN'

Elie Halévy, the still-influential older authority on the Smith–Bentham school, declares in *The Growth of Philosophic Radicalism* that 'the doctrine of utility is not, in origin and in essence, a philosophy of liberty' (p. 84). As if anticipating Foucault, Halévy finds damaging evidence in Bentham's words concerning pupils in a panoptical school:

'Call them soldiers, call them monks, call them machines, so they were but happy ones, I should not care.' I cited this passage myself, while I also pointed out the self-questioning irony at work in the surrounding context. Bentham asks

whether the liberal spirit and energy of a free citizen would not be exchanged for the mechanical discipline of a soldier, or the austerity of a monk?—and whether the result of this high-wrought contrivance might not be constructing a set of *machines* under the similitude of *men?*

Halévy refers to these queries without taking them seriously; for him, they are queries raised only to be dismissed. Down the line in this vein, Douglas Long, in his book *Bentham on Liberty*, finds something essentially 'illiberal' in the very manner in which Bentham conceptualizes liberty: 'what Bentham called liberty others would call subjection' (pp. 9–10). More recently, summing up, Douglas Peers says, 'the authoritarian streak running through utilitarian dogma has long been noted' ('Imperial Epitaph', 208).

However, this judgement has increasingly been brought under review by scholars of Bentham and Benthamite theory. Philip Schofield, F. Rosen, and P. J. Kelly challenge Halévy; Janet Semple challenges Halévy, then Foucault.[1] Schofield refutes any idea of Bentham's late, sudden, fortuitous, or self-inconsistent 'conversion' to democratic political doctrine. He traces a steady logical development that made Bentham a strong advocate of majority rule.[2] Rosen studies the contribution of Bentham's *Constitutional Code* to the forging of democratic institutions and underscores the liberal significance of Bentham's emphasis on protecting the securities of the citizen. He declares that 'the security that [Bentham] seeks to establish is not enslavement, but a realm of personal freedom where each person can define and pursue his own idea of happiness so long as he does not endanger the security and subsistence of others. It is also a realm of political action where the critical searching voices of the people deal with the transgressions of their rulers'.[3] Kelly reaches similar conclusions from study of Bentham's manuscript writings on civil law. Semple sees liberal implications in Bentham's contributions to prison reform, and, even if his Panopticon might give us pause, she says it is not to his design for a prison but to his *Constitutional Code* and other writings on government that we should look to grasp his conception of democracy.[4] Likewise Stephen Engelmann protests the notion deriving from Foucault on the Panopticon that Bentham is a 'statist architect of unfreedom'.[5] Lea Campos Boralevi lists many categories of oppressed beings for whom Bentham stands up as defender—from women, Jews, sexual nonconformists, and slaves to animals.[6]

But revisionists still have not carried the day. I would instance the collection *Mill and the Moral Character of Liberalism*, especially views expressed by Peter Berkowitz, Richard Ashcraft, Eldon Eisenach, Nicholas Capaldi, and Bernard Semmel. Capaldi describes a Bentham who is deterministic and deficient in understanding of freedom as an internal condition, and a Mill who expands his thinking far beyond this (pp. 94–5—a view Capaldi carries into his biography of Mill, pp. 58–60, 65, 72). Semmel describes a Bentham with little insight into the inward life and uncommitted to freedom, and a Mill who turns away from this 'narrow and inadequate' philosophy (pp. 61–2). Kelly has it right in saying that critics' approval of Mill typically turns on the premiss 'that he is an interesting and subtle thinker to the extent that he abandoned "Benthamism"' (p. 6). In this light, Mill's mental crisis as a young man of 20, when he took it upon himself to reflect on his education under James Mill, appears to be a full-blown oedipal rebellion against his father and his father's school, and his points of criticism in his essay on Bentham appear to be damning judgements. This is even though Mill himself notes the misleading weighting on the critical side in his treatment of Bentham in the essay, compared to his undue favouring of the positive side in the companion essay on Coleridge, and though he attests to his rebound back to Bentham after a period of some reaction (*Autobiography*, 227, 237).[7]

It is true that Bentham waves aside consideration of free will. '*Entre nous*', he writes to a correspondent, 'I don't care two straws about liberty and necessity at any time. I do not expect any new truths on the subject: and were I to see any lying at my feet, I would hardly think it worth while to stoop to pick them up' (*Memoirs*, x. 216). He calls the subject too speculative for him, and he is, as Mill calls him in the Bentham essay, a most practical-minded philosopher.

Mill, too, declines to discuss liberty and necessity in 'On Liberty'. He does discuss the subject in *A System of Logic*. He says it is impossible to distinguish agent from patient as a matter of logic; the distinction depends solely on choice of words. In Mill's explanation, a falling stone is as much an agent as the earth with its gravitational pull, and the stone can be said to move by properties in itself as truly as it can be said to be moved by properties in the earth. Mill gives human examples of interactions of the senses and mind with physical phenomena, and examples of person-to-person social interactions. Between eye and brain and light there is acting and being acted upon. Between student and teacher there is acting and being acted upon. So Mill argues that while we are determined by conditions outside ourselves, we are agents as well as patients, and we can feel free in partly choosing to determine the conditions that will determine us. 'Things are never more active than in the production of those phenomena in which they are said to be acted upon' (vii. 336). This is a good line but hardly one to settle the matter for long. Proving free will may be a philosophic task better let lie, as Bentham quips.

Amanda Anderson is not persuaded by Mill's proof, but she thinks he sets forth a leading preoccupation of the age in concern over agency. She in great part associates troubles over free will with Mill's Benthamite–Smithian tradition.[8] Indeed, Bentham's springs of human action as arranged in tabular form can seem fixed, axiomatic, automatic in functioning. Malthus depicts people as almost irresistibly ruled by sexual instinct, even to their ruin. Smith has a vision of human beings situated within a huge system. One's own self is just one point of self-interested desire among myriad others. Each of us is dependent on those others for much-needed utilities of sympathy and reputation—these things looming large for Bentham as well as Smith. Each is likewise dependent on those others for many more utilities—dependent for our dinner on the self-interests of brewer, baker, and butcher. Brewer, butcher, baker, and we ourselves all function within a market that none fully comprehends and none controls, a system of division and subdivision of labour of regional, national, and global extent, elaborately mechanized, a vast, complex concatenation of actions and reactions governed by abstract general laws. In a market controlled only by the invisible hand, persons in it are so controlled, or so they can seem.

I would add, though, that troubles over freedom and necessity are to be found not only in Utilitarian political economy but in contemporaneous Romantic philosophy as well. Fichte's ideas, considered in Chapter 3 for their bearing on vocation, also have a bearing here. In search of freedom—release from determinism—materialism resorts to idealism. Idealism, turned solipsistic and drained of freedom of a meaningful kind, resorts once again to materialism. Fichte struggles to reach some resolution. For him, to conceive of other people as real and free to act on things and on oneself sets limits on our own freedom, while it is also the condition of conceiving of ourselves as real and free to act on other people and things. Carlyle's Gospel of Work is thus Romantic and Utilitarian in affirming liberty in full cognizance of paradox. Carlyle preaches liberty—to pursue vocation, to work—in the face of constraint: 'Compassed round with Necessity; yet is the meaning of Life itself no other than Freedom, than Voluntary Force' (*Sartor Resartus*, 183). This might be Mill. Might it be Bentham? Well! But I do believe that Utilitarian political economy is acutely aware of constraint on liberty as a problem and much more than passingly concerned with protecting, and, indeed, drawing out 'the liberal energy and spirit of a free citizen'.

'ON LIBERTY' AS UTILITARIAN TEXT

Acknowledging his tradition, in 'On Liberty' Mill makes utility his 'ultimate appeal'—'utility in the largest sense, grounded on the permanent interests of man as a progressive being' (p. 224). In Mill's lexicon, the term utility carries a defined philosophic meaning. It means pleasure or happiness, the 'well-being' that appears in the title of his third chapter, 'Of Individuality, as One of the Elements of Well-Being'. Utility means satisfaction of 'liking'—as in the repeated phrase 'doing as we like'. Liking involves 'desires and impulses' 'feelings', 'preferences', 'inclinations'. It involves the 'raw material of human nature' (pp. 263–4) or the deep springs of human action, recognizable from Bentham, Smith, Malthus, Ricardo, and James Mill. What *we* like is fundamentally important, and Mill means what the individual likes; so self-interest is fundamentally important. Mill refuses to glorify passive obedience, submission, or a tendency to make an 'idol of asceticism' (pp. 255–6). He tilts at Christianity precisely on its ascetic side. This would be the Pauline Christianity anathematized by Bentham in 'Sextus' and *Not Paul, but Jesus*.[9] Doing as we like *is* subject to limitation, but only, according to Mill's 'one very simple principle', so as 'to prevent harm to others' (p. 223). This reads very much like an echo of

Bentham in his 'Manual of Political Economy': 'Leave them to live as they like, under the single condition of not injuring one another' (p. 73).

Mill appeals to utility with reference to individuals but also with reference to society at large. This fits his thinking very closely to the mode of Bentham and Smith, which is concerned with individual benefits and wide social benefits, with personal bettering of condition and overall growth of welfare and wealth. So Mill makes the case that liberty is good for one, and all. This is not, in fact, an easy case to make, as will become clearer later in this section.

Certainly Mill's topic of freedom of thought and expression is a familiar one for Utilitarianism. Recall Bentham's opening of the Panopticon to 'the great *open committee* of the tribunal of the world', among other provisions for the functioning of the Public Opinion Tribunal. Recall Mill Sr's 'Liberty of the Press'. (Utilitarians would back the likes of Trollope's *Jupiter*.)

Freedom of behaviour and way of life is a topic that might be expected as well. Mill defends eccentricity. He gives examples of eccentric behaviour that would be likely to call forth disapproval and defends the drinker (like Mr Sleary), on whom we may frown but should not force sobriety. This is a bold stand, if not as mischievous and teasing as Bentham's defence of a taste for push-pin, nor as daring as Bentham's defence of eccentric sexual behaviour—the 'solitary mode', the 'Attic mode'. Of course, 'On Liberty' was published, and the 'Sextus' material was not. Publishing was not yet free enough for that. Mill does go so far as to defend Mormon polygamy if voluntary for wives and husbands in a society founded to lift the sanctions that Mormons faced elsewhere.

To back the eccentric is to back individuality and the notion, as found in Bentham, that different minds are different. Not only are they different, but their difference is a good thing. Mill's thinking links to Smith's on the division of labour. Smith does not press the notion of innate difference in talents very hard. Instead, he says such difference is 'in reality, much less than we are aware of' (i. 28). He is far from postulating hereditary suitability for one occupation or another, a sort of caste idea. This opens prospects of mobility across types of work and across class. But the human impulse to truck, barter, and exchange makes it effectual to divide up tasks instead of each person's doing everything for him- or herself. The specialist saves time and works more productively, making more products obtainable all around, for the greatest happiness of the greatest number. Division of labour takes advantage of what difference exists, increases that difference, and 'renders that difference useful' (i. 29). Ricardo applies the idea to nations. Each specializes according to comparative advantage (*Principles*, 133–40). Mill applies the same idea in arguing for diversity among individuals in 'On Liberty'. To take advantage of existing diversity in thought, expression, and style of life and to multiply such diversity is to render difference useful. More utilities—ideas, discourses, models of living—are produced and go on offer at the site of exchange.

The best condition of exchange in each circumstance is freedom, laissez-faire. Laissez-faire foils monopoly by fostering competition. It has been often observed that Mill employs the language of competition in 'On Liberty'. He speaks of collision of opinions, struggle between combatants, competing experiments in ways of life. He does not propose a system of disinterested intellectual gift-giving in debate nor require advocates on each side to relinquish self-interest and self-will any more than the butcher, the brewer, or the baker. In a position close to his father's in support of passionate expression whether of praise or protest ('Liberty of the Press', 32–3), Mill endorses argument from conviction and strong reactions, including negative reactions. His doctrine of tolerance does not mandate large measures of forbearance. Judgements may involve 'the opposite of admiration', indeed 'distaste' or 'contempt', identifying folly, 'lowness or depravation of taste', or 'inferiority' in alternative ideas, statements, and behaviours. This may lead to disagreements, charges, cautions, or sundered relations ('On Liberty', 277–8). Mill does not look to ban Smith's moral sentiments of judgement or Bentham's moral sanction. He does not shy away from recognizing that people may feel antipathy as well as sympathy and that they may well 'like' to disapprove and may, on some occasions, be right to do so. (He would not insist that people approve of the woman's request to be ferried out on dangerous waters in Eliot's novel.) He argues against imposition of a standard of inoffensiveness of expression. This would be likely to be unequally applied and to prove more restrictive to representations on behalf of unpopular positions. Between what is popular and unpopular, the latter will be almost by definition the more offensive. Mill does not stipulate that human beings should purge their language of dyslogistic usages. But his own example suggests that speakers gain in persuasiveness when not *over*-dependent on loaded word choice, whether dyslogistic or eulogistic. They reap the benefit of their own choice—free choice—of well-weighed, well-deployed expression.

So exchange thrives in conditions of liberty, stymieing monopoly, stimulating division of labour or diversity, rendering difference useful, and increasing the range of products—ideas, expressions, styles of life—on offer in the marketplace, which is advantageous to all. In this sense Utilitarian political economy makes liberty instrumental to utility.

Bentham does not place liberty on his table of the springs of human action as *itself* a utility. In his 'Manual of Political Economy' he does refer to constraint on free agency as a pain (p. 33). This implies that free agency is a pleasure, or utility. But I would agree with scholars like Engelmann and Kelly, who, while bent on reclaiming Bentham's reputation for liberalism, are content to note the usefulness in the sense of instrumentality of liberty in Bentham's conception and his lesser emphasis on personal autonomy as compared to Mill.[10] Bentham rejects designation of liberty as a natural right, according to the 'fiction' or 'figure' often found in the discourse of the American and French revolutions. And for him, any liberty instituted by law involves coercion, or limitation of freedom to impose on others, and might just as well be known under the term security.[11]

Smith speaks warmly and often in favour of 'perfect liberty' (i. 73, 79, 116; ii. 606), not for itself but for its economic benefit. For him (and Bentham largely follows Smith in the 'Manual of Political Economy'), a free market, uncontrolled by private monopolies or government, decolonized, with as few as possible restrictions, best coordinates supply and demand and sends labour and capital to where they can prove most productive. A free market puts the greatest number and variety of utilities into exchange. It best limits wages and profits to just enough return on labour and capital to constitute incentive to work, save, and invest, and so best holds prices near the cost of production in a manner consistent with the labour theory of value. As regards this mainline position of classical economics, Malthus expresses a reservation. He prefers an exception to free trade when it comes to a basic foodstuff like corn because of the value to the nation of protecting its ability to feed itself in event of emergencies (*Essay* (1803 edn.), 165–79). Ricardo, however, advances laissez-faire doctrine. He calls for flows of commodities, labour, and capital 'unfettered by artificial restraints' (*Principles*, 172, and see 132, 318). (He does temper his position on behalf of grain, calling for gradual reductions in protection, p. 268). In the wake of Ricardo, political economy becomes progressively bolder in pressing for free trade, whose signature legislation is the Repeal of the Corn Laws under Peel.

Ricardo makes the remark that by scarcity the price value of commodities may be raised, but by abundance, riches (p. 276). Classical economists are deeply concerned with riches, the wealth of nations, and not only with individual fortunes. Certainly, they come to recognize that private and general betterment can be at odds. This recognition is especially owing to Ricardo's incorporation of Malthus's theory of population into his own theory of rent, and it gains scope and impetus with the Mills. There is a growing perception of monopoly advantage to holders of agricultural land who control the food supply while population and demand for food rise. Such a situation may well produce higher prices without greater abundance, or riches. The whole land-owning class (Dedlocks hand in hand with Chancery lawyers and Barchester clerics) may well prosper at the expense of the capitalist and labouring classes. Countermeasures are possible—such as Corn Law Repeal and later radical land-tax policies. However, the overarching argument is and remains that that economy will be richest that is best structured to build the benefit of all on the benefit of each.

Like Bentham, Mill forgoes argument from a natural right to liberty. Like Bentham and the economists, he does not suppose that liberty comes of itself. Laissez-faire requires restraints to be imposed on monopolist and government powers. Mill proposes restraints on censorship and other impositions of legal sanctions on certain beliefs and behaviours, and he advises against imposing prohibitively heavy moral sanctions. He is close to his forebears in making liberty highly instrumental to utility. To my mind, he differs from them in the extent to which he makes liberty *itself* a utility, a pleasure of Benthamism.

For instance, he refers to the possibility of considering 'individual spontaneity' as something of 'intrinsic worth'. This would be to consider 'the free development of individuality [as] one of the leading essentials of well-being' (p. 261). There is a tally with calling liberty a 'personal want', next in strength to desire for subsistence, in *Political Economy* (2: 208). Not in 'On Liberty' but in his other great essay that defends freedom, 'The Subjection of Women', Mill yet more overtly and eloquently describes the feeling of liberty as a pleasure. He speaks of 'personal independence as an element of happiness'. He reminds any male reader how he felt when he emerged from boyhood and was released from the tutelage and control of elders, however loved and loving they might be. 'Was it not like the physical effect of taking off a heavy weight, or releasing him from obstructive, even if not otherwise painful, bonds?' (pp. 336–7). In this view, men—and women—not only like the things they do when they do as they like, but they like— they 'indulge' in the 'luxury'—of being *able* to do them ('On Liberty', 270). (Think of Mr Harding escaping the Archdeacon by train and enjoying his freedom in London.) Mill ends 'The Subjection of Women' by hailing freedom as 'the principal fountain of human happiness... in all that makes life valuable to the individual human being' (p. 340).[12]

So Mill goes further than Bentham and prior political economists in characterizing liberty not only as serviceable to utility but as a utility in its own right. However, in 'On Liberty' he does *not* cast it as a near-universal object of desire (by contrast to his earlier characterization in *Political Economy*). In fact, 'On Liberty' acknowledges that many people do not care much about feeling they can do as they like. They do not care to be eccentric and prefer the centric pleasures. They are satisfied to be governed by custom and do not hanker after individuality, original-ity, and genius. In one of Mill's sharpest sayings, 'Originality is the one thing which unoriginal minds cannot feel the use of' (p. 268). Thus he locates conformity to custom in China and the East and *also* in Western democracies. He ratifies Alexis de Tocqueville's perception in *Democracy in America* of a special danger within democracy itself of the tyranny of the majority. Mill says the spirit of improvement in modern Western societies is not always a spirit of liberty (p. 272). He observes that modern improvements like those in communications—new paper-making technology, steam-powered printing, railway transport, all cheapening and widening dissemination of newspapers and other publications—may bring individual thought and action under the heavy influence of what is generally thought and done. 'The mind itself is bowed to the yoke' (p. 265).

Still, as a Benthamite, a Smithian, Mill must be concerned with the welfare of all as well as the welfare of each. He must derive the former from the latter when on the face of it the two appear to diverge. He must demonstrate a sharing of benefits from liberty without presuming a sharing of desire for it. This is the special challenge he faces in making his case. He meets it with impressive feats of eloquence and reasoning. He sets out with apparent modesty to assert his one simple principle. At the same time he makes clear the boldness of his undertaking—to justify liberty on very different grounds of intrinsic and instrumental worth. Besides galvanizing one set of readers by means of passionate testimonials to the satisfactions of individual freedom, he must rationally demonstrate to another set of readers, 'those who do not desire liberty, and would not avail themselves of it, that they may be in some intelligible manner rewarded for allowing other people to make use of it without hindrance' (p. 267).

LIBERAL SPIRIT AND ENERGY: FORCE OF WORDS AND ARGUMENT A FORTIORI

Mill is far from hard, dry, and Gradgrindian as a writer, though few commentators discuss his stylistic power—making me appreciate those who do, such as his editor John Robson, along with Ann Robson, and Mill's successor in economics, William Stanley Jevons.[13] Mill shows Bentham's sharp awareness, if not his sometimes exaggerated wariness, of language. He begins his essay ruling out misnomers such as the 'so-called' Liberty of the Will and goes on to provide his own redefinition, Civil, or Social Liberty. It may be worth comparing this to his grappling with terminology early in his essay 'Utilitarianism'. This example illustrates the constructed, made-up (in Bentham's sense 'fictitious'/'figurative') nature of verbal naming, with the problems entailed yet the necessity for purposes of thought and communication, and the pleasures that may come in as well (in Bentham's sense elements of expression that are 'ornamental'/'impressive'). Mill remarks that the term 'Utilitarianism' as the name for a school of thought has been open to misconstruction, and he believes it was he himself who first brought it into use. However, he does not recall but upholds the term as one that 'supplies a want in the language', and he employs self-referential irony or paradox to call attention to his own care as a writer to convey its meaning exactly, without prejudice, without 'tiresome circumlocution', but with force (pp. 209–10 and n.).

So in 'On Liberty', to accomplish his far from simple task, Mill employs many devices of rhetoric and argumentation. Indeed, these are integrally bound up with his ideas. They 'triumphantly enforce' them.

His rhetoric often serves to voice and to excite liberal spirit and energy, that is, feelings of the sort experienced in exertion of voluntary force. Mill writes with fervour about desires and impulses. These become keywords, as does the word 'energy' itself: 'Strong impulses are but another name for energy. Energy may be turned to bad uses; but more good may always be made of an energetic nature, than of an indolent and impassive one' (p. 263). He says of good discussion that those engaged and those listening should 'feel the whole force' of it. They should be able to imagine the stance and the stakes on both sides to gain 'a vivid conception and a living belief' (pp. 245–7). In rhetorical terms, Mill uses *energia* of verbal style to urge free thought and behaviour that are not 'inert and torpid' but 'active and energetic' (p. 262).

Repetition adds emphasis, as in recurrent references to doing and liking that reinforce the message of 'doing as we like'. Mill sharpens attention and adds force to particular words. For instance, he reverses the usual connotation of 'eccentricity' to make it a good thing. 'Infallibility' is an unexpected word choice, but it fits when Mill makes us realize that to silence discussion means no other than to claim infallibility. There is vivid figurative language. People are not machines, automatons, cattle under the yoke, apes, or tailors' forms more easily fitted with opinions than coats. The ideal is not to mould minds and lives like a Chinese lady's foot. The mind is a muscle and is improved only by being used. Debate is struggle, combat, collision. Mill uses provocative, paradoxical phrases like 'tyranny of the majority', 'tyranny of opinion', and 'moral police'. Sometimes he writes with hard-hitting bluntness: 'All attempts by the State to bias the conclusions of its citizens on disputed subjects, are evil' (p. 303). Sometimes he exquisitely hones his syntax to draw subtle but crucial distinctions and encompasses complex ideas in consummately self-complete complex sentences: 'Though the customs be both good as customs, and suitable to him, yet to conform to custom, merely *as* custom, does not educate or develope in him any of the qualities which are the distinctive endowment of a human being' (p. 262). Mill uses first-person references to himself and his aims and difficulties to enhance the sense of his living conviction and effort to convey it. He uses rhetorical questions to add point. He catches attention by challenging the 'pleasant falsehoods' of stock maxims like 'truth always triumphs over persecution' (p. 238). But he also generates many maxims or *sententia* himself. He does so with precision of word choice and command of syntax for sharply, exquisitely delimiting concepts, and with repetition of words and balance of phrasing for delivering just the right emphasis. He makes a show of *brevitas*. Here are a few quotable quotes from 'On Liberty':

The only freedom which deserves the name, is that of pursuing our own good in our own way. (p. 226)

His own mode of laying out his existence is the best, not because it is the best in itself, but because it is his own mode. (p. 270)

The principle of freedom cannot require that he should be free not to be free. (p. 300)

With small men no great thing can really be accomplished. (p. 310)

The human faculties of perception, judgment, discriminative feeling, mental activity, and even moral preference, are exercised only in making a choice. He who does anything because it is the custom, makes no choice. (p. 262)

He who lets the world, or his own portion of it, choose his plan of life for him, has no need of any other faculty than the ape-like one of imitation. (p. 262)

It really is of importance, not only what men do, but also what manner of men they are that do it. (p. 263)

Conformity is the first thing thought of; they like in crowds; they exercise choice only among things commonly done: . . . until by dint of not following their own nature, they have no nature to follow. (p. 265)

The last four citations come from a run of four pages. 'On Liberty' is impressive for energetic bursts like that and for a sustained stamina of style that keeps the memorable quotes coming. I have been attending to the level of word-to-word, sentence-to-sentence rhetoric and demonstrating devices for expressing and exciting the sort of feeling for liberty that Mill believes some people experience. But, as I indicated, Mill is also writing for those others who remain more or less torpid and inert, low in liberal spirit and energy or inclination to exert voluntary force. As regards them, he cannot expect so much from the power of powerful rhetoric. It may not arouse fellow-feeling with liberty as itself a utility. He must carry his points to this group at the level of argument.

Of course, 'On Liberty' is full of powerful reasoning. It is a showcase for argumentative devices. I will give some sampling of these but move through them quickly to spend more time discussing one that I think works particularly well for Mill's purposes. This is argument a fortiori.

The essay excels in clarity of proposition. It moves from thesis statement to main supporting points in sequence after sequence. It features logical structure by means of timely and explicit definitions of terms and domains of analysis, orderly divisions and subdivisions or *digestion* of argument, clear chapter layouts, conceptual forecasts, main-point enumerations, mid-course recapitulations, and concluding summaries. While a master of *brevitas*, Mill also amplifies. He is tirelessly, relentlessly thorough. The essay on his simple idea runs to some ninety-three densely packed pages. Mill puts the Socratic method that he advocates on display; over and over he presents idea, objection, and answer to the objection. He uses *concessio*. He gives evidence, often historical examples. He bolsters his authority through exhibition of wide learning. He cites others for authority, notably Tocqueville and Bentham, free-press advocates, and expositors of political economy. He gives topical illustrations.

Now to underscore the force of persuasion Mill achieves through argument a fortiori. This works both to overpower logical objections of readers of the unsympathetic sort *and* to impress—enliven and please—sympathetic readers by a pure display of the author's strength of mind, subject mastery, and logical prowess. The strategy is to infer likeness from lesser to greater or greater to lesser cases. The effect is to glean strength from an unlikely quarter. For example: if even the authoritarian Roman Catholic Church finds it worthwhile to appoint a devil's advocate to argue the counterposition, how much more can democratic societies expect to benefit by insuring open discussion. Or: if even the wise and virtuous Marcus Aurelius failed to see the merits of Christianity and became its persecutor, and if even Saul, before he was Paul, did the same, how much less can ordinary people be sure they are in the right when they condemn new ideas. Or: if the feeling which prompts calls to halt railway travel on Sunday out of respect for religion may seem of little account, it is less only in degree than religious prejudices that inspired past bloody persecutions. There is a show of force when Mill says he will choose examples least favourable to his own position to prove his points. Belief in God, a future life, and commonly received doctrines of morality would appear to offer strongholds of certainty to most people in the Britain of the day and would seem in no need of a guarantee of freedom to allow them to be further debated. Yet even here Mill makes it his business to demonstrate the advantages of free discussion and the dangers of its lack. There is a show of force when Mill backs such seemingly weak candidates for tolerance as eccentrics, drinkers, and Mormon polygamists. I would say there is a show of force when he pitches his overall case for liberty not only or primarily to those with feelings to draw them towards it, but to those low or lacking in such feelings and poor prospects for persuasion. Mill writes in a manner strongly evocative for the first sort of readers and gives overmastering reasons to the second.

In capsule, some people will find vital satisfaction in thinking, saying, and doing as they like, and those who care less about the experience of liberty will be gratified by its results. That is because liberty prompts critical reflection on many views, including one's own, and a sifting through to get closer to the truth and to reliable grounds of action. Scope for individuality, originality, and genius encourages experiment (or projection), which incubates new ideas, discourses, inventions, institutions, and modes of living. The best of these will tend to be culled from the rest. And these will tend to become available to benefit not only the independent-minded individualist original geniuses but the conformist non-geniuses too. So liberty serves everyone instrumentally as well as being a pleasure in itself to some.

Actually, while he sees people as diverse, Mill would not distinguish so sharply between original and unoriginal minds as some of his statements might suggest and as I might sometimes suggest in the terms of my own analysis. According to the theory of division of labour, no one is an all-around genius, nor capable of taking strong pleasure in freedom of thought, expression, and action in every arena. In this sense everyone depends on someone else's being a genius enjoying his or her freedom in one or another of many arenas.

And there is Mill's belief in 'man as a progressive being' to suggest his hope that more people may come to truly relish individual freedom, as well as relish the fruits of the freedom they leave open to others. Liberty may be recognized as a 'fecund' utility that is subject to and repays cultivation. A notion of cultivating pleasures exists within Bentham's theoretical frame, but Mill considers it more fully. This is in his 'Utilitarianism' essay. There he describes a process of habit formation that involves both consciousness and feelings. In this process what is at first mainly understood as a means of happiness may come to be experienced as a significant part of happiness (pp. 235–9). And surely, through the force of his rhetoric and argument Mill aims to excite some spirit and energy of feeling for liberty not only among those presently well disposed to this, but among those less well disposed who also need to be given many reasons why liberty does them any good.

TRIUMPH AND CRITICAL THINKING

'On Liberty' is triumphant but not triumphalist in its ideas and expression, for it calls attention to elements that remain hard to resolve within its own frame of understanding. Mill participates in a tradition that is liberal, spirited, energetic, experimental, projective, and critical. Liberal critical thinking—free, multiple in perspective, and self-examining—is clear to see in the essay's last chapter, 'Applications'. Mill looks for limit points in practice for his principle of liberty, and many limits are admitted. These include acceptance of government restrictions on liberty to prevent fraud by adulteration, to enforce sanitary precautions, and to protect workpeople in dangerous occupations. Mill goes on to trickier questions—how about restrictions on sale of poison? on prostitution? on management of brothels? He presses to the boundary line where there are good arguments on both sides. He fine-tunes compromise positions. So while it is an undue infringement on liberty to protect the drinker from himself by restrictions on the sale of alcohol, it is acceptable to place a tax burden on drink that partly discourages its consumption on the grounds that taxes for support of government have to fall somewhere and can justifiably be directed to bear more heavily on unhealthy items of sale.

One of Mill's most striking proposed limitations of liberty involves a means test for marriage. This derives from his embrace of the Malthusian analysis of the population problem and its toll on individuals, particularly children, and on general wage levels and broad working-class prosperity and self-sufficiency. Mill goes beyond Malthus. Malthus retains liberty in marrying, subject to the possible consequence of poverty for large families when recourse is limited to bare-bones relief under new Poor Laws (*Essay* (1803 edn.), 226). But—*forbid* marriages?

Mill comes across as tough-minded to the point of hard-hearted here. He maintains that freedom to wed may be held to the harm test. He might not license improvident marriages (like those of two generations of Skimpoles?) that are liable to cause great personal suffering as part of general economic and social ills of overpopulation (ills produced outside marriage, too, as illustrated by the children born with claim to nothing in *Bleak House*).

Mill moves along to other applications that present difficulties, where liberty is far from simple to uphold. The liberty of some groups is to receive less protection. Children are not fully included under the principle, nor are people in 'backward states of society' as yet unacculturated to freedom and in their 'nonage' (p. 224). Massive policy matters are at stake in these instances. I refer to compulsory universal education, which obviously trenches on the liberty of children, and to imperialism, which obviously trenches on the liberty of colonial subjects. Utilitarian political economy gives strong backing to educational mandates and more mixed theoretical support to empire, though its imperial involvement is substantial at a practical level. The latter instance of apparent illiberalism within liberalism is especially likely to disturb us. In Chapters 6 and 7 I will have more to say on empire and will take up the vexed question of liberal imperialism. Meanwhile 'On Liberty' goes into more detail on education as regards the balancing act between freedom and compulsion.

This brings to mind the worry-point for Bentham. Panoptical efficiency in the teaching of children would be a benefit, but attendant loss of 'the liberal spirit and energy of a free citizen' would be a cost. As I have argued, Mill goes further than Bentham in considering liberty itself a utility; so more is on the line for him, and he pushes his critical thinking further. We see a delicate and quite precarious balancing of factors in his discussion. The government should require all to be educated and pay for the poorest students, but it should not centrally control the schools. It might set exams to be passed, but not the curriculum. Exams should test for knowledge of intellectual systems, but not for adherence to one or another. Exam records should be made available as information for employment purposes, but not be required for employment *per se*. They should not function as part of a state-controlled programme of certification. Many means are needed to keep schools diverse and to offer choice to individuals.[14]

I will not go on with examples from the chapter on applications but shift to a second illustration of critical thinking traceable throughout the essay. Less overt, yet evident enough, this involves Mill's probing of the downside of a force for good that is a much-vaunted one within his school of thought. With naming of utility as his ultimate standard, with references to Bentham and political economy, with identifiers like calling himself 'the last person to undervalue the self-regarding virtues' (p. 277), Mill lets his affiliation be known. Yet one of the major targets of 'On Liberty' is the tyranny of the majority, whether by democratic vote or public opinion. With this, Mill takes a critical stance on Bentham's majority rule (ultimately and ideally meaning universal adult suffrage) and on Bentham's great open committee of the tribunal of the world or Public Opinion Tribunal. This form of rule and this tribunal operate in a broad sense panoptically, by means of the moral sanction. The moral sanction (like Smith's moral sentiments of judgement) derives from people's interest in how others see them, sympathetically or unsympathetically, approvingly or the reverse. The moral sanction informs the political sanction through the vote, and, outside the vote, it constitutes the power of opinion. Like Bentham, Mill's father James advocates majority rule and a free press as engines of democracy that promise great individual and social benefits. But in the face of this, J. S. Mill raises concerns about coercion and conformity within democracy itself, coercion and conformity that derive precisely *from* majority rule and widely disseminated majority opinion. The words 'majority', 'opinion', and 'moral' shade from eulogistic to dyslogistic in their new association with 'tyranny' and 'police'. I call such language new, but it could also be pegged as a more elaborated and urgent articulation of Bentham's own wry expression of scruples concerning potential for ill as well as good in the panoptic idea.

Indeed, Bentham followed Smith and Malthus, while he also argued with them on occasion, and he commends his own ideas to further testing through discussion and experience. With his population theory, Malthus took an important step beyond Smith. He and Ricardo debated points with each other. Ricardo used Malthus to rethink aspects of Smith, notably on rent. James Mill catalysed this new thinking and sharpened its point by targeting it to reform practice, as I argue in Chapter 7, and also passed along such thinking to his son as the ground for another radical departure. It is an important innovation upon his tradition for J. S. Mill to cast liberty as a utility, but for him to speak in critical terms of the power of the ballot and public opinion in democracy strikes a particularly contestatory note. It gives strong expression to a far from dogmatic thought process, one that is critical, free-ranging or liberal, self-reflexive, self-adaptive, and characteristic of Mill's whole school.

I will conclude with a last instance of a critical mode. At stake is the fundamental principle of utility. Here I do not claim that Mill explicitly subjects the principle to examination or that he raises a point that is readily recognizable as a point of debate within his school. Still, the ideas informing his case for liberty, and informing the way he puts his case, bring a perplexity as regards utility into view. And Mill's emphasis on critical thinking opens the door for a reader to carry such thinking further.

Smithian–Benthamite theory postulates strong energy of desire, strong impulses of self-interest at the springs of human action. There is a presumption of vitality in inclinations and likings. But Mill posits a liking of liberty that is strong only in some and otherwise weak. While his essay affirms an idea of progressive human development, it does not identify particularly promising prospects for cultivation in most people's feelings for liberty. Such is the sense conveyed through the essay's whole structure of rhetoric and argumentation. As Mill addresses readers desirous of liberty and readers far less desirous of it, a larger point takes shape: that 'the general average of mankind are not only moderate in intellect, but also moderate in inclinations: they have no tastes or wishes strong enough to incline them to do anything unusual' (p. 271).

A good deal in Utilitarian political economy concerns incentive and actually exposes the fact that the boundlessness of desire premissed by Smith and Bentham cannot be *too* much relied on. Pursuit of self-interest may need considerable prompting. That is why, for instance, private property in the products of labour must be justified, even at the expense of an equalizing of fortunes that would carry benefits for the greatest happiness of the greatest number, because prospects of individual wealth motivate work, capital savings, and investment, plus Malthusian moral restraint, thus leading to increased production and consumption. That is why bequests must be allowed, regardless of the theory's egalitarian leanings, because ability to pass on wealth raises incentive for saving and capital accumulation. That is why usury laws must be lifted, even at the risk of encouraging prodigality, because this raises incentive for projection. That is why laissez-faire must be legislated through Repeal of the Corn Laws, because this raises incentive for competition by discouraging monopoly. And why new Poor Laws must be instituted, despite present severity towards the poor, because this raises incentive for self-betterment and lowers incentive for early marriage and creation of large families in reliance on public aid.

So it sometimes appears that individuals are not so self-activated by self-interest. Smith had been concerned about inertia and torpor in workers in a factory system of division of labour. Bentham had wondered about loss of liberal spirit and energy in panoptically schooled boys. Mill's *Political Economy* contains lengthy passages on the indolence of Irish workers under rack-renting farm conditions. Desire of bettering their conditions does not seem to come with them from the womb and leave them only when they go into the grave. The Irishman is quite stultified:

If he were industrious or prudent, nobody but his landlord would gain; if he is lazy or intemperate, it is at his landlord's expense. A situation more devoid of motives to either labour or self-command, imagination itself cannot conceive. The inducements of free human beings are taken away. (ii. 319)

The problem is not sloth that is accountable to race but rather to economic circumstances that arrest energy and endeavour. Freedom appears in the passage as a corrective, for it opens up motives to action. Motivation is the goose that lays the golden egg, but, we may gather, it requires encouragement. Often Utilitarian political economy does not so much count on desire as search out ways to raise awareness of it as a potent resource and to elicit and expand the feeling of it. The worst would be for the fire of craving to be so tamped down as to go out. The repression, sublimation, distortion, diminution, even death of desire I discussed in *Hard Times* may be called Smithian–Benthamite (before they are Freudian) concerns.

For Mill, pecuniary interest has considerable vitality among human interests, and this seems to be a factor drawing him to political economy. Among objects of desire, he does not entirely exalt economic advancement in the world, but he does find in this a large measure of motivational appeal. So 'On Liberty' locates in business an arena, almost alone in the period, for exercise of energy on a large scale (p. 272). Compare that to an observation in *Political Economy*:

That the energies of mankind should be kept in employment by the struggle for riches, as they were formerly by the struggle of war, until the better minds succeed in educating the others into better things, is undoubtedly more desirable than that they should rest and stagnate. While minds are coarse they require coarse stimuli, and let them have them. (iii. 754)

In 'Utilitarianism' Mill lauds mental-emotional cultivation, acculturation, habituation that gradually intensifies feelings around 'fecund' utilities, ones especially capable of generating more utilities. His key example is not liberty in that essay; it is virtue, and he speaks at most length about love of justice. But rather surprisingly, yet tellingly, he offers love of money as a clear, everyday illustration of the developmental process he has in mind. Money (meaning the money-form—coin, paper, or credit) is manifestly of value only for allowing us to purchase the things we want, things quite other than money; yet money comes often enough to be eagerly sought after and enjoyed for its own sake, too (pp. 235–9).[15]

I think of Sleary saying, 'You *mutht* have uth . . . make the betht of uth; not the wortht!' Mill's lesson seems similar—to judge some of the worst in us as not so bad if it shows energy of desire.[16] We must have this. At times both Dickens and Mill show fear of its demise and affirm what stimulates and develops it, however coarse.

Mill advocates ramping up the desires of the working class. He wants to see them raising their expected standard of living rather than 'peopling down' to a flat, too easily satisfied standard of subsistence (*Political Economy*, ii. 341–2). He increases emphasis on a point also found in Ricardo and Malthus. Ricardo says 'friends of humanity' must call for stimulation of working-class desires, for without 'a taste for comforts and enjoyments', where is the incentive to limit family size in a scheme of self-betterment (*Principles of Political Economy*, 100)? Malthus speaks of the people of England, compared to people elsewhere, as having stronger desires for conveniences, comforts, and self-betterment '(that master-spring of public prosperity)'. From such a mentality comes willingness to endure pains—of work, savings and investment, and sexual restraint—for the sake of the payoff in pleasures. Therefore Malthus wants to see 'the spread of luxury . . . among the mass of the people' (*Essay* (1803 edn.), 267, 321). But he is not altogether hopeful. He observes that 'few things are more difficult, than to inspire new tastes and wants, particularly out of old materials'.[17]

Perhaps desire for liberty, like desires for other utilities, may develop under inducements. Mill's case for liberty, in its crafting for a double readership, gives a glimpse of something provocative but unresolved. Desires often presumed to be widely shared primal fires, deep springs of human action, may sometimes be weak or barely active at all, and in need of calling forth and cultivation.

NOTES

1. Schofield, *Utility and Democracy* (also countering Dinwiddy, 'Bentham's Transition'), 79–80, 82, 137–8; Rosen, 'Eric Stokes, British Utilitarianism, and India' (also countering Eric Stokes, *English Utilitarians and India*), 20–1; Kelly, *Utilitarianism*, 4; Semple, *Bentham's Prison*, 320–1.

2. Schofield refutes the idea of 'conversion' by James Mill. According to Schofield's analysis, Bentham's conceptualization of sinister interest as this operates in lawyers paved the way towards his recognition of sinister interest as it operates in legislators as well. That is, absent controls, rulers will tend to advance their own interests at the expense of those they rule. Democracy offers controls through the political sanction of the vote in combination with the moral sanction of public opinion. These sanctions are to function by way of both check and encouragement. They give those in power an interest in doing less by way of disservice and more by way of service to the public, so as to maintain and enjoy their own power, with circumscribed but still remaining opportunities to benefit from that power themselves (pp. 137–40).

3. Rosen, *Jeremy Bentham and Representative Democracy*, 221.

4. Semple, *Bentham's Prison*, and see Ch. 2 n. 14.

5. Englemann, *Imagining Interest*, 9.

6. Boralevi, *Bentham and the Oppressed*. See also Crimmins, *Secular Utilitarianism*, on Bentham's defence of various kinds of religious dissent, and Crompton, *Byron and Greek Love*, 251–83 and Crimmins, ch. 9, on his defence of sexual nonconformity.

7. See Ch. 2 n. 27; Ch. 7.

8. Anderson, *Tainted Souls and Painted Faces*, 22–38.

9. Hamburger contends that Mill's ultimate object is to attack Christian belief (in favour of the Religion of Humanity) and that the need for free speech to allow such a provocative subject to be raised grounds his interest in liberty. This is interesting for calling attention to a critique of Christianity. However, I part company with Hamburger when he pins Mill's critique of Christian ethics to a critique of 'selfishness' (*John Stuart Mill*, 43). Mill

has too much stake in Utilitarianism and political economy, and Utilitarianism and political economy too much stake in self-interest for that.

10. Engelmann, *Imagining Interest*, 16; Kelly, *Utilitarianism*, 92.

11. 'Liberty then is neither more nor less than the absence of coercion. This is the genuine, original and proper sense of the word liberty. The idea of it is an idea purely negative. It is not anything that is produced by law. It exists without law and not by means of law. It is not producible at all by law, but in the case where its opposite *coercion* has been produced [by law] before. That which under the name of Liberty is so much magnified, as the invaluable, the unrivalled work of Law, is not *liberty*, but *security*' (University College London, Bentham MS box 69, fo. 44, cited Long, *Bentham on Liberty*, 74).

12. Liberty as itself a utility for Mill does not figure in works, for instance, by Dworkin (ed.), *Mill's* On Liberty; Riley, *Mill on Liberty*; Hamburger, *John Stuart Mill*; Levin, *J. S. Mill*; West (ed.), *Mill's Utilitarianism*; D. A. Lloyd Thomas distances himself from the idea of liberty as an end in itself in Mill ('Rights, Consequences', 178). Brink thinks Mill's liberty is not, at any rate, a 'dominant intrinsic good' ('Mill's Deliberative Utilitarianism', 166). Rees sees conceptions of liberty in Mill as both a good in itself and a means to happiness, a view I share, except that I do not say only the second would be 'strictly utilitarian' (*John Stuart Mill's* On Liberty, 76–7). I am closer to Baum, who believes Mill considers liberty so fundamental to happiness as to be desired as part of that end (*Rereading Power*, 144–5, citing 'On Liberty', 224, 'Utilitarianism', 235, 212). Re Baum, see also n. 16 below.

13. The Robsons ('"Impetuous Eagerness"') catch the passion of his early Radical journalism. Jevons, one of the shapers of neoclassical economics, is a considerable critic of Mill and acknowledges more debt to Bentham; still he speaks of the easy and enticing flow of Mill's sentences and ideas, which bear the reader along despite questions and contradictions ('John Stuart Mill's Philosophy Tested').

14. Gutmann ('What's the Use of Going to School?') and Gardner ('Liberty and Compulsory Education') shine a strong light on quandaries for Utilitarianism re freedom and compulsory education.

15. It is I, not Mill, who introduce Bentham's terminology of fecundity. To speak of fecund utilities is, in part, strictly applicable, in another part, only in a more roundabout way. Mill lines up love of virtue and love of money in equivalence to each other, and, more briefly, in equivalence to love of power and love of fame. He then qualifies, drawing a distinction between the first and second of these pairs. At a primal level, power and fame offer immediate pleasure, so they are utilities, and they are prone to

produce more utilities, so they are fecund utilities. Virtue and money are primally 'indifferent', only sought as a means to other satisfying ends, so they are not at first utilities, but they, too, are prone to produce utilities down the line. So there is fecundity of a sort; and feedback processes of association may turn virtue and money into sources of immediate pleasure in themselves, thus utilities, and thus, going forward, fecund utilities. Bentham provides a place in his theory for generative, self-fostering processes of mind and cultivation, which would only be consistent with his philosophic commitment to ideas of progress, improvement, critical thinking, the felicific calculus, and choices for maximizing utility, and consistent with his practical commitment (to name a relevant reform cause) to education. Certainly, Mill goes further than Bentham in analysing the complex mental-emotional dynamics of progressive self-development and habit formation.

16. Mill's perceived differences from Bentham in 'Utilitarianism' have been 'the subject of an extensive literature, much of it highly critical', says Wendy Donner ('Mill's Theory of Value', 124). The debate often plays out over Mill's language of 'quality' versus 'quantity' in utilities ('Utilitarianism', 211–13). I see this as a distraction since Mill uses 'quality' to mean 'kind' (category as defined by properties) in a way compatible with Bentham's usage of the word 'quality' ('Ontology', 197, 199, 202). That there are different kinds of utilities is non-controversial in Benthamite theory. More controversial are Mill's claim that 'some *kinds* of pleasures are more desirable and more valuable' and his terminology of 'higher' pleasures and 'higher faculties' of a cultivated sort. The question arises, is Mill an elitist? (As the question arises, is Bentham—defender of push-pin—an egalitarian enemy of all cultivation?) Donner gives an interesting answer on Mill. She argues that he valorizes the power of cultivation and gives examples of cultivated utilities that are highly valuable, but without declaring fixed priorities; she therefore concludes that the spirit of his theory is 'radically egalitarian' ('Mill's Utilitarianism', 271–2). John Skorupski entertains a similar idea (if tentatively): that Mill allows for differences between people, while believing all people capable of cultivation, and therefore allows for differences, but still equivalent value, in the pleasures they cultivate ('The Place of Utilitarianism in Mill's Philosophy', 57). Donner and Skorupski point to examples in Mill such as love of justice and a sense of dignity, and they add examples of their own such as caring and relationship and poetry and chess. These sound pretty exalted. I think Mill moves in a more egalitarian direction when he places love of money, also love of power and fame, in parallel to love of virtue in order to illustrate the complex activities of mind that constitute cultivation. Also

consider Baum. As I indicated in n. 12, he is one of the few critics to identify liberty and happiness in Mill's conception. He cites 'Utilitarianism' for a reference to love of liberty and personal independence (*Rereading Power,* 144–5, 'Utilitarianism', 212). He does not address the controversy re elitism raised by the passage in its language describing some pleasures and faculties as 'higher'; nor does he, while making a reference to the passage in 'Utilitarianism' that explains the process of cultivation ('Utilitarianism', 235–6), delve into that process. Like Skorupski, he points to Mill's example of a sense of dignity, in this case to place it in parallel to Mill's examples of love of liberty and personal independence. Again, the comparison sounds rather exalted. But Mill presents what may well sound like lowlier correlates in the same breath: pride, love of power, love of excitement, love of health. Still, re the egalitarian–elitist continuum, it may be worth mentioning a couple of facts: for the vote, Bentham calls for ability to read and to write enough to sign one's name; Mill calls for ability to read, write, and do some arithmetic, while he sees merits in plural voting for those with higher education, members of the liberal professions, and perhaps some others who can demonstrate comparable knowledge and ability (both want votes for women) (Bentham, *First Principles Preparatory to Constitutional Code,* 96–7; Mill, 'Considerations on Representative Government', 470, 474–7, 479–81).

17. Malthus is challenging Ricardo's acceptance of Say's law that increased capital investment will be met by increased demand for the supply produced (Ricardo–Malthus letter exchange 24, 26 Jan. 1817, vii. 121–2). Malthus says that capitalists, with their propensity for saving, are unlikely to provide sufficient consumer demand and that workers may choose leisure over working, earning, and spending, and/or sexual satisfaction and big families over expanding their consumer tastes. So 'it is true that wealth produces wants; but it is a still more important truth that wants produce wealth. The greatest difficulty in civilizing and enriching countries is, to inspire them with wants' (*Principles of Political Economy,* 359–67, 459). Mill follows Ricardo, arguing against Malthus (and Thomas Chalmers and J. C. L. de Sismondi) (*Political Economy,* 2: 66–8). He says that with increased capital investment, the overall amount of wages to the workforce will increase, and workers will increase demand for the increased supply they have produced. There are two possible paths to this result. If the working-class population rises, individual wages will not rise (only overall payments made to more workers), but there will be more mouths demanding an unchanged level of supply-per-mouth (presumably until a Malthusian correction checking population growth). Or if the working-class population remains stable, individual wages will rise, and an unchanged number of mouths will demand more supply-per-mouth.

Mill's economics holds out hopes for the latter. Gagnier refers to a postulated possible deficit of working-class desire in classical-school economics, in contrast to fuller commitment to insatiability of desire in the neoclassical school, her main claim (*Insatiability of Human Wants*, 26–7, 4). Herbert discusses the worried Malthusian position (*Culture and Anomie*, 126–8), and Kreisel makes use of Herbert, pursuing an application to *Mill on the Floss*. Gallagher indicates that concern about consumer satiety in neoclassical economics is traceable to such a concern in the classical school—she sees more continuity than sharp difference between schools (*Body Economic*, 123–5, 127–8). I think there is greater overall belief in unbounded desire in classical economics than Gagnier suggests and greater overall belief in possible gratification of desire than fits Herbert's emphasis on anomie or Gallagher's on satiety and other dissatisfactions. Also see Ch. 1; Ch. 2 nn. 1, 3; Ch. 4 n. 13.

6

Time and the Textile Industry

Gaskell and Tagore

This chapter takes up one more deep-level principle of Utilitarian political economy, though it is one that is not very discretely addressed in the theory but runs throughout it. This is the principle of time. In previous chapters I have placed principles in relation to actualities, but here I give more sustained attention to actualities, to history. I trace the development of the pre-eminent industry of the Industrial Revolution, linked to trade at home, abroad, and in the empire. This is the textile industry.

Economic theory and economic history support Carlyle when he observes that 'Society [is] founded upon Cloth'. No doubt this might be said in any period but never with more literal as well as symbolic meaning than in this one. The Philosopher of Clothes hails Arkwright's spinning machine and Watt's steam engine, operating together at the vanguard of the Industrial Revolution and empowering UTILITARIA, though a monster in need of due restraint, to challenge the *ancien régime* of Church and aristocracy and usher in a new age. Economic theory and history also provide a reminder of the foundational principle of pleasure in a Society founded upon Cloth—considering, as Carlyle has it, that the first purpose of Clothes is Ornament and to view them is a source of Wonder. And theory and history shed light on the principle of time—considering, again in Carlyle's terms, that 'no fashion will continue' (*Sartor Resartus*, 47).

Following an initial section on theory, I trace a history of the cloth economy and examine representations of this fast-paced economics in novels by Elizabeth Gaskell and Rabindranath Tagore. Gaskell's *Cranford* and Tagore's *The Home and the World* may seem an odd pairing, and I overstep a strict period boundary to treat the latter, which dates to 1916, while it is set some ten years before. But I think the two novels considered together make vividly apparent a huge, world-spanning scope of change. Gaskell and Tagore portray small feminine home spheres—one early Victorian, one just post-Victorian, one British, one Indian—each concerned with pleasures of cloth and clothing, each enmeshed by cloth and clothing in the larger more masculine world of economics and empire, each greatly changed in the process, and most markedly so in changed relations between women and men and low and high in social rank.

'SOCIETY FOUNDED UPON CLOTH'/CLOTHES-AS-ORNAMENT/'NO FASHION WILL CONTINUE'

Doubts about desire like those I touched on at the end of the last chapter do not go very far in Smith. Certainly, when it comes to dress, Smith identifies a vigorous, unflagging desire. While desire for food precedes every other, it is limited by the capacity of the stomach, whereas desire for dress, along with building, equipage, and household furniture—'the conveniencies and ornaments' of life—'seems to have no limit or certain boundary' (*Wealth of Nations*, i. 181). This makes desire of this type a very important economic force. Therefore a Smithian adaptation of Carlyle might state that A Great Deal of the Wealth of the Nation is founded upon Cloth. The economics of dress gives Smith some of his most famous passages. He illustrates division of labour in his description of the pin-factory, and supply and demand in his observation that 'a publick mourning raises the price of black cloth' (i. 14–15, 76). Marx perhaps nods to Smith in using English needle-makers to exemplify the leading edge of division of labour (p. 200). Marx himself writes pages and pages about ten yards of linen and a coat, by which he explains the labour theory of value, exchange value, and the money form.

It is true that clothes sometimes raise questions in economic theory. Malthus lays emphasis on demand for foodstuffs and the danger of shortfall, given his law of population. By comparison, the coat business may suggest a mere dressing up of Dandy, Drone, or prodigal. Mill uses the tailoring of a coat to explore the vexed question of productive versus unproductive labour and productive versus unproductive consumption. He comes out sparing the tailor's labour from a negative judgement under these terms and lets the judgement fall instead on the consumer, who may enjoy wearing a fine coat but produce (or save) nothing.

Still it was textiles that became Britain's industrial leader and agriculture that it subordinated, as marked by Corn Law Repeal. Identified with pains of work, capital savings, and sometimes sexual restraint, the Victorian economy was nevertheless very much devoted to and very much profited by pleasures. Textiles are needed coverings, but they are more than that. They please the senses and aesthetic taste and offer social and erotic pleasures of self-expression, self-display, and the winning of others' regard. They illustrate the strong purpose of industry to supply Clothes-as-Ornament—'conveniencies and ornaments'—to bring pleasures of Benthamism to market.

A market in pleasures supplying demand 'with no limit or certain boundary', the textile market was expansive and dynamic, a market following fashion, where no fashion will continue. It set a pace of change that calls attention to the temporal principle that runs throughout Utilitarian economics.

As a general principle, that of time is not easy to capture in key theoretical statements. Bentham gives some theoretical prominence to time by naming four time factors as determinants of utility. These are 'duration', 'propinquity', 'certainty' (in expected realization), and 'fecundity' (in generation of future utilities) (*Morals and Legislation*, 38–9). Malthus identifies a mental habit indispensable to economic success as ability 'to reason from the past to the future', 'to look before and after' (*Political Economy*, 195). Jevons, in accordance with classical theory, observes that 'time enters into all economic questions. We live in time, and think and act in time; we are in fact altogether the creatures of time' (*Political Economy*, 65).

In that the temporal principle enters in everywhere and meshes with the rest of the principles of Utilitarian political economy, I have already attended to various considerations of time. Thus: pleasures and pains are greater or lesser the more lasting or fleeting they are, the more imminent or delayed, the more certain or uncertain, the more or less generative and subject to cultivation for the future. Critical thinking is forward-looking and developmental over time. The projector projects in time. Pains of work and capital savings for investment—including

lending at interest—represent temporally calculated delays of gratification. So does 'moral restraint'. Division of labour means its articulation
along a timeline of stages of production. Capital embodies past labour
in forms capable of being stored and accumulated over time, and capital
investment puts that past labour to work augmenting present labour.
Capitalists set firmer dates for payment than those in a gift economy.
Economists frown on indefinite delay, deadlock, hoarding (Chancery,
Krook's Rag and Bottle non-shop, Mrs Glegg's clothes-chest). They do
not favour slow turnover (like that of land by inheritance within the
landlord class). They smile on liquidity, brisk investment (Tom's and
Mrs Glegg's staking of Bob Jakin), and brisk trade circulation (Mrs
Bagnet's shop, Bob's pack-goods sales). They track individual betterment and growth of national wealth by temporal increments in running
accounts. Time layers economic mentalities and practices one upon
another (capitalist upon gift-exchange modes). It is time that tells how
freedom bears results and reveals the workings of the invisible hand.

Further temporal considerations are worth adding here and are well
brought out by economists' commentaries on textiles. Malthus points to
the rapid innovation that is 'very strikingly exemplified' by mechanization in the cotton industry. He links this to the rapid growth of
Lancashire mill-towns like Manchester and to cotton's rapidly rising
value to the economy as goods become cheaper and consumption
increases at home and abroad (*Political Economy*, 311–12). His remarks
also make evident the rapid expansion of international trade. Ricardo
addresses such trade in his doctrine of 'comparative advantage', exemplified by exchange of British cloth for Portuguese wine. As he explains,
in an international trade that is free, each nation gains by producing
what it can most efficiently produce and trading that for whatever else it
wants that is most efficiently produced elsewhere (*Principles*, 133–40).
However, factoring in time, Malthus observes the volatility involved.
One innovation spawns another, conditions of production and exchange alter, supply and demand fluctuate, and comparative advantage
shifts. Again, textiles provide the example. Malthus observes the distress
of Spitalfields silk weavers facing the rising vogue for muslin. He
anticipates decline in the US export of raw cotton to Britain and
increase in its own cotton spinning and weaving (*Essay* (1803 edn.)
187, 144). No fashion will continue.

But let me move now from theory to history.

'NO FASHION WILL CONTINUE'

Students of Victorian literature and culture are likely to be familiar with a number of facts of textile history, but in context of Britain or India, industrialism or imperialism, considered more or less separately. I think a more interconnected account of facts familiar and not so familiar more fully conveys the reach and momentum of change. So I sketch a chronology to take us to the period of *Cranford*, set mainly in the 1820s–40s.

In Britain wool was for centuries the pre-eminent textile. Old fifteenth-century Hiram of *The Warden* had been a wool-stapler; so had Mr Glegg of *The Mill on the Floss*, the one wealthy enough to endow a pensioners' hospital, the other to enjoy a prosperous retirement. St Ogg's and its hinterlands supply 'soft fleeces' for ship cargo (p. 101). Mr Deane marks his success in the world by wearing fine woollen broadcloth.

Mrs Tulliver cherishes her linens, linen being a fibre often brought from Scotland or Ireland as well as from the Netherlands or elsewhere on the Continent. She does not want Tom to go to school so far away that she cannot 'wash him and mend him', or else he might as well have calico as linen shirts. The loveliness of linen consists in its whiteness, maintained by bleaching to hold off the 'yallow' (p. 9).

Wools and linens involved inland transport and, in the case of linens, import from Europe. British woollens went out. So there was international trade, which came to encompass trade within the empire and large-scale import of non-indigenous fibres into Britain, most notably cotton. Mrs Glegg disapproves of the increasingly widespread wearing of woven cotton stockings, while she is tempted by Bob Jakin's packgoods of calico and muslin. Mrs Pullet refers to her valuable 'Indy muslin'.

Cotton cloth came at first from India, during the early days of the East India Company, founded in 1600. The Company's initial object was to get in on the spice trade that had proved very profitable to Indian, Arab, then Portuguese merchants and the Dutch East India Company. Portugal and the Netherlands developed a triangular trade, buying Indian cotton cloth to carry to Indonesia for barter for pepper, cloves, nutmeg, and mace, which were then brought back to Europe. Britain found another opening for profit in buying cotton cloth for direct import to Britain and Europe.[1]

James Mill gives an account of the business in his *History of British India*. This covers the period from 1600 up to the 1818 publication date of Mill's book, during a good part of which time India was the greatest exporter of textiles the world had ever known.[2] Calico and other woven manufactures were the East India Company's chief trade goods, along with raw silk, diamonds, tea, porcelain, pepper, drugs, and saltpetre. Mill describes a system employing mainly native intermediaries supplying materials or means of purchasing them to village producers, with further capital outlay to sustain them while at work, and providing for completion to standards, on schedule, for prearranged prices, and transport to Company warehouses, called factories. Because of insecurities under the weakening Mogul Empire, these factories were developed as armed strongholds (pp. 339–42). Thus the securing of the textile trade led towards Britain's build-up as a military and ultimately governmental power in India.

There was no even British–Indian, wool–cotton balance of trade. Wool was too warm for hot India plus dull-coloured and hard to wash. The comparative advantage was on India's side. For the British, Indian cotton offered lightness and brilliant colour—its greatest advantage being capacity to hold its colour when washed. It also offered novelty and cheapness. One main dye was madder for red—also black—held fast by chemical interaction with a pre-applied mordant. The other main dye was notably colourfast indigo. The most elegant goods were painted (with the mordant), less fine ones block printed. For calico (from the town name Calicut) or chintz (from Sanskrit *chitra*: variegated, or vernacular non-Aryan *chitta*: spotted cloth), designs were mostly floral or with small florets or spots. There was also fine white muslin from Bengal. At first Europeans were eager to get furniture fabrics, then increasingly piece goods for clothing. I may capture the array in brief by listing names for cotton materials and clothing types taken into the English language from India: besides calico, chintz, and muslin—percale, gingham, khaki, dungaree, seersucker, madras, pajama, sash, bandana.

Beyond cottons there were fine Bengal and other silks. There was access to Chinese silks via trade in Indian cottons, indigo, and opium. And there were mountain-goat's wool weavings, notably Kashmir shawls. The Mogul Emperor Akbar created a vogue for these in the late sixteenth and early seventeenth centuries, Napoleon gave one to Josephine, and they were the rage in England from the latter eighteenth century to the middle of the nineteenth. Cashmere is another word taken into English. So is shawl.

The economy of cloth took a turn in 1700. The sought-after textiles of India prompted a transformation in British textiles that set the course for the Industrial Revolution. In 1700 a ban was placed on use in Britain of printed cottons, also silks, from the East, especially calicoes. Plain white cotton cloth could still enter the country. The law was meant to protect British woollen and silk interests from Indian competition. It was a manifestation of non-laissez-faire thinking (of the same sort that caused Parliament in 1678 to require burial of the dead in wool!). The legislation of 1700 was preliminary to full-scale illegalizing of all painted or printed cottons from 1721 to 1774. In response to the 1700 legislation, British concerns developed techniques for decorating the plain white Indian cotton cloth that could still be imported up to an Indian standard of colourfastness and with a price advantage from increasingly effective mechanized block-printing. Thus when faced with the legislation of 1721, the industry in Britain had reached a point to see profit in provisioning itself with the white cotton cloth that was needed as ground for the printing that it could now do. It dodged the 1721 ban on all printed cottons by developing cotton-linen weaves on which to print.[3]

Arkwright's frame mechanized the spinning of cotton. Significantly, Arkwright was a petitioner for the 1774 repeal of the ban on printed all-cotton cloth. Arkwright's 1775 improvement on his machine led to the production of cotton thread suitable for knitting frames of the sort that made cotton stockings widely available (to be criticized by Mrs Glegg).[4]

Innovations followed in weaving, especially through the laying on of steam. The earliest power loom with commercial viability dates to an 1802 patent. There were innovations in printing by engraved copper rollers from the mid-1780s and a breakthrough in the process of bleaching dating to the end of the eighteenth century. Following from an 1823 experiment with indigo, synthetic aniline dyes became available, ultimately to be produced from coal tar and displacing natural dyes in the 1850s.

While prohibition of the import of Indian calicos was relaxed in the latter eighteenth century, it was only after the trade had succumbed to Britain's seizure of comparative advantage through her industrial revolution in cotton.[5]

As for silk woven goods, there was a ban on their import from the late seventeenth century, aimed largely at protecting British silk-weaving against French competition (at the high end of the market) and against Indian, then British, competition in cotton calicoes (across the market spectrum, reaching ever further towards the low end). In 1826 Spital-fields interests let this protectionist ban go (making do with a substantial import duty on silk cloth) in exchange for lowered import duties on raw and thrown silk as these materials for supply of the home industry become obtainable from Bengal. This stimulated the industrialization of silk weaving, which increased its advantage relative to the French industry largely at the middle to lower end. The effort to hold out against calicoes in the broad middle and low end of the cloth market was futile and ended.[6]

And as for Kashmir shawls, by the first decade of the nineteenth century they were being imitated at Paisley in Scotland. By the 1850s high-tech Jacquard looms were supplying demand at cheaper and cheaper cost. There were shawls in cotton and silk as well as wool and coloured by aniline dyes. Here volatility is especially evident. Having gained advantage in the market, Britain proceeded to saturate it, making shawls commoner and commoner till the fashion ran its course and died out in the 1880s. This fashion did not continue.[7]

One more change indicator and change agent to mention is the railway-building that was initiated in service to the far-reaching, fast-moving economy of cloth. The first line was laid from Manchester to its port of Liverpool in 1830. But now it is time to go to *Cranford.*

CRANFORD

Gaskell's *Cranford* gives us a view of the cloth economy from the vantage point of the early Victorian period in Britain. Cranford is a village close to Drumble, that is, Manchester, the ultimate Coketown or Cotton-opolis. The elderly spinsters and widowed ladies who form the high society of the village dislike the 'horrid cotton trade' (p. 106) of

Drumble, as they do the coming of the railway. However, theirs can well be considered a Society founded upon Cloth, with a foundation, to be sure, that is not stable but shifting. Clothes-as-Ornament loom large for these ladies, and changing cloth economics refashions their lives and community. In my reading, the cotton trade, no longer so 'horrid'-seeming by novel's end, brings economic change for the better to Cranford and social change for the better as well.

Cranford is known for odd and charming vignettes such as that of the cow dressed in grey flannel and the washing of fine old lace in milk with the subsequent business of getting the cat to disgorge it. Fabrics abound. We hear of fine coloured silks and rustling pure black silks (for the toniest widow's weeds), black bombazine (wool-silk for the more plebian widow), chintz, cotton prints instead of summer silks (so easy to wash), mousseline-de-laine (wool or wool-cotton), gay shawls (for working-men's wives and daughters, no doubt Kashmir-imitation Paisley), crochet-work, gigots, bright petticoats, calashes, red silk umbrellas, all kinds of bonnets. We hear of the pounds per annum it costs to dress the Brown sisters—£2 more a year for the younger Miss Brown, still pretty and marriageable. We become very aware of the importance of dress as an object of desire in Cranford, and of the importance of economics to satisfying that desire. The Cranford ladies are stinted in means and must practise 'elegant economy' if they are to enjoy their 'aristocratic', 'blue-blooded' style (pp. 42, 41, 108).

The novel is constructed to set small, old-fashioned, 'aristocratic' Cranford off against big, modern, 'vulgar' Drumble, with its 'horrid' cotton trade. The narrator, Mary Smith, a frequent visitor to Cranford, is the daughter of a Drumble businessman and views the village with affectionate amusement at its anti-vulgarian quaintness.[8] At the same time that the novel sets Cranford off against Drumble, it sets the ladies of Cranford off against men. The ladies are likened to Amazons. They are anti-man, as they are anti-vulgar. They almost persuade themselves that to be a man is to be vulgar (p. 45). But Gaskell probes a confusion here when she causes the ladies to reflect that, after all, their own gentlemen fathers were men. The Cranford–Drumble, female–male binaries turn out to be problematic. Cranford's ladies are not so entirely cut off from Drumble, with its 'vulgar' and 'horrid' economics; nor are they so entirely cut off from men. It is just that they would like Cranford's economics to be 'elegant', and Cranford's men to be gentlemen.

Critics typically see a cherishing of old-style ladylike Cranford in Gaskell's novel. Or they see regretful acknowledgement that its days are numbered in the face of an encroaching modern, masculine, capitalist world. Sometimes they see an account of self-preservation through strictly limited adaptation.[9] In any case, critics often dwell on Cranford's miniaturist charm. Elizabeth Langland reminds us to watch out lest we regard the feminine sphere as small or even trivial in importance.[10] Langland thinks the ladies deploy effectual cultural capital through their socially expressive modes and manners. However, she treats the feminine cultural capital of Cranford as if it were indeed separate from and opposite to the masculine material capital of Drumble. Like others, she is content to set off Cranford and Drumble, women and men. She speaks of the 'sufficient' ladies of Cranford.[11] I would say that only wryly does Gaskell call the ladies 'sufficient' (p. 39). On the contrary, as we initially observe them, they are isolated and straitened in circumstances, enduring 'general but unacknowledged poverty' (p. 41), gallantly attempting to maintain their old style and status on their own, but not succeeding too well. Gaskell represents the diminution of the ladies' former means by the falling away of the gentlemen who provided them. New means and new men come to Cranford by way of Drumble and, beyond that, India and world-imperial trade, especially in cotton. In large part the new men, as was true of the old, are the providers, but altered economic conditions bring more opportunity for the ladies to provide for themselves, and for some less-than-genteel Cranford inhabitants to better their conditions. Gaskell invites us to recognize that little old-fashioned Cranford exists within a large and a changing world and that it gains when it opens itself to wider new connections.

Miss Matty Jenkyns, younger daughter of a Church of England rector, remains unmarried, as does the elder Miss Jenkyns, due to a lack of suitably high-class suitors in town. Because their gentlemanly father's Church living died with him and they are without the support of gentlemanly husbands, the Jenkyns sisters' incomes are much reduced— to return on investment of the small capitals left them by inheritance. Nevertheless, still very much the lady, Miss Matty imitates the headwear of the most aristocratic member of her circle, the Honourable

Mrs Jamieson, a Governor's daughter, relict of the younger brother of a Scotch peer, a Baron's daughter-in-law. Mrs Jamieson keeps up her ties with county families and is proud to have a titled sister-in-law, Lady Glenmire. She maintains a grandly powdered butler. This is even though she must skimp on high-priced sugar at her tea parties, just as the rest of the Cranford ladies must make the best of fine caps instead of new dresses, of saving candle ends and bits of butter, of subsisting on 'fragments and small opportunities' (p. 54). There are many things 'we wished for but could not afford' (p. 175).

Struggling to sustain itself in its old ways, Cranford is defensive against what appears new-fangled and external to it. The ladies are nervous about the coming of the new railway and the coming of new railway reading, too. Miss Jenkyns upholds Samuel Johnson and a traditional Latinate style as against the new rage, Dickens. Cranford remembers the days of danger of attack by the upstart foreigner Bonaparte. In the novel's present-day plot there are various characters who seem like invaders, and they are men. First Captain Brown comes to town, then his namesake Signor Brunoni (Samuel Brown), then the long-lost Jenkyns brother, Peter. Indeed the railway proves dangerous and kills Captain Brown. Miss Jenkyns suspects a tie to his Dickens-reading. Another man is not an outsider but has a taste for going outside; he is also old-fashioned but inclined to modernize. This is Mr Holbrook, a yeoman farmer who had not stood high enough in the social order to be a proper suitor to Miss Matty, though she loved him long ago. He still lives in an old farmhouse but travels abroad to Paris and reads the latest poet, Tennyson. He, too, dies, seemingly brought down by foreignness and modernity. Signor Brunoni, the magician with the novel foreign name and novel foreign tricks, learned in India, is the avatar of Captain Brown and causes a panic over rumoured robberies reminiscent of the Bonaparte scare. But he does not turn out to be so threatening, nor does he die. The same is true of Peter Jenkyns when he, like another Brunoni, makes an entrance from far-away India and as a very new man by Cranford standards.

Though fearful of what is new and foreign, Cranford nonetheless harbours tastes for the latest exotic fashions. This hints at some residual openness to the larger world and to change. The Cranford ladies remember dates in relation to the year in which one of them bought her Indian muslin gown. The Jenkyns's mother had been thrilled to receive a white silk *paduasoy*[12] from her husband-to-be, and she was sorry her mother did not give her a wedding present of a soft Indian shawl—perhaps a Kashmir. She might have received some comfort in her sorrow at her son Peter's running away from home had she lived long enough to receive the large, white, soft shawl he later sent her from India. Miss Matty fancies dress goods in an Indian-launched vogue for strong colours and patterns, such as a silk in lilac with yellow spots and another in sea green. She longs for nothing more than a sea-green turban. When Signor Brunoni appears in Turkish costume, she is delighted to see him confirming a new Eastern style: 'You see, my dear, turbans *are* worn' (p. 134). Such venturesome taste is an indicator for venturesome actions that follow in Matty's story and that typify her brother Peter's story throughout, when we come to learn it. The taste is in clothes; the plot plays out over cloth economics.

After Matty's finances dwindle from straitened to desperate with the failure of the Town and Country Bank,[13] she receives some help locally, but it is access to new, larger-world—Indian—resources that saves the day. First she is helped out by subscription among her friends—a form of gift-giving that is characteristically feminine, entailing considerable self-sacrifice on the part of these mostly already strapped ladies. But then she takes a bold step. She becomes an agent of the East India Tea Company, investing and working in her own tea-shop. How things change from novel's start, when 'none of us spoke of money because that subject savoured of commerce and trade, and though some might be poor, we were all aristocratic' (p. 41)!

How does the tea get to Matty except by railway from Drumble and Liverpool and by ship (more and more likely steamship) from India and China? Tea represents the briskly advancing modern commerce of global, imperial scale, as does cotton. Critics note Matty's departure from standard sales practices and often suggest that she upholds Cranfordian values that are anti-Drumble, anti-masculine, anti-business.[14] Yes, she gentrifies the déclassé ambiance of retail by discreet signage and location of her enterprise in her home. She gives away comfits to children, sometimes warns customers against the health hazards of her own green tea, and finds ways to divide the custom with Mr Johnson's shop without cut-throat competition. Yet it is worth noticing that both shops profit as they carve out marketing niches, Matty specializing in high-class Congou and Souchong and Mr Johnson in commoner but in-demand Gunpowder and Pekoe. Mary Smith supports opening the shop, and her Drumble businessman father helps with financial arrangements, accounting, and advice. Matty turns a £20 profit in the first year. The return is better than what she might have made from teaching or fancywork with her scant, outdated lady's education and skills. £20 represents a real boost in income in the context of the some £162 annual investment proceeds on which she used to live, now reduced to £13. And Matty likes the employment.

So Matty does well seeking to repair her fallen fortunes by means of the Anglo-Indian tea trade. However, it is the Anglo-Indian cotton trade that is her ultimate financial resource. Long-lost Peter comes home from India with fortune enough to dress his sister in Indian muslin and pearls and to support her in comfort. His story very much tells of an orientation to the wider world and a move from the old economy to the new.

Peter grew up disrespectful of genteel Cranford, a player of practical jokes, most memorably in the form of a sartorial outrage. He fell foul of his gentlemanly father by dressing up in his elder sister's clothes, cradling a bundle like an (illegitimate) baby Jenkyns in his arms. Instead of following his father into the Church, aided by the 'gift' of a Church living from his aristocratic godfather (p. 93), Peter decamped for Liverpool, the Navy, the Napoleonic Wars, then India, where he made his substantial fortune as an indigo planter.[15] Back in Cranford, he presents a new look, one that is 'so very Oriental' (p. 211), with the foreign cut to his clothes, his dark tanned skin, and habit of sitting cross-legged. Still a joker who does not stand on his dignity, he tells tall tales of the East—of shooting cherubim in the high Himalayas. He rejects aristocratic Cranford past and embraces 'vulgar' Drumble and the 'horrid' world-imperial cotton trade during this period when Britain, rapidly innovating, was rapidly gaining comparative advantage.

Upon his return Peter himself is not regarded as 'vulgar' or 'horrid', as he once would have been as an indigo man, a cotton-dye man, and, for that matter, as a man. He takes his place as favourite and presiding figure for a Cranford that is economically refashioned—and socially refashioned as well. By means of millinery, low people like the Miss Barkers rise in society. Coming from backgrounds as ladies' maids, they open a business catering to ladies' fashions and eventually dress better and spread a better table than their former fine clientele. They get to be well enough off to retire and enter the ladies' circle. Signor Brunoni also rises. He uses his stint as a sergeant in India to advance his career as a showman and becomes less an alarming upstart and alien than a star performer in Cranford. Miss Matty's servant Martha rises to become her former mistress's landlady, and a country girl of the Hoggins family rises to become Mrs Fitz-Adam, able to afford the largest charitable contribution to Miss Matty in her time of need. Mrs Jamieson's titled sister-in-law Lady Glenmire might be said to fall in becoming mere Mrs Hoggins, the village doctor's wife. However, Mrs Hoggins rebounds, for she flanks Peter on one side while Mrs Jamieson flanks him on the other at the novel's final, festive social gathering.

The scene is the Assembly Room, in the past a meeting-place for county families, thereafter emanating a 'mouldy odour of aristocracy' (p. 133), but now a place of popular entertainment where Signor Brunoni appears, thanks to Peter's arrangements, before a socially mixed, gender-mixed assembly as Magician to the King of Delhi, Rajah of Oude, and Great Lama of Thibet.

The novel's happy ending is defined by an increase in prosperity for Cranford that carries with it considerable class-levelling and opportunity for women. It is true that ex-servants the Miss Barkers like to exclude those from similarly low backgrounds from their roster of customers, that ex-servant Martha still acts more like the servant than the mistress in a household that is now hers, and that Matty bows out of shopkeeping when her brother can support her. Yet Gaskell links change that is progressive in socio-economic and gender terms to participation in a world-scale, rapidly changing economy of cloth.

'NO FASHION WILL CONTINUE'

Going on with the economic chronology, I will briefly cite Gaskell's *North and South*, which presents a mid-century cotton mill-town, Milton. The novel portrays both mill-hands and a Carlylean Captain of Industry, a latter-day Arkwright (p. 83), sympathetically. The workers suffer from the hazards of breathing in cotton fluff and losing work in a trade downturn. The Captain of Industry, Mr Thornton, likewise suffers from vicissitudes of trade and loses his mill under pressure from a strike. But the Hale family from the traditionalist, aristocratic, agricultural South comes to admire the 'grandeur' of northern modern industrial Milton (p. 70). I applaud Susan Zlotnick for weighting the positive far more than is usual in her reading of the novel. Her emphasis is on Milton as a place of progress in prosperity, productivity, and independence for women. She attends to women of the working as well as middle class. Milton's workers dress well, many of them women who prefer mill jobs to being servants. Among middle-class women in the novel, Mr Thornton's mother is a close adviser on matters of management, and Margaret Hale ultimately expresses her desire to marry Thornton by proposing to invest her inherited capital in his projected new undertaking. She puts him back in business.

Leonore Davidoff and Catherine Hall detail similar patterns of business consultation and investment by middle-class women.[16] Nancy Henry catalogues a range of women investors in Victorian fact and fiction.[17] (Remember Mrs Glegg.) But it is in the working class that the industrial revolution in textiles shows its most feminine face. Pamela Sharpe confirms women mill-hands' love of dress and their better pay for mill work than domestic service. She notes women's mobility in the textile trades.[18] Females over 13 comprised the majority of employees in the Lancashire cotton industry. Factory spinning came to be controlled by men, but women and girls worked as carders, blowers, drawers, slobbers, rovers, and piecers. In weaving women were winders and wrappers, again typically supervised by men. But in north-eastern Lancashire there were women power-loom weavers and women who continued to work after marriage, earning piece-rates equal to men's and seeing narrowing wage differentials.[19] Harriet Martineau, a Victorian feminist and proponent of political economy, speaks in favour of expanding work opportunities for women in industry and against 'the jealousy of men in regard to the industrial independence of women'.[20]

Reforming Factory Acts of 1833 and 1844 increased the regulation of child labour and pressed the agenda of public education by requiring increased hours of school per day. Textiles set the model for other industries in this regard. With Forster's Education Act of 1870 under Gladstone and later laws strengthening it, child labour was further restricted. Labour regulations also encompassed women, and there was backing by male workers in the Ten Hours Movement from the 1840s. Women's and children's hours set a limit to hours of factory operation per day and thus to men's hours.[21] Assessing the situation in 1860, W. O. Henderson says Lancashire textile workers stood at the head of the British working class.[22]

Certainly Gaskell, like Dickens, depicts labour–capital conflicts in the 1850s. There were hard times, and harder ones followed during the cotton famine caused by the American Civil War. Whatever its liberal implications for British women and the British class system, cotton also reminds us of reverse implications—of US slavery for raw materials, of empire for trade. J. S. Mill speaks of the forbearance of Lancashire workers aware of the grave cause of their distress from reading in the press about Abolition and the Civil War (*Political Economy*, iii. 763). John Bright, Liberal MP from Manchester, then Birmingham, a backer of free trade and extension of the franchise, championed the North.[23] Certainly Utilitarian political economy opposes slavery—for killing work incentive to the detriment of productivity and, in turn, to the detriment of consumption. Mill develops a more fundamental basis of opposition when he conceptualizes liberty itself as a utility. This makes denial of liberty a direct subtraction from the sum of pleasures. In this period cotton cultivation increased in India, also in Egypt. Both were spared slavery though not colonialism in connection with cotton.[24]

By the 1870s Lancashire labourers and owners recognized the benefits of collective bargaining, and by the 1880s real wages were rising. By the early twentieth century Lancashire workers were among the most unionized and powerful in Britain. Women predominated in factory finishing jobs, and they were important in silk and lace works.[25] Carol Morgan reports women workers' union participation and heavy involvement in the women's suffrage movement.[26]

As regards sewing, a recognizable female path of advancement was from servant to needlewoman, as illustrated by *Cranford*'s Miss Barkers. Male tailors struck in 1834 to resist women's entry into the field, but tailoring greatly expanded in the 1840s, and Carlyle's Tailor became ever more likely to be a Tailoress. There was slop-work, notorious for bad labour conditions, and marketing of more and more ready-mades. In the 1830s–40s Benjamin Hyam pioneered low-profit-margin bulk tailoring, and the Macintosh firm began producing its popular weather-proofs. Elias Howe's, then Isaac Singer's, sewing machines speeded up production from the mid-century.[27] Cotton ready-mades included stockings, underwear, stays, drawers, nightclothes, linings and stiffeners for tweeds off the peg, shirts and neckcloths, shirt fronts and cuffs, ladies' 'costumes', and fustian, dungaree, and corduroy work-clothes.

Scholarship debates the question of the working-class standard of living and the extent of its growth in the nineteenth century,[28] while for the middle class there is little doubt of a major increase. Leaving other measures to the side, let us consider clothes. The price of clothes fell from early on in the Industrial Revolution, and workers bought more of them.[29] Sarah Levitt describes a rising sartorial standard for the population at large during the century.[30] The less-than-wealthy wore cotton instead of wool or linen or silk, machine-made net instead of fine old lace, bright mechanically printed calico instead of hand-painted Indians, printed cotton shawls instead of Kashmirs, natty ready-made tailoring with cotton underpinnings instead of bespoke suits. They had more changes of clothes and more bed linens (bedcottons), curtains, and tablecloths, more washability and more to wash.

Mary Schoeser notes the 'vulgarization' attending this boom. Many industrial, mass-market goods were cheap and 'shewey'.[31] Indeed considerable scorn has been expressed up to the present day for Victorian clothes—with their bright colours, voluminous yardages, busy patterns, paddings and trimmings, penchant for the exotic, and quickness to follow fashion trends. Thad Logan points out this element of scorn for Victorian furnishing fabrics and interior design—featuring curtains, upholstery, trailing tablecloths, fringes, embroideries, antimacassars, doilies, etc. I join her in questioning whether we should be so scornful.[32] A certain misogyny lurks in this attitude, along with a disdain for bourgeois tastes. Furnishings and clothes were typically chosen by women and were undoubtedly a source of pleasure to women—sensuous, aesthetic, erotically charged, a means of self-expression and display of social identity and standing, a means of garnering admiration. Enjoyment of Clothes-as-Ornament would extend to men, too, and, irrespective of gender, to the new rich, the new middle and lower-middle classes, the new working classes in a democratizing Society founded upon Cloth. Miss Matty likes her bright colours, Eastern or Eastern-style novelties: turbans *are* worn.

The industrial revolution in textiles refashioned Britain. And far places. Import of Indian cottons spurred British industrial innovations for purposes of import, imitation, and substitution, leading in time to an entire reversal of comparative advantage that made Britain rather than India the great exporter of cotton goods. British cotton export accelerated from the turn to the middle of the century and ballooned as a percentage of overall export. Sales extended to Europe, North and South America, Australia, Africa, and Asia, above all, India. By the outbreak of the First World War 80 per cent of Lancashire cotton output was for export, 45 per cent of that for India.[33] The Government of India set lighter duties on export of raw cotton to Britain than to other countries, to the benefit of Lancashire, and Lancashire pressured the Government of India to hold the line on duties on import of cotton goods into India and saw abolition of these duties in 1882.[34]

Lancashire did not meet all its goals, nor was Britain actively averse to India's own industrialization of textiles. S. R. B. Leadbeater describes contributions by British experts and some investment of British capital in largely Indian-owned spinning and weaving concerns from the 1850s. Gujarat's Ahmedabad was the 'Manchester of India', along with Bombay. The industry grew if it did not thrive, given British competition. Leadbeater's account proceeds to the period of India's resistance to imperial rule through resistance to the economy of cloth, that is, to the *swadeshi* movement of boycott of foreign goods.[35] This major instrument of Indian nationalism was formulated to protest the Conservative Lord Curzon's Partition of Bengal of 1905, and it was taken up by Gandhi in 1920 when he promoted the *charka* and *khadi*, the spinning wheel and homespun, hand-loomed cloth. Thus symbolically India rejected colonial dependence by rejecting industrialism in textiles. Certainly, it was a symbolism that was politically helpful. India won independence in 1947. However, such symbolism and accompanying implementations were less helpful economically. They considerably inhibited India's development of a modern textile industry. Large northern mills suffered setbacks while spinning remained in the south. Power-loom weaving was mostly limited to dispersed, village-based, small enterprises. In consequence, Indian producers were no match for Britain and other rapidly industrializing competitors.

In the East in the first four decades of the twentieth century, Japan, South Korea, Hong Kong, Taiwan, and what would become Pakistan played better catch-up than India. Setting value on traditional methods and slow to innovate, India favoured low-tech, low-end, low-profit import substitution over modernization and high value-added export, and favoured market protection over laissez-faire.[36] India lost her comparative advantage as the world's premier cloth exporter, lost it to Britain, and then lagged behind other countries that afterwards pulled ahead of Britain herself in the economy of cloth.

THE HOME AND THE WORLD

In Rabindranath Tagore's *The Home and the World* we see the economy of cloth in the latter days of the history I have sketched, and from the Indian side. This novel by the Nobel-prize-winning Bengali writer is set just past the century's turn when Curzon's Partition of Bengal met resistance in the *swadeshi* movement. Like *Cranford*, Tagore's novel features a small, feminine, traditional home sphere set off against, while more and more integrating with, a wider masculine, modern socio-economic-imperialist world. We observe great change in either case, though change that involves more loss in Tagore's than in Gaskell's novel. Indeed changing cloth economics bore harder on colonial India than imperial Britain. Yet in Tagore's account, what has carried loss carries potential for gain as well,[37] in both economic and social terms.

The home is the traditional *zenana*, the women's precinct of the house behind *purdah*. The world is modern male-dominated cloth economics and empire outside. We get the first-person narrations of the novel's main characters: Nikhil, a prominent Bengali *zemindar*, in many ways modern and Westernized,[38] an advocate of *swadeshi* in its non-militant form of voluntary boycott of foreign goods and promotion of Indian production; Nikhil's friend, Sandip, likewise quite modern and Westernized, the leader of a more militant *swadeshi* of violently enforced boycott; and Nikhil's wife, Bimala, encouraged by both men to leave the *zenana* and, when she does, drawn into conflicted, largely disastrous involvements with Sandip and his cause. The points of view of these subtly rendered characters are far from easy to resolve, they speak in poetically elusive language, each of their accounts is marked by internal contradictions and ironies, and the novel's ending is open and inconclusive. I lack scope as I conclude the chapter for comprehensive analysis of this complex work but will explore one of its most provocative aspects: its twofold narrative lines, what I call its *swadeshi* and its feminist stories of change, which play out in the world and in the home.

In the *swadeshi* story the anthem of Indian nationalist resistance rings out against cotton-milling Manchester: 'The mills of Manchester [are to] sound their own dirge to the tune *Bande Mataram*' (p. 128).[39] While cloth is important within the feminist story—there are references to dresses and ornaments from European shops, low-necked English bodices, embroidery in English patterns, 'many-coloured garments of modern fashion' (p. 22), a gold-bordered white sari with a fine short-sleeved muslin jacket, and an earthen-red sari with a broad blood-red border—such passages do not call attention, as is the case in *Cranford*, to obvious money matters of wherewithal to afford fine clothes. Rather, this story concerns a wife's ceasing to live shut away from the world in the *zenana* and ceasing to 'take the dust' of her husband's feet in token of worship and service in an arranged marriage.

The two storylines suggest some connection between bids to emerge from subordination. But what meaning should we draw, considering the very different powers being challenged in each case? What connects an Indian challenge to British industrial-commercial power and an Indian challenge to an Indian domestic institution? I find an answer in observing both stories' concern with political economy at the base-level of theory. Nikhil, with his modern, Westernized education—he is a holder of the BA degree now reading for the MA—has conversations with his respected old teacher that show his grounding in classical-school principles. These provide the basis for his brand of *swadeshi*. And as part of the modern, Westernized education Nikhil is offering his wife—he has brought in the governess Miss Gilby—he himself is giving her lessons in political economy (p. 26). These figure into his campaign to persuade her to leave the *zenana*.

The principles behind cloth economics in the world bear implications for the less evidently economic sphere of the home. In the *swadeshi* story Nikhil embraces utility, the pleasure principle, pursuit of desire, self-interest. He wants to improve his country's material well-being, undercut by Britain's comparative advantage, especially in textiles. He, like his friend Sandip, wants to increase the wealth of the nation, 'to fill our country's coffers' (p. 37). The friends share such a goal, though Sandip is not the systematic follower of political economy that Nikhil is, and the two do not see eye to eye on the best *swadeshi* practice.

Still, Sandip serves as a particularly vociferous spokesman in the novel for the pleasure principle, for desire and against asceticism. He is not ashamed to admit to 'covetousness' and willingness to snatch if need be. His mantra is 'I want...; I want...; I want...' (pp. 45–6, 38, 130, 48). Sometimes he accuses his friend of being too half-hearted in what he wants for India, instead 'infatuated with the glory of bankruptcy' (p. 47), unwilling to pursue *swadeshi* to its extreme. On occasion, Sandip finds Indian models for unbridled desire. One is Ravana, the demon abductor of *The Ramayana*. But to make a hero of Ravana breaks with standard Indian interpretation, and Sandip more readily associates vindication of desire with Western thought. He says desire finds better accompaniment in the music of an English military band than of Indian festive pipes. He is critical of any lingering ascetic strain in himself: 'I was born in India and the poison of its spirituality runs in my blood... the madness of walking in the path of self-abnegation' (pp. 81, 80).

In the feminist story Sandip also speaks and acts on behalf of desire. That Bimala's passage from the home to the world is a passage towards passion becomes evident in her meetings with Sandip. Clothes-as-Ornament—especially the white and the earthen-red saris—are erotically charged here. They are charged as well with intimations of public adoration and political power as Sandip gives Bimala a vision of herself, dressed in Indian rather than British garb, as a female avatar of the motherland—Kali, Durga, the Shakti of Delight.[40] Sandip says: 'Let [Bimala] gradually come to the conviction that to acknowledge and respect passion as the supreme reality, is to be modern—not to be ashamed of it, not to glorify restraint' (p. 62).

But Nikhil gives fuller conceptual articulation to the cause of desire in the feminist story. He wants his wife to leave the *zenana* and even to leave the ancestral estate for a new life with him in Calcutta. The reason is, above all, that he wants her to be free to desire him. 'Up till now Bimala was my home-made Bimala, the product of the confined space and the daily routine of small duties. Did the love which I received from her ['taking the dust' in worship and service], I asked myself, come from the deep spring of her heart...?' 'One must give up all claims based on conventional rights, if one would find a person freely revealed in truth' (p. 41). Nikhil pushes Bimala towards a liberty she has not sought for herself. This accords with the logic I discussed in the last chapter that makes freedom necessary to deep energy of desire. Nikhil endures great pain in finding that it is not himself but Sandip who is Bimala's chosen object, and not his but Sandip's *swadeshi* that thrills her. He has moments when he endeavours to let Bimala go as his own object of desire. The ascetic side to Nikhil that Sandip has noticed comes out. Here drawing on Indian tradition, Nikhil ponders the Buddha's wisdom in teaching his followers 'to cast out our desires from our minds' (p. 134). However, Nikhil never actually repudiates his scheme to emancipate Bimala. His idea here is Western and stands in contrast to an Eastern idea. In his image, it offers an alternative to the binding of the Chinese woman's foot (p. 22). By the same token, it offers an alternative to the *zenana*. And the novel confirms that the constraint of the *zenana* is harsh. It does so in the words of a secondary yet significant character, one who has long lived within that constraint. This is Nikhil's sister-in-law, the Bara Rani. Having entered the house as a child-bride, endured marriage to a difficult husband, and passed into the bereft, devalued state of a widow, a childless one, the Bara Rani declares: 'I would not live my life again—not as a woman! Let what I have had to bear end with this one birth. I could not bear it over again' (p. 190).

While there is a Western strain in both Sandip's and Nikhil's affirmations of desire, of pleasure, Nikhil affirmation is more systematic. He hews to the principles of political economy. In the feminist story he invokes the pleasure principle and the principle of liberty in a teaching that upholds the free pursuit of utility for each self. In this way, his aspirations for his wife match his aspirations for *swadeshi*. In the *swadeshi* story, he invokes the pleasure principle and the principle of liberty in a teaching that upholds free-market laissez-faire. Unlike Sandip, Nikhil does not consider it his role to control the market that operates on his estate. He will not forbid trade in foreign goods. He condemns the burning of foreign-made shawls and the forcing of merchants to sell Indian ones. He opposes coercion of uncooperative traders by the sinking of their boats. He believes that each agent in the market has an independent interest equal in standing to any other, and that each knows best what that interest is and should be free to pursue it: '"Are you determined not to oust foreign articles from your market?" "I will not," I said, "because they are not mine."' This stance is supported by Nikhil's teacher: '"Because he, whose is the loss, is the best judge"' (p. 103).

In this setting it is poor, low-caste, and Muslim traders who are liable to lose as peddlers of Manchester goods, and poor people, many low-caste or Muslim, who are liable to lose as customers for cheap, serviceable, attractive Manchester cloth. The novel shows that forced boycott cuts not only against the British but against Indians low on the social scale. It points especially to a dangerous anti-Muslim trend in Sandip's movement—recall that Bimila is to embody the motherland as a Hindu female divinity.[41] For Sandip, though in some sense he is an advocate of freedom—for his country, for a woman in the *zenana*—only some people's free pursuit of their interests matters. But for Nikhil, Muslims, lower castes, the poor, women, and everyone else—the greatest number—are selves best left free to act on their own interests as they see them, even if the buying and selling of British cloth has taken and still takes a toll on India's economy, and even if his wife prefers her husband's friend to her husband and the one's version of *swadeshi* to the other's.

Let me go beyond laissez-faire, however, in my account of Nikhil's *swadeshi*. In addition to boycott of non-Indian goods, always provided it is voluntary, he wants more production of Indian goods. Various details delineate Nikhil the projector, the innovator. The temporal principle is very observable here. Nikhil looks to modernize. He would be interested in assisting an inventor of a new loom or rice-husking machine. He once tried to invent an apparatus for extracting date juice to process into sugar. He establishes a bank to help finance new enterprises. He brings Indian-milled yarn into the local market and has considered investing in a cotton mill. 'Why not try to build up something?' Nikhil asks Bimala in a discussion of the economics of *swadeshi* (p. 27). This contrasts with Sandip's more purely negative stance of rejection and destruction of what others have built up.

Nikhil wants to build up something in feminist terms, too. Again he pins his hopes on utility and liberty and is willing to take his chance on time and change. 'I must not lose my faith: I shall wait. The passage from the narrow to the larger world is stormy. When [Bimala] is familiar with this freedom, then I shall know where my place is' (p. 45).

But Nikhil's efforts do not lead to very successful results in either the *swadeshi* or the feminist narrative. As his teacher regretfully points out, the Indian-milled yarn is expensive; therefore Nikhil has to buy it up himself and start a weaving school. All he can expect is to loom cotton fabrics so pricey, though flimsy, that they might as well be cloth-of-gold. He would be the only buyer able to afford them. Or should they ever gain a quality commensurate with their price, they might succeed only in being bought by foreigners. Nikhil concedes that though he would be willing to lose his own money on a cotton mill, he does not want to be a cause of loss to poorer shareholders. Sandip's rather than Nikhil's version of *swadeshi* wins a following. And Bimala emerges from the *zenana* to involvements with Sandip and militant boycott, putting her freedom to dangerous uses in sexual and political terms, and financial terms as well. To raise money for the cause, Bimala steals gold from the household treasury. This is a reserve held for the Bara Rani. Bimala's theft makes clear that the home, not only the world, has its economics, in a woman's scant access to money and scant choice in deploying it, richly as she is clothed and provided for. To take the gold means loss, not so much to her husband, as to a woman—the Bara Rani—such as she herself had been when she lived within the traditional female role. The point emerges that a woman who is not the recipient of money from a male source, a form of gift, can only take it as a thief, at the expense of another dependent woman. This amounts to a sort of self-robbery. Contrite, Bimala seeks to replace the stolen gold by selling her jewels through Sandip's young follower, Amulya. This fails; Amulya undertakes another theft; he is apprehended. Disillusioned with Sandip, Bimala is beset by mounting guilt when the robberies she has been involved in add to the unrest surrounding militant boycott, triggering aggrieved Muslim looting and arson at novel's end. Amulya is killed, Nikhil badly injured.

Yet despite the culmination of the *swadeshi* and the feminist narratives in catastrophe, the novel cannot so easily be called anti-*swadeshi* or anti-feminist.[42] It evokes considerable sympathy for Nikhil's version of *swadeshi*, with its commitments to laissez-faire in trade, innovation in production, and the regaining of comparative advantage. And it evokes considerable sympathy for Bimala's stormy passage in leaving the *zenana*. Desire springs up in her. She takes free action, sexual, political, and financial. She makes misjudgements, lacks options, transgresses, suffers for the suffering she has helped cause, attempts restitution. We come to understand the daunting magnitude of change she experiences: 'I feel as if I have passed through a whole series of births, time has been flying so fast.' We understand her disorientation: she is like a fish set free in the sky. We understand her frustration with change that is obstructed, uneven, and partial, and respond to her note of sadness when she asks, 'Why do not men change wholly when they change?' (pp. 136–7, 185).

Bimala takes a step backwards in her passage when, seeking to restore the bond with her husband, she 'takes the dust' of his feet. He tries to draw her to his breast but does not insist. It seems, again, he does not want to be the one to choose for her. Before the riot intervenes, Nikhil and Bimala had been set to travel to Calcutta, and this would not represent a step backwards but forwards. In a remarkable development, the Bara Rani, the figure of the traditional woman, refuses to be left behind but declares that she too will leave the *zenana* for Calcutta. The Bara Rani would in some ways bring tradition with her—she jokes with Nikhil about the luggage women make men carry so as not to allow them to travel too light. But then too, she asserts a claim on Nikhil that is not strictly traditional. It is not the claim of the sister-in-law on the brother-in-law as patron or provider, but the claim of the former child-bride on the playmate she found in her husband's little brother, who is now her only remaining object of affection and interest in life. Tagore gives us a glimpse in an unexpected quarter of a woman who is tightly bounded in her narrow home but proposes to pass through to the outside world, who is free enough in spirit to desire and to claim something for herself and to choose a new way of life. Nikhil says: 'When I saw the Bara Rani make ready, with all her belongings, to depart from this house of ours, all the ties that bound us, to their wide-spreading ends, felt the shock' (pp. 189–90). The novel is open to this passage, this change.

In his essay 'Nationalism in India' Tagore calls himself 'not an economist'. Yet he describes the world-imperial economy as a huge force that India must contend with through her own 'industrial originality'. He does not want India to become a primarily agricultural country. He expresses the belief that she has something to offer and should do so by productive work, despite possible failure and suffering (pp. 153, 149, 134). This can justify Nikhil's enterprises, though they falter. Taken further, it can justify his risky inducements to Bimala to leave the *zenana* and her risky involvements once out, and justify Bimala's and the Bara Rani's willingness to venture forth to an unknown new life. In his essay on 'Woman', Tagore advocates women's engagement beyond the domestic sphere and their contribution to outside affairs and to their country (p. 218).

Compared to *Cranford, The Home and the World* shows very different proportions of cost and benefit flowing from the fast-paced Anglo-Indian cloth economy. But with more or with less confidence and cheer, both novels affirm change. The heavy cost of change for Indian textiles is clear in *The Home and the World*. Yet Tagore suggests that the principles carried along with the actualities of the cloth economy hold promise for the future for the world and the home. They can be built on for economic revival, improved prospects for the lowly by reason of poverty, caste, or religion, and advances for women that will benefit their husbands as well. In the light of subsequent developments in textiles, in which other countries—though not India[43]—pursued free trade and industrial innovation and ultimately gained comparative advantage over Britain, we may deem Tagore prescient when he causes Nikhil to remark that, even for the British and their empire, 'history is not yet ended' (p. 37). No fashion will continue.

NOTES

1. John Guy, *Woven Cargoes*, 11–17; Irwin and Brett, *Origins of Chintz*, 3.
2. Irwin and Brett, 1.
3. Lemire, *Fashion's Favourite*, 30–42, 24; Schoeser, '"Shewey and Full of Work"', 189.
4. Timmins, 'Technological Change', 42; Levitt, 'Clothing', 157, Edward Baines, from *History of the Cotton Manufacture in Great Britain* (1835), in Freedgood (ed.), *Factory Production*, 70–82.
5. Irwin and Brett, 6.
6. Martineau, *History of the Thirty Years Peace*, i. 475–9; Lemire, *Fashion's Favourite*, 16; Davidoff and Hall, *Family Fortunes*, 409.
7. Gillow and Barnard, *Traditional Indian Textiles*, 117; see Price, *Selected Design Techniques*; Chaudhuri, 'Shawls, Jewelry'.
8. See Gillooly on the emotional tone—distanced amusement and pain at Cranford's marginality seen at such a remove (*Smile of Discontent*, 126).
9. The first two alternatives articulated by Gillooly (p. 126) and Hilary Schor (*Scheherazade*, 85). Cass speaks of both nostalgia and lament, Cranford's 'pastoral charm' along with its 'unwanted metamorphosis' in face of 'sinister capitalist infiltrations' ('Scraps, Patches, and Rags', 418–19, 432, 429). Knezevic offers considerable specificity in his observation of capitalist inroads into Cranford, while he thinks the novel demonstrates the ability of a class regime of gentility to co-opt what threatens it and to preserve itself 'more or less intact' (*Figures of Finance Capitalism*, 111, 102).

10. Langland, *Nobody's Angels*, 114, a view different, for instance, from Tim Dolin's, which is that by encapsulating itself as a feminine separate sphere, Cranford 'reduces its institutions to teaparties and its commodities to trinkets' (*Mistress of the House*, 46).

11. Langland, *Nobody's Angels*—a subtitle within discussion of the novel is 'The Sufficient Ladies of Cranford'. Cf. Rosenthal, who calls Cranford a feminist utopia that assimilates and defeats patriarchal, commercial, technological encroachments ('Gaskell's Feminist Utopia', 92).

12. A heavy French-woven dress silk (Rosemary Crill, Deputy Curator, Indian Department, Victorian & Albert Museum).

13. The 1844 Bank Charter Act increased stability through improved means of supplying country banks from London and increased regulation of the ratio of reserves to circulating notes, though the Act did not always achieve it aims—see Daunton (*Progress and Poverty*, 346–51), Poovey (ed.), *Financial System*, 22–3.

14. Andrew Miller says Matty's shop 'subverts the space of exchange' as a 'resolutely domestic' space that 'bases its economy on gifts rather than on financial gain' (*Novels behind Glass*, 116). Langland places Matty and her shop on the side of cooperation vs. competition and holds that the Cranford ladies 'challenge the values of... industrial capitalism' (*Nobody's Angels*, 124, 122). Likewise Colby ('*Some Appointed Work to Do*', 67). Knezevic speaks of accommodations on Matty's part that leave her standard of gentility only 'a slightly more relaxed version of itself' (*Figures of Finance Capitalism*, 100).

15. This would be after the 1813 Charter renewal ending the East India Co. exclusion of other projectors. Though Knezevic notes the imperial connection re Matty's tea-shop, he notes it in only general terms re Peter's indigo plantation. He speaks of Peter as 'a colonial version of the territorial aristocrat' and treats the sale of his land as his source of wealth and a 'drain of capital' from India. He overlooks the connections of indigo to cotton, trade, industry, Drumble, railways, and vulgar vs. aristocratic class standing (pp. 104, 106).

16. *Family Fortunes*, 272–89, 301–12.

17. '"Ladies do it?"'.

18. Sharpe, *Adapting to Capitalism*, 52, 115, 42.

19. Winstanley, 'Factory Workforce', 126–30; Morgan, *Women Workers*, 44–5; Freedgood (ed.), *Factory Production*, 14–16.

20. 'Female Industry', 63; see also her *History of the Thirty Years Peace* (iv. 216), stating that restrictions on work hours represent restrictions on earning power. Martineau wrote the popular *Illustrations of Political Economy*, and the women's suffrage leader Millicent Fawcett wrote

Political Economy for Beginners and *Tales in Political Economy*; also see Searle (*Morality and the Market*, 142–6) on the interest of other Victorian feminists in political economy, including Bessie Raynor Parks, Barbara Bodichon, and Jessie Boucherett.

21. Morgan, *Women Workers*, 45–64; Freedgood (ed.), *Factory Production*, 14–16.

22. *Lancashire Cotton Famine*, 1.

23. Trevelyan, *British History in the Nineteenth Century*, 332.

24. David Levy (*How the Dismal Science Got its Name*) urges recognition of political economy's anti-racist, anti-slavery position. He notes Mill's vehement rejection of Carlyle's Gospel of Work in its unsavoury (later-career) application to Jamaican freed slaves that comes close to endorsing labour compulsion. See Carlyle, 'The Nigger Question'; Mill, 'The Negro Question'. Levy also details Mill's leadership in bringing Governor Eyre to account for his bloody quelling of the 1865 Jamaican ex-slave uprising. Carlyle took the other side. See Henderson, *Lancashire Cotton Famine*, on the stimulus to Egyptian cotton production in the 1860s. After the building of the Suez Canal in 1869 Disraeli bought controlling shares in 1875; bombardment of Alexandria and establishment of a Protectorate in Egypt followed in 1882 under Gladstone. Security for Mediterranean routes linking Britain to Egypt and to India through the Suez mattered to Lancashire.

25. Winstanley, 'Factory Workforce', 138–40, 128; Sharpe, *Adapting to Capitalism*, 50–6.

26. *Women Workers*, 63.

27. Sharpe, 66–7; Davidoff and Hall, *Family Fortunes*, 241; Levitt, 'Clothing', 168–9, 172–4.

28. Sharpe (*Adapting to Capitalism*, 145) sets E. P. Thompson's finding of a decline in the quality of life for workers against Lindert and Williamson's finding of their net real wage gains. Daunton (*Progress and Poverty*, 439–41) considers a pessimistic assessment more justified for 1770–1820, a more optimistic one after that. Rubinstein's view is roughly similar. He says the working-class standard of living grew in the Napoleonic period, stagnated to 1850, and rose thereafter for a clear improvement by century's end. He correlates the period of stagnation with that of maximum population growth and associates improvement with slower population growth, advances in technology and mechanization, decreased taxes on the working class, growth of world markets, and declining trade barriers (*Britain's Century*, 293–4). Voth indicates that, considering the population boom, it is remarkable that living standards held steady to 1850 ('Living Standards', 271, 293–4), while Boyer charts a clear rise in the second half of the

century and to the 1930s ('Living Standards', 280, 312–13). Floud points to a major rise in the standard of living across the board from 1830 to 1914. Goods and services increased sevenfold, while the population doubled, and the average person was nearly three and a half times better off. There was no long-term overall increase in unemployment. Rising incomes correlated with falling family sizes. In 1914 'the comfort, which … had been the preserve only of a small part of the population, had spread to the majority' (*People and the British Economy*, 3, 10, 46, 186).

29. Voth, 'Living Standards', 283.
30. Levitt, 'Clothing'.
31. Schoeser, ' "Shewey and Full of Work" '.
32. Logan addresses 'the all-too-misogynistic devaluation of women's lives and works' (*Victorian Parlor*, 101) as regards home décor. She draws some connection to anti-bourgeois views, citing Veblen and Baudrillard (pp. 83, 86, 90–2). I also discuss aesthetic levelling, 'vulgarization', or democratization in Ch. 2 and nn. 25, 30, and touch on it at the end of Ch. 4 and in Ch. 7.
33. Mary Rose, Introduction to *Lancashire Cotton Industry*, 9–10; Dupree, 'Foreign Competition', 270.
34. Henderson, *Lancashire Cotton Famine*, 37–41; Bose and Jalal, *Modern South Asia*, 81–2.
35. Leadbeater, *Politics of Textiles*.
36. Dupree, 'Foreign Competition', 283–92; Leadbeater, *Politics of Textiles*, 12; Specker, 'Madras Handlooms', 215–16; Bose and Jalal, *Modern South Asia*, 103, 106.
37. In broad terms I align with Sarkar ('*Ghare Baire*', 144–5) and Battacharya ('*Gora* and *The Home and the World*', 140) in emphasizing an orientation towards modernity.
38. Bose and Jalal (*Modern South Asia*, 90–101) speak of Tagore's own selective incorporation of European thought, neither full-scale accommodation nor reaction.
39. A song by Bankim Chatterjee that became the national anthem.
40. Sangeeta Ray points out the attraction towards power, along with the sexual attraction (*Engendering India*, 116).
41. Underscored by Nandy (*Illegitimacy of Nationalism*, 1–9), and see Bose and Jalal (*Modern South Asia*, 98). See Sarkar on interlinking religious, caste, and class inequities, all challenged in the novel ('*Ghare Baire*', 148–52). Elsewhere, as in 'Nationalism in India' (pp. 117, 137, 139–40), Tagore identifies caste inequity as the worst problem. See Ch. 7 on Utilitarian political economy's disapproval of caste.

42. Re *swadeshi*, Nandy calls Tagore's position anti-imperialist patriotism, contrasted to militant nationalism (*Illegitimacy of Nationalism*, 1–9). Sarkar agrees to a considerable extent ('*Ghare Baire*', 144). Ray speaks of an ambivalent position, quite sympathetic towards Nikhil's *swadeshi* (*Engendering India*, 119), rejecting Sandip's. Re feminism, for Koljian, Tagore suggests that woman's world is the home ('"Durga ... "', 127). Ray perceives sympathy towards Bimala's emancipation in terms of education but lack of overall support for her as a new woman, given the indictment of her participation in Sandip's politics. Battacharya sees some positive treatment of women's emancipation through anti-colonial involvement, even with its conflicts ('*Gora* and *The Home and the World*', 139–41). Sarkar calls Nikhil's determination to respect Bimala's autonomy the dominant note in the novel (p. 167).

43. Tagore had no faith in Gandhi's promotion of textile handcrafts as an instrument of Indian emancipation (Bean, 'Gandhi and Khadi', 371).

7

Utilitarian Political Economy and Empire

Mill as Liberal Imperialist

Like the economy of cloth with which it is linked, British imperialism in India is an arena of huge historical importance. This chapter treats writings on India by Bentham, with parallels in Smith, and by Thomas Babington Macaulay, James Mill, and J. S. Mill. Like the chapter before, this one gives sustained attention to historical actualities. It goes into most detail on Indian developments, while also tracing their relevance to developments in Britain. With this, it offers a broad last look at principles of Utilitarian political economy as they inform practice, along with reminders of commonalities between writers in the tradition of Bentham and Smith and other Victorian writers who are usually set apart from them and more often than not deemed their foes. But to conclude in this way is to put Utilitarians and political economists to a hard final test. Recalling the principle of liberty, in particular, we may well wonder what to make of a liberal tradition that is closely associated with empire.

DOING HIM JUSTICE

Mill writes as a defender of empire in his 'Memorandum of the Improvements in the Administration of India during the Last Thirty Years' and 'The Petition of the East-India Company'. These date to 1858. This is the year following the Indian Mutiny or Sepoy Rebellion, which violently challenged the legitimacy of British rule. It is the year preceding publication of 'On Liberty', where Mill writes as a defender of freedom. Speaking on behalf of the East India Company as Examiner of Correspondence after a career going back to 1823, Mill declares that 'they are satisfied that posterity will do them justice' ('Petition', 80) How are we to understand Mill as liberal and imperialist? How are we to do him justice?'

Edward Said speaks of Mill's 'illiberalism about India' (*Culture and Imperialism*, 163). Uday Singh Mehta holds that the terms of his book's title, *Liberalism and Imperialism*, go all too fittingly together and that Mill belongs to a liberal tradition that shows its authoritarian colours in serving empire. Jennifer Pitts portrays a liberalism that is not imperialistic in its original thrust but must be charged with a 'turn to empire' with the Mills, Sr and Jr.[1]

One may certainly cite anti-imperialist statements by Bentham as well as Smith. Bentham's essay addressed to the 1793 French National Convention seems to say it all: 'Emancipate your Colonies!' Colonialism on the face of it fails to meet France's revolutionary ideals of liberty and equality, declares a vehement, radical Bentham. The French, though high-principled democrats in Europe, must look like sinister aristocrats in the foreign territories that they rule (pp. 291–4). Bentham's argument turns on Utilitarian ideas of social and political justice and on economics straight out of Smith. Articulating positions in line with *The Wealth of Nations* (ii. 610–30), Bentham identifies monopoly as the first object of colonialism—a nation's effort to profit by ruling market conditions in foreign places—and he inveighs against it. Like Smith, he holds colonialist enhancement of the wealth of the nation to be illusory, when reckoned against cost in governance and military enforcement. It is not the sum total of national wealth, nor of wealth accruing to home and colony counted together, that is enhanced, but the wealth of special interests. Imperial monopoly is to the advantage of particular producers and merchants, but to the disadvantage of many others—producers, merchants, and consumers in the colony, producers and merchants at home not engaged in colonial trade, consumers at home, and taxpayers in both places, especially at home, who pay for the imperial infrastructure. On cue from Smith, Bentham instances the British–American trade that proved itself able to thrive *after* US independence. Still, as Smith says, one cannot be very sanguine in expecting a nation to dismantle existing institutions that feed its pride and pay well to some, though at the expense of many (ii. 616–17). And while the essence of Bentham's advice on colonies is 'to get rid of them', he admits that this presents difficulties, practically speaking. He says with regard to French holdings in India: 'You may find yourself reduced by mere necessity to what we should call here a practical [much circumscribed] plan' (p. 311).[2]

So despite its theoretical underpinnings, Utilitarian political economy does not maintain a firm anti-imperialist stance. On the contrary, its imperial involvement is great. This is evident in Mill's career and that of his father James, who brought his son into the Company and preceded him in the powerful Examiner's position. James Mill's *History of British India* helped him win Company appointment in 1819 and became standard reading at the Company's training college at Hailey-bury. Mill the younger describes the work as 'saturated... with the opinions and modes of judgment of a democratic radicalism then regarded as extreme' (*Autobiography*, 29). Friend and champion of Bentham, intellectual resource to and backer of Ricardo in advancement of Utilitarian political economy a next step beyond Smith and Malthus, James Mill held the East India Company Examiner's post from 1830 until his death in 1836 and exerted great influence during the strongly Utilitarian liberal Whig Governor-Generalship of Lord William Bentinck from 1828 to 1835, with which Thomas Babington Macaulay was also associated.

Yes, there is a connection between liberalism and imperialism. But I do not perceive in this a contradiction only to be resolved by ceasing to look for a root meaning of liberty in the term liberalism or a deep concern for liberty among its proponents. Standing behind Mehta's view of J. S. Mill, James Mill, et al. is the line of scholarship I have previously discussed that minimizes the importance of liberty as a principle in the tradition. This has been brought into question by Bentham scholars like Schofield, Rosen, Kelly, Semple, and Boralevi. Arguing the consistency between Bentham's commitments to utility and to democracy, Schofield addresses Bentham's thinking on empire as well, and he finds Bentham 'in general sceptical about the benefits of colonial rule' (*Utility and Democracy*, 201). Here Schofield expresses agreement with Pitts, and Pitts stands up for Bentham, also for Smith, though not for the Mills, as liberal critics of imperialism. Still, mainline opinion still prevails and guides judgement of liberals' involvement with empire. Rosen points to the ongoing influence of Eric Stokes's *The English Utilitarians and India*. As he says, 'Stokes adhered closely to

Halévy's argument that utilitarianism was fundamentally an authoritarian doctrine, and he provided the additional argument that the Indian context enabled the authoritarian element to be revealed most fully' ('Eric Stokes, British Utilitarianism, and India', 21).

Lynn Zastoupil saves Mill from censure of this kind by distancing him from Utilitarian political economy. He presses the idea that Mill's attitude changed under an alternative Burkean/Coleridgean/Romantic influence, strengthened through the influence of certain Anglo-Indian administrators.[3] Thus despite differences between Mehta and Zastoupil, they share a familiar viewpoint.[4] Both give an impression of Utilitarian abstraction, dogmatism, inattentiveness to Indian experience and even disdain for it, and unselfquestioning, unchecked willingness to impose authority in the name of progress. We find charges of 'reliance on abstract maxims', 'narrowness', 'naiveté', and deficit of sympathetic imagination (Zastoupil, *John Stuart Mill and India*, 190, 31, 40, 49, 180, 193, 117, 76–7 and 'India, J. S. Mill, and "Western" Culture', 131, 137), or—in very hostile language—imposition of 'unreflective prejudices that masquerade as thought' (Mehta, *Liberalism and Empire*, 97).

Above all, it is open-mindedness that Mehta misses in Mill—because Mill is a Utilitarian. It is open-mindedness that Zastoupil lauds in Mill—because Mill departs from Utilitarianism. It is also open-mindedness that Pitts misses in Mill—though, as she sees it, this is *because* he departs and is not Utilitarian enough. She speaks of Mill's 'apparent determination to ignore the complexities of Indian society', his two-dimensional viewpoint, lack of curiosity, lack of imagination, lack of sympathy: 'For Mill, then, once a society was deemed backward, there was little more about it that one needed to know' (*Turn to Empire*, 133–4, 140).

Unlike Mehta and Pitts, Zastoupil believes Mill emerges from such a blinkered state of mind to wider, more sympathetic comprehension and even willingness in some instances to learn from India. He treats historical specifics of the East India Company administration. He also calls for attention to 'the neglected story of the influence of the colonized on the colonizer' ('India, J. S. Mill, and "Western" Culture', 130). His is a specificity that I value and a call that I heed. Neither Mehta nor Pitts deals much with particular policies of the Raj. They are suspicious of its 'improving' reformist aims and concern themselves very little with the merits, demerits, or some mixture of the two in given reforms. Nor does either entertain the idea of Indian influence. But a good deal of current work in post-colonial studies stresses attention to historical, contextual specifics and to interactions in the 'contact zone', to 'hybridity' and the 'intimacy' of enemies, in phrases of Mary Louise Pratt's, Homi Bhabha's, and Ashis Nandy's.[5] Scholarship increasingly reveals that dominion did not transfer all agency to the colonizer. It increasingly explores how the colonizer as well as the colonized was shaped by imperial interchange. My own brief history of the economy of cloth shows interchange at the material level—think of the British market for Indian cottons, then the British and Indian markets for Britishized Indian, that is Manchester, cottons. Of course, dry, hard closed-mindedness such as Mehta, Zastoupil, and Pitts attribute to Mill's tradition and/or to Mill must limit interchange at the intellectual level (affecting the material level, too). For a response, let me hark back to the critical thinking in Utilitarian political economy.

I believe that Smith–Benthamite thinking is critical, not a blockage but a conduit for interchange, indeed that it finds special challenges and opportunities in the imperial situation, that these foster its interactive, developmental dynamic, and that Mill does not abandon but carries forward such a mode of thought. As I see it, this critical mode opened the way for Britain herself to be changed in bringing change to her colony. Undeniably, change wrought under imperialism involved damages, and damages loom large in many discussions of empire. But, with some other post-colonial scholars—a notable example for me is Eugene Irschick[6]—I am interested in cultural production as well, as this may sometimes be more neutrally or even positively conceived. Altogether, my aim is to gauge what may be deemed liberal in implications for India, and for Britain.

So I devote the next section to demonstrating the factor of critical thinking in Mill's writings on India, also in Bentham's. I then move to sections on key policy rationales of the Raj concerning equalization of persons; the penal code; education; and government revenue collection and land tenure. The first three reveal a flow of influence mostly from British ideas, the last an important backflow of Indian ideas. Here, arguably, we see liberal imperialism at its most liberal.

CRITICAL THINKING AGAIN

Concerning India, Mill acknowledges context, contingency, and compromise. It would be off the mark to call him abstract and dogmatic. For that matter, he might be more open to the charge of special pleading (as I might, in making his case). Like Bentham, also Smith, he recognizes the tenaciousness of existing institutions, even though subject to change.[7] He calls government by the East India Company 'very much the growth of accident' ('The East India Company's Charter', 36–7). In Mill's time a major function of the Company had come to be regulation and amelioration of the massive, unplanned impacts of the trade it had fostered, going back to the early days of the cloth economy. Arkwright looms, Watt's steam engines, Coketown, and Drumble were Facts not Fancies. Dating to the 1813 charter, the Company had lost its commercial monopoly; dating to the 1833 charter, it had lost its commercial function altogether. India saw the entry of many 'projectors'—such as Gaskell's Peter Jenkyns. Mill recognizes Company rule as one of military force on behalf of a foreign power, many of whose people have a will to dominate and exploit Indians. For that reason, 'the Natives of India need protection against the English'. 'Our empire in India, consisting of a few Europeans holding 100 millions of natives in obedience by an army composed of those very natives, will not exist for a day after we shall lose the character of being more just and disinterested than the native rulers and of being united among ourselves' ('Minute on the Black Act', 14–15).

Mill describes Indians as 'not ripe . . . for representative government' ('East India Company's Charter', 49). This is what alienates Mehta so that his whole judgement turns on it and he hardly touches on other policies. Much the same can be said of Pitts.[8] Mehta charges 'indefinite temporizing' (p. 111). To my mind Mill does take a temporal view. The time-sense is an important part of the thinking, including the critical thinking, of his school. Calculations of utility take into account increments of realization, odds and trade-offs at each stage, along with durability and 'fecundity' for the future. Mill sees Indians as emerging from a long rule of despotism and custom only in the aftermath of empire under the Moguls, as this was superimposed on an immemorial Hindu system of caste hierarchy and monarchical rule. But he also sees Indians as 'constantly becoming fit for higher situations' till 'the time arises when the natives shall be qualified to carry on the same system of Government without our assistance' ('East India Company's Charter', 63, 65).

The right of the British Raj is thus relative—as in the phrase 'more just and disinterested than'—and time-bound. The language of Mill's *Autobiography* captures 'the necessities of compromise' he learned in his Company job, 'to obtain the best I could' and on occasion 'to be pleased and encouraged when I could have the smallest part of it', 'to effect the greatest amount of good compatible with... opportunities' (p. 87).

As I have said and will repeat, Utilitarians have been painted as absolutists à la Gradgrind in a legacy from Bentham of abstract system-building. One may point to some of Mill's own charges along these lines in his essay on Bentham. These are oft-cited in a way that ignores Mill's later acknowledgement of overstatements on the negative side and his firm declaration of ongoing affiliation with Bentham.[9] Recall also that in the Bentham essay Mill characterizes Bentham as a seminal thinker of the age precisely by virtue of his difference from purely speculative philosophers. 'His was an essentially practical mind' (p. 81). It was practical abuses that drew Bentham to become the great subversive and questioner of all things established. The flavour of critical thinking in Utilitarianism comes across in Mill's essay where he assesses Bentham's doctrine of majority rule. Mill does not back this in the same form that Bentham had done. As discussed in Chapter 5, he is more urgently concerned than his predecessor with safeguarding individual liberty against the tyranny of the majority operating through the ballot and public opinion. Still, he presents Bentham's position as justified within a provisional perspective, 'on the whole right, not as being just in itself, but as being less unjust than any other footing on which the matter [could] be placed' at the given time (p. 108). In expressions like these Mill presents Utilitarian proposals as socially situated, subject to limits of practicability, and adaptable over time.

Bentham gives a nod to practical difficulties in the colonial situation. Even in his Jacobin-toned call to France to emancipate her colonies, he temporizes. He does so in the name of liberty. 'Would the tree of liberty grow there, if planted? Would the declaration of rights translate into *Shanscrit*? Would *Bramin, Chetree, Bice, Sooder,* and *Hallachore* meet on equal ground? If not, you may find some difficulty in giving them to themselves' (pp. 310–11). Bentham pays attention to context and historical moment. He pays attention to 'The Influence of Time and Place in Matters of Legislation', in the title of another piece of his concerning India. Mill salutes the contextualist, time-sensitive, practical-minded reformist philosopher by citing this piece in his essay on Bentham.

In 'The Influence of Time and Place in Matters of Legislation' Bentham considers the transplantation of British law to Bengal.[10] He does not here question whether there *should* be such a transplantation. On balance, he expects good from it. In that sense he is a liberal imperialist. But he argues that such good will not come from imposition of British views as absolutes but from adaptation to the Indian situation. I would second Allison Dube's account of Bentham's 'general purpose . . . to emphasize that any transferal of laws must be supported by a diligent examination of, and respect for, the circumstances and sensibilities of those to whom the laws will apply'.[11] With this goes another relativizing of perspective. The Indian situation will set British law in a light to show what is not worthwhile in it, as well as what is. The essay is full of typical Bentham railings—foretaste of Dickens's *Bleak House*—against the inutilities kept alive in the British legal system by the practitioners whose interests they serve:

> Would you see the worth of any established body of law in its genuine colours, transplant it into a foreign clime: The vicious parts of it (that is, speaking of any system as yet in being, the great bulk of it,) no longer veiled by partiality, will display themselves in their genuine weakness and impropriety. (p. 184)

We see the reflection directed back upon British practices that Javed Majeed likewise points to in James Mill.[12] Bentham says that a great deal of English law will be 'bad everywhere' and will 'not only be, but appear worse in Bengal than in England'. From this relocated vantage point he anticipates that new possibilities will appear for 'a system . . . which, while it would be better for Bengal, would also be better even for England' (p. 185).

New possibilities did appear, and India became a spawning ground for major reforms, for colony and for home country in turn. As J. S. Mill says, 'the foreign dependencies of the empire will enjoy the benefits of many reforms, long before the much more compact masses of private interest which oppose themselves to such changes at home, will permit the mother country to share in them' ('Penal Code for India', 21).

The sections that follow on key policy rationales show how India provided a context for reform. For the most part British ideas were the main agents of change. But the critical thinking of Utilitarian political economy also opened the way for Indian ideas to exert influence.

EQUALIZATION OF PERSONS

Mill declares it a foremost honour of the East India Company's government that 'it has acknowledged no such distinction as that of a dominant and a subject race' ('Petition', 82). This accords with the anti-hierarchical, individual-interest and freedom-promoting trends of Utilitarian political economy, which are trends in the wider culture and its literature as well—there in Dickens, in Carlyle in his way, in Trollope, Eliot, Gaskell, and Tagore. Each person's pleasure or pain counts equally into the sum of welfare, and each person's free pursuit of self-interest, pursuit of desire, contributes to the greatest happiness of the greatest number. The doctrine is disposed against distinction of persons for privilege or disability by group, especially by any group defined by inherited birthright, by blood or race. It would place the hereditary Dedlocks on a level with the illegitimate orphans Esther and Jo. Such a doctrine confirms and intensifies itself in the Indian context by antithesis. Thus Bentham backs off from the idea of emancipating an India that still binds and rank-orders her people by inherited caste. And some of the harshest passages in what has been judged to be a harsh treatment of India in James Mill's *History*[13] concern caste, 'the unfair and odious distinctions among men, created by the Hindus' (p. 81). The kinds of things that incite Mill's most vehement diatribes are, for instance, Brahmins' occupational advantages, lighter punishment under the law, exemption from taxes, preferential interest rates, and special legal protection in marriage (for husbands, that is) through severity of punishment for a wife's adultery in proportion to caste adulteration (pp. 45–8, 52–3, 80–3, 100).

James Mill's tone can truly be virulent on the Hindus. It can also shift to a tone of admiration on the Muslims. Here we see his attention to Indian traditions in a play of respect for the one strengthening him in antagonism towards the other, and by this reaction strengthening him in his Utilitarian convictions:

The Mohammedans were exempt from the institution of caste; that institution which stands a more effectual barrier against the welfare of human nature than any other institution which the workings of caprice and of selfishness have ever produced.

Mill lauds the fact that for Mohammedans,

all men are treated as equal. There is no noble, no privileged class. Legally, there is no hereditary property, as the king is the heir of all his subjects. The only thing which creates distinction, is office. . . . For office, there is no monopolizing class. Men from the very lowest ranks of life are daily rising to the highest commands; where each of them is honoured, in proportion not to the opulence of his father, but the qualities which he himself displays. (p. 305)

As for James Mill, 'caste' is a repugnant word for J. S. Mill. He condemns any English presumption of innate superiority and right to rule as caste feeling: 'It should be proclaimed that the English who resort to India or any other foreign possession, to make their fortunes, are naturally inclined to despise the natives and to seek to make themselves a ruling caste.' Mill says that this is something to be resisted, and that the Company should be honoured for resisting it ('Minute on the Black Act', 15).

By such expressions James and J. S. Mill favour a historicist rather than a race/caste interpretation of present Indian subordination to the British.[14] Ideas of universal human nature and its differential development according to time and place combine in this statement of Mill Sr's: 'Notwithstanding the diversities of appearance which, in different ages and countries, human nature puts on, the attentive observer may trace in it an astonishing uniformity with respect to the leading particulars which characterize the different stages of society' (p. 106). It is by such thinking that Mill Jr can look forward to progress leading some day to the end of the British Raj. While it governs, Mill counts as advances steps towards equalization of persons under the law. His 'Memorandum of Improvements' records abolition of slavery. Macaulay set in train legal mechanisms to undercut masters' impunity, indirectly ending slavery, which was directly banned in 1843 (Clive, *Macaulay,* 447).

The 'Memorandum' also records abolition of *sati*. Ascetic subordination and sacrifice of one self to another, one interest to another, in the all-too characteristic form of feminine subordination and self-sacrifice for the sake of a man, is a concern of novels by Dickens, Trollope, Eliot, and Tagore, and it called forth high-profile opposition from Utilitarians in opposition to the Hindu immolation of widows. The Bentinck government outlawed *sati* in 1829. Further reductions of women's disabilities appearing on Mill's roster of improvements are suppression of female infanticide and legalization of the remarriage of widows in 1856.

Another instance of equalization of persons appears in the Black Act of 1836, placing Indians and Britons on the same footing under the law. The act abrogated a British privilege of appeal to the Supreme Court and exemption from civil trial in local courts with native judges (Clive, 333–7). Macaulay spearheaded this measure in the face of loud opposition from Anglo-Indians. In words from his speech on the East India Company's charter renewal of 1833, 'God forbid that we should inflict on her [India] the curse of a new caste', one with special legal prerogatives (p. 157). The word 'caste' drives home his Utilitarian point.

In another area equalization of persons advanced significantly, though not going so far as the Black Act to put British and Indians on a par. I refer to developments in the Indian Civil Service. The Indian Civil Service departed from a gift-economy or patronage model. In testimony to a committee of the House of Lords in the lead-up to the 1853 charter renewal, Mill praises advancement according to fitness rather than patronage. 'There is hardly any government existing in which there is so little personal jobbing.' What would be eulogistically termed livings by 'gift'—of the sort Trollope critiques in the old Church establishment and Gaskell's Peter Jenkyns rejects—fall under the dyslogistic term 'jobbing' in a new vision for government employment. Entering into this frame of judgement would be the labour theory of value and the Gospel of Work; repudiation of the Drone philosophy and of Unworking Aristocrats and Plumstead Episcopi sinecurists; with respect going instead to Iron Master Rouncewell, Captains of Industry, a shopkeeping Cranford lady, and Dame Durden, the Busy Bee. Mill explains that the change in the Indian Civil Service has resulted almost more fortuitously than by design. While there is still patronage in initial appointments, it is largely exercised by the Company's Court of Directors, a body unconnected to Parliament and Britain's ruling class. The flow of jobs is to the middle classes, but, after initial appointments, patronage largely gives way to merit promotions. In a statement with affinities to his father's on Mogul freedom to rise in office by merit, not favour, Mill says: 'the son of a horse-dealer is as likely to qualify himself in the subordinate situations for succeeding to the higher as the son of any one else' ('East India Company's Charter', 37–8).

Mill's East India Company perspective informs his 1854 advocacy of civil-service reform in Britain. He says he looks forward to the step from gift-patronage to appointments by competitive exam as a 'great and salutary moral revolution' ('Reform of the Civil Service', 207). While Trollope questions the efficacy of selection by exam, he too favours a 'cleaner' method than patronage. Developments towards reform followed an incremental, convoluted, and variously compromised route.[15] Open competition by exam was established in India under the 1853 charter and in England by Liberal Prime Minister Gladstone's Order in Council in 1870.

Still in India we see only partial progress towards openness to merit regardless of person. Thus Mill's 1852 charter-renewal testimony approves of the 1833 charter's Macaulay/Bentinck liberalization, removing legal disabilities that would bar Indians from holding any appointment. Mill still backs barring Indians from the covenanted service, which operates by a routine of regular promotions leading to the highest offices. He explains that while some natives may be appointed to very high positions outside normal channels, he does not consider Indians generally fit enough yet to be put into regular expectation of rising to the top. He takes the pains of frustrated ambition and resentment of a glass ceiling seriously and expresses concern about morale. He maintains go-slow caution and declares his faith that natives are constantly becoming fitter for higher situations beyond the very responsible work they now perform, such as most of the administration of justice (especially in Bengal and Agra), subject to appeal, and deputy revenue collection.

THE INDIAN PENAL CODE

Consideration of the penal code links to that of equalizing persons, as the code brings English and Indian under one law. The need for a single code had never been more apparent than at the time of the Black Act, after the influx of English into India following the 1833 charter when an Anglo-Indian clamour for legal privileges had to be quelled. Macaulay finished drafting the code in 1837. In 1858 Mill's 'Memorandum' anticipates its final enactment as well as enactment of codes of civil law and civil and criminal procedure. Together these would constitute 'the most thorough reform probably ever yet made in the judicial administration of a country' (p. 114). Mill's support goes back to his 1838 article for the *Westminster Review*, where he praises Macaulay's work as an experiment in Benthamite judicial philosophy. Besides holding Hindus, Muslims, and English alike accountable, the code demonstrates that Bentham's ideal of encapsulating the whole law within a single written text might be achieved in practice, with clarity of language to make it intelligible not only to men of law but also to the general public. Aims would be to divest lawyers and judges of power to make law through interpretation of precedents, and to control access to law through exclusive command of a specialized legal discourse, a means of maintaining the profits of expertise. A further aim would be to make the code a 'popular book' in which the public could learn the definitions of justice by which it was to live. This is an anti-Chancery conception, and, broadly speaking, a panoptical conception (in a Benthamite, not Foucauldian sense). It favours unobstructed two-way sightlines between the law and the public. Mill says Macaulay advances the great man's purposes, sometimes even surpassing 'the sagacity of Bentham' ('Penal Code for India', 28).

Macaulay follows Bentham on the law though his record shows him at times a Whiggish critic of Utilitarianism. In his *Edinburgh Review* articles of 1829 he disputes James Mill's ideas on representative government, but he calls Bentham a 'great man' (p. 79) in jurisprudence. James Mill himself earns Macaulay's praise as the author of *The History of British India* ('Government of India', 139), and Mill vouched for Macaulay to become Legal Member of Council. Mill called for the drafting of a 'clear and unambiguous digest of law' (*History*, 510), and Macaulay met the call with reforms 'such as would make old Bentham jump in his grave'. Beyond Benthamite code-creation, Macaulay had Benthamite procedural reforms in view, 'oral pleadings—examination of parties—single-seated justice—no institution fees' (Clive, 429–30).

James Mill is often as scathing as Bentham, or Dickens, in his remarks on British law:

As the vulgar of every nation think their language the natural one, and all others arbitrary and artificial; so, a large mass of Englishmen consider English law as the pure extract of reason, adapted to the exigencies of human nature itself; and are wholly ignorant that, for the greater part, it is arbitrary, technical, and ill-adapted to the general ends which it is intended to serve; that it has more of singularity, and less capacity of adaptation to the state of other nations, than any scheme of law, to be found in any other civilized country. (*History*, 398–9)

This illustrates judgement turned back on British practices. What should be recognized as well is an opening of the eyes to Indian alternatives.

In court procedure Mill Sr declares that 'the advantage is all on the side of the Indian systems'. Hindu as well as Muslim traditions gain his approval by contrast to the technicality-bound home system. With harsh indictment of British procedures, Mill points out the advantages of simplicity in native practices. He approves of the discretion allowed the judge in mode of proceeding and the widest admission of evidence and use of cross-examination. Certainly he offers many sharp criticisms of native judicial practices, but within a frame of comparison to evils in the British system which, by multiplying procedures, renders the course of law long, confusing, treacherous, and expensive. On expense, Mill draws a wickedly invidious comparison, worthy of Bentham or Dickens. Payment is levied in the form of bribes in India and of fees in England. But fees look almost worse because they find their opportunity in procedural complications that increase chances of infractions, so that a 'double performance of the ceremonies, [with] double payment of the fees, is one of the most remarkable features of the English system of procedure'. Indian venality may economize time at least and stand less in the way of justice, as justice delayed is justice denied (*History*, 318, 66, 320–1).

Guidelines from James Mill indicate that new legislation should not neglect India's own usages (Clive, 428). Macaulay's work reflects such a viewpoint, open to admit points in favour of a foreign system. The penal code acknowledges that in legislating for India the British exert a will to change their colonial subjects. Still 'it is our duty, while their opinions and feelings remain unchanged, to pay as much respect to those opinions and feelings as if we partook of them' (*Indian Penal Code*, 'Notes', 318). For Macaulay, an insult to religion must be punished based on the sense of injury felt by the faithful, setting aside judgement of the faith. In this sense caste is to be respected, little as the British, especially Utilitarians, like it and much as they in some venues decry it. They gained critical perspective in sometimes having to countenance what they liked worse in India than England, as well as sometimes discovering what they liked better.

Macaulay's code went through adaptations and was not ultimately promulgated until 1862. It remained largely in force through the next century. Macaulay wrote in a letter to James Mill that he hoped the example of a code for India would spur the English to undertake law reform on their own behalf (Clive, 438). The forward course of reform in England was strong but incremental, many-faceted, and without fulfilment of the grand goal of comprehensive codification. There was an overhaul of criminal law from the 1820s under Peel as Home Secretary. The Court of Chancery, stronghold of procedural abuses, became a prime target of reformers from Bentham to Dickens. Markers of reform are the 1826 Commission report, 1850 Chancery Act, 1852 Chancery Procedure Act, and 1873 Judicature Act.

EDUCATION

On education East India Company policy looks perhaps its least liberal. The best-known element is educational 'diffusion', by which England presumed to teach India in English, apparently taking no lessons home to itself. Tagore's characters learn English, read English books, study political economy. For better or worse, that is diffusion. Yet back-diffusion is another result of the Company's educational policy. Altogether, the policy carries some liberal implications.

The teaching of English and English literature to Indians is the least vigorously backed element in J. S. Mill's account of education. The famous—or infamous—proposal for English studies is Macaulay's 1835 'Minute on Indian Education', calling for Westernization and Anglicization. Macaulay says he has found nobody 'who could deny that a single shelf of a good European library was worth the whole literature of India and Arabia'. He proposes to form educated natives to be interpreters to the millions, 'a class of persons, Indian in blood and colour, but English in taste, in opinions, in morals, and in intellect' (pp. 722, 729). The proposition was co-masterminded by Charles Trevelyan, who wanted natives to 'become more English than Hindus' (Clive, 409).

Mill's 'Memorandum' is sparing of comment as it reports the shift in emphasis in the Company's educational efforts. The shift was away from preserving classical Oriental learning and providing training in Muslim and Hindu law important for the courts; it was towards introducing study of English in the higher places of instruction under government influence and widening education in the vernacular. Mill attributes the shift partly to the spontaneous action of the government in India, partly to direction from home. Buried in this account is his own history of objections to the English-studies component that, once instituted in India, was unstoppable in London (Clive, 384–423). Mill's draft dispatch of 1836—which was overridden—shows him deeming it chimerical to expect the mental cultivation of the people to take place in a foreign language. He does value modernization and diffusion of European knowledge. But he considers the greatest need to be for Sanskrit and Arabic scholars able to create new terms for science and philosophy, which can then feed into the various vernaculars. He does not want these scholars to be alienated by disrespect for their learning and lost to good service as translators and teachers to the people. Mill questions the benefit of producing students who aim only at getting government jobs through knowing English without more meaningful wider influence ('Previous Communication 1828').

In this matter Zastoupil presents Mill's thinking as divergent from his father's. He interprets it in relation to Mill's youthful 'mental crisis' as evidence of an oedipal rebellion involving deep questioning of the tradition his father had taught him and greatly altering his whole subsequent course of thought.[16] Yet James Mill also had doubts about English as a medium of instruction in India. This is according to his 1832 testimony to a Parliamentary select committee supporting vernacular translation and opposing replacement of Persian by English in the courts. Majeed says that 'in the debate between the Anglicists, orientalists, and vernacularists in India, [James] Mill took a vernacularist stance' (*Ungoverned Imaginings*, 140–1). Compared to his father, the younger Mill speaks with greater respect for the traditional learned class and its role in expanding education. Still, I find that father and son are quite consistent as anti-Anglicists with their foremost commitment to educational diffusion through the vernaculars.[17]

The Mills are linked as Utilitarians in placing value on wide dissemination of knowledge—something akin to schooling for Dickens's humble Sissy and Esther, sorely lacking to Jo. And the Mills are linked in backing a free popular press or Benthamite Public Opinion Tribunal—something akin to Trollope's *Jupiter*. James Mill declares that a government serves only itself 'by constant, strenuous, and wicked endeavour' to control the press, but it serves the people by lifting controls and opening itself to outside scrutiny and advice. Also, if it wants to encourage reading, the way is to give people things to read—'there is one effectual measure for this purpose; and there never was, and never will be another; and that is the freedom of the press' (*History*, 538, 581). Even the law is to be a popular book. Both Mills are more convergent with Macaulay on a free press and the law as an open book than on education in English. Following a Bentinck bent under his successor Metcalfe, Macaulay saw through the formal freeing of the press by abolition of the licensing system (Clive, 323). In his 1852 charter-renewal testimony J. S. Mill says the dangers some thought would ensue did not materialize (pp. 70–1). Of course, freedom of expression is a paramount value in Mill's 'On Liberty'.

Mill's 'Memorandum' indicates further aspects of educational policy. Besides the English-studies element, Mill describes efforts towards greater inclusiveness, such as counteracting prejudices against female education, stimulus to education through open civil-service exams, extension of vernacular education, direct central-government backing, with funding, guidelines, and inspection, and support of secular instruction. This is a broadly Utilitarian educational agenda for India that carries significance for Britain.

Gauri Viswanathan has pointed out that English as a school subject came earlier to India than England. I would add that civil-service reform also came earlier to India than England, and that when it did arrive there, this helped along English studies. English (linked to commercial) studies were to constitute preparation for the middle and lower levels of the civil service, in contrast to classics for the top level. While classics still retained a position of privilege in this scheme, its decline was only delayed in relation to the rise of English studies. And in England, as was not the case in India, study in English did not vie with but *was* study in the vernacular. Also following after government efforts to sponsor, fund, inspect, and expand Indian education—Trevelyan in particular cherished a vision of comprehensive national education for India (Clive, 360)—came Forster's Education Act, which mandated state responsibility for universal public education in England. Forster's Act was passed in 1870 under Gladstone, the same year as Gladstone's Order in Council establishing the Home Civil Service. School attendance requirements and public funding were added in 1880 and 1891.

One more aspect of the historical pattern is the earlier placement of education under secular auspices in India than in England. Viswanathan explains the rationale in the Indian context. From its early days the East India Company had maintained religious neutrality. That meant that with Anglicist educational reform, secular English texts could be taught, whereas the Bible could not. Some thought the teaching of English works might indirectly teach a Christian outlook. Still, a Christian missionary educator like Alexander Duff observes with concern that government schooling in India is a 'field for testing the non-religion theory of education' (Viswanathan, *Masks of Conquest*, 65). Forster's Act represents a further application of the non-religion theory of education. It gave the State rather than the Church ultimate educational responsibility. This aligns in a basic sense with Utilitarian resistance to the sway of the Church establishment and of Church principles. In political, economic, and class terms, such resistance bears against Chancery with its biblical seal; it bears against Barchester. In ethical terms, it bears against Pauline asceticism, teachings of the kind repudiated by Bentham and Mill, deeply questioned by Dickens and Eliot, laughed at by Trollope, and not nearly so compatible with Carlyle's teachings as is usually supposed.

To sum up, Anglo-India contributed in circuitous ways to the emergence in England of a state-supported system of universal education, levelling and secular in tendency. It expanded the curriculum beyond the Greek and Latin learning associated with class privilege to encompass vernacular English studies, and it fed a reformed, more meritocratic, work-based civil service. It was not Church-run.[18] There is a lot to call liberal in this.

REVENUE COLLECTION AND LAND TENURE

Even the most aggressive diffusion involves back-diffusion, as seen in education. Still the backflow there is most clearly of British ideas returning from India to Britain, changed in the process, but with little influx of Indian ideas. More such influx is observable elsewhere. I have argued that Hindu caste thinking spurred reaction in favour of relative Mogul egalitarianism, which provided an analogue and reinforcement for liberal belief in equality of persons. I have argued that Indian conditions sharpened the Benthamite critique of British law, and, in addition, that this sharpened Benthamite attention to Hindu and Mogul alternatives, especially regarding legal procedure. Still, there is a sense that alternatives were sought out that would fit preconceptions.

Regarding revenue collection and land tenure in India, liberal imperialism certainly brought Utilitarian political economy to bear. But here we find the sharpest critical awareness of British misapprehensions, mistakes, and need for adjustment, the most dynamic development of thinking over time, and the boldest incorporation of Indian ideas. As in other areas of reform, Britain changed in changing its colony. Here we see a most liberal direction of change.

Collection of revenue is Mill's lead point in the 'Memorandum'. The government relied on land for its prime revenue source. This allowed for various extensions of free trade that Mill catalogues, such as abolition of the tobacco monopoly and steps towards phasing out the salt monopoly. James Mill had approved of ending the Company's monopolist standing (*History*, 363–9), and, of course, free trade is dear to political economy. Political economy—along with Carlyle—backs Corn Law Repeal, as it—along with Tagore—backs laissez-faire markets. But according to J. S. Mill, it is the land revenue system, over and above its facilitation of free trade, that represents 'the first great monument which the British rule in India has exhibited' ('Memorandum', 98). James Mill likewise hails the importance of this system. He calls attention to the moment when Clive, after the 1757 battle of Plassey, shifted function from that of the servant of a trading company to, in effect, the holder of territory as land revenue recipient under the Mogul emperor. This was a prelude to the moment when the Company mandated Warren Hastings 'to stand forth Duan', or revenue collector, in 1771, still putatively within the structure of the Mogul empire. Regularizing land revenue collection was the main object for Lord Cornwallis when he replaced Hastings. James Mill declares that the British takeover of the revenue effected a 'revolution' greater than the European reader can easily conceive (*History*, 373, 408–9).

Both James and J. S. Mill present Cornwallis's 'permanent settlement' of the revenue of 1793 as a mistake and one from which the Company learned. The mistake was one of misunderstanding existing Indian practice. At its most forgivable this was due to ignorance and at its least forgivable due to British prejudice involving national pride and class bias. James Mill asserts that though there might be some valid objections to the Hindu system, these 'arise rather from the mode, than the essence' (*History*, 135). J. S. Mill explains this essence as a conception of the sovereign as the universal landlord under the Hindus and then in adaptation under the Moguls (*Political Economy*, ii. 321–2).

In the Indian system payments on land are made to revenue gatherers who are the emperor's representatives, sometimes with hereditary claim to office. But the British erred in essence to institute these officials, or *zemindars*, as landlords. James Mill several times castigates Company officials for their blindness to conditions in the country that they ruled. He quotes Sir Henry Strachey to this effect and quotes another Company servant who observes that 'we generally... see Indian affairs, with English eyes; and carry European notions into Indian practice' (pp. 549–50, 484). Mill himself blasts

the overweening estimate, which our countrymen are prone to make, not only of their own political contrivances in India, but of the institutions of their own country in the mass. Under the influence of a vulgar infirmity, That *Self* must be excellent, and everything which affects the pride of *Self* must have surpassing excellence, English institutions, and English practices, have been generally set up as a standard, by conformity or disconformity with which, the excellence or defect of every thing in the world was to be determined. (p. 539)

The grand example is the superimposition of a British class conception onto Bengal by making *zemindars* into great landlords: 'the legislators were English aristocrats; and aristocratical prejudices prevailed' (*History*, 494). Mill, the son, sets forth his father's strong words on behalf of a strong claim: that 'there was an opportunity in India, to which the history of the world presents not a parallel' (*Political Economy*, ii. 321).

The opportunity lay in merging the Indian conception of land tenure and revenue with new thinking in political economy. Ricardo's theory of rent, which I have touched on before in relation to Dickens, J. S. Mill, and Carlyle on landlords, comes into prominence here. This theory appears in Ricardo's 1817 *Principles of Political Economy and Taxation*. It adapts the Smith tradition to accommodate Malthus on population and owes something to James Mill. James Mill saw the potential in his friend's ideas, urged him to write them up, and provided a steady stream of editorial help. Mill's *History* and Ricardo's *Principles* are the close to contemporaneous products of a close intellectual exchange. Mill invokes rent theory, as seen in a footnote acknowledgement in the *History* (p. 136). However, he does not just apply it as a ready-made, received idea. He finds confirmation in the Indian context for what was at the time a theory at a fledgling stage, and he reconceptualizes it in that context in a way that greatly expands its import.[19] There is an interactive innovation of ideas, then passed along to spur the further thinking of the younger Mill.

Rent is the unearned increment that derives from the quasi-monopoly advantage in owning land. Land is a finite resource that rises in value as it becomes scarcer in relation to population growth. Land is of variable fertility, and rent is the differential in proceeds accruing to the holder of fertile land, ever rising compared to proceeds accruing to the holder of the least fertile land that will still repay cultivation. Landowners 'grow richer, as it were in their sleep', says J. S. Mill (*Political Economy*, iii. 819). They do so without labour and without investment of capital (capital conceived in accordance with the labour theory of value as past labour saved, accumulated, and put to work again augmenting present labour). Landowners grow richer by a natural advantage. As Mill says: 'No man made the land. It is the original inheritance of the whole species' (ii. 230). Political economy after Ricardo figures wages to labour and profit to capital investment as returns on laborious and thrifty 'making', but not rent on land. Thus no man but the species should rightfully gain from it. And thus the instructive example to Utilitarian political economy of an Indian system placing ultimate real property rights in the sovereign, the state.

Political economy proposed to adapt the Indian system. There were elements to correct to make the state's demand of rent fair (tied to actual fertility), regular, certain, and stable over a long period. The object was not only to sustain the major source of state revenue but to help large numbers of people and the whole agrarian economy through promotion of small landholdings. Though the government might be ultimate landowner, that was not to prevent individual proprietorship in the sense of vested rights in landholding and alienability of those rights. Fair rent for each plot was key, accompanied by long leases at predictable rates and rights against eviction. The state undertook to leave some of the value of rent with the cultivator. Mill describes a government demand of two-thirds of rent in the North-western Provinces and one-half in newer settlements. The political economic purpose: to spur energy of desire, increasing incentive by widening freedom of opportunity and bringing 'the motives to exertion, and to the exercise of intelligence, which property gives, to bear upon those on whom the prosperity of agriculture most depends—the actual cultivators of the soil' ('Memorandum', 102).

The 'Memorandum' recounts the Company's history of trial and error in land revenue collection since Cornwallis's permanent settlement in Bengal. It lauds the advance from investiture of *zemindars* as great hereditary landlords to recognition of the *ryot*, or peasant cultivator, as the proprietary unit, subject to payment of the government demand. The pioneer of this system was Thomas Munro in Madras. Mill especially praises him, along with his collaborator Alexander Read. Assessment techniques for land value by productivity were not yet fully capable of generating fair rent rates in the Madras application, but Mill stresses acquisition of the knowledge necessary to correct former errors and progress in applications in the North-western Provinces. In these provinces the British also moved from understanding *ryotwar* tenure to understanding tenure on a village-community basis. It took a critical leap to perceive the village as the primary Hindu unit for governance and land management, as it had taken a leap to understand the sovereign as the ultimate landlord. Mill details further reforms in the Punjab, Bombay, and Madras, whether making the *ryot* the direct payer of rent or the village community for him. He speaks admiringly of the tenacity of Hindu ideas about land, kept alive even in Bengal, where the blunder was made of creating British-gentry-style *zemindar* landlords.

There 'traditionary feeling' counteracts the official system, which Mill hopes to see modified (p. 96).

Respect for 'traditionary feeling' has not been much acknowledged in British rule in India when it comes to Utilitarians. Certainly not by Mehta. Certainly not by Pitts with reference to the Mills.[20] Zastoupil does note some respect for Indian traditions on the part of J. S. Mill but credits this largely to a break with his Utilitarian heritage.[21] Zastoupil presents a Mill who came to believe 'that his father and Bentham were wrong to see only evil in established political institutions' ('India, J. S. Mill, and "Western" Culture', 131). According to this interpretation, Mill's oedipal struggle with 'narrow-minded' Utilitarianism sent him to Coleridge plus the Saint-Simonians and various Anglo-Indian administrators tagged by Zastoupil as Romantic/Burkean—all of whom helped Mill gain an open mind and give more credence to Indian actualities and traditions.

Differences exist between father and son, but, again, I do not believe they cut so deep. Thus in the matter of revenue James Mill salutes Thomas Munro, pioneer of the *ryotwar* system, and one of those Anglo-Indian administrators from whom, in Zastoupil's contention, John Stuart learned to think differently from his father.[22] James Mill praises Munro among a select few others who are able to reconceptualize the revenue by being 'sufficiently enlightened to see the things which were before them with their naked eyes: and not through the mist of English anticipations' (*History*, 125).[23] If the younger Mill could join Munro in looking past English prejudices to recognize merits in traditional Indian practices, so could the elder Mill. This is because the two Mills participated as Utilitarians in 'enlightened' critical thinking.[24]

Quite in line with his father, Mill salutes the Munro-initiated *ryotwar* system of Madras, followed by the adapted village-community system in the North-western Provinces. He presents his father as vindicated in having excoriated the creation of British-aristocratic-style *zemindar* landlords under the Bengal permanent settlement. J. S. quotes James at length in support of the very Indian system of 'proprietary rights of the sovereign' procuring the 'greatest portion of interest in the soil' to the 'immediate cultivators' (*Political Economy*, ii. 321; *History*, 494).

Revenue collection on land was a hugely important part of British rule in India. It was a revolution when the East India Company took it over, according to James Mill, and, according to J. S. Mill, this led to creation of a great Company monument. The reformed revenue policy prevailed. It outlasted the East India Company and the British Raj itself. There was some eclipse immediately after Company rule ended and India came directly under the British Parliament in 1858. But this was temporary. Sir George Wingate, a disciple of J. S. Mill, used his *Political Economy* to persuade Indian authorities to retain the system in 1862. Sir James Strachey used a passage from Mill's 'Memorandum' to justify Indian land revenue as rent in his book *India* of 1888, which remained a semi-official handbook for more than twenty years.[25] The reformed system was introduced in Bengal in 1885, and post-Independence, beginning in 1951, applied to all-India.[26]

Stokes says that this system was often perceived in England as 'un-English'. This in spite of the fact that British business interests might have been expected to prefer land instead of trade to form the state's main revenue base. In Stokes's characterization it appeared 'un-English' for being 'authoritarian' (*English Utilitarians and India*, 128). This holds with his view—a still prevalent view—of 'the simple authoritarian logic of the Utilitarian mind' (p. 80). What should be recognized as well is that the revenue system was 'un-English' for being part-Indian.

But is it to be judged as 'authoritarian'? Gradgrindian? Panoptic and carceral? Or is it to be judged as liberal? Certainly, the state wielded a large authority to gather information on land productivity and value and to set rates and collect on them. For Utilitarian political economists the liberal justification would lie in the critical openness that gave rise to the policy and its 'improving' and liberatory thrust—in extending proprietary rights to peasants, the mass of the population, boosting the greatest happiness of the greatest number by boosting their freedom and incentive to work, save, limit debt and family size, and invest in farm improvements, thus boosting their productivity and profit. This should serve their individual self-interests and increase the wealth and welfare of their society and the treasury of its government. According to the doctrine of rent, landholders would not even trade off private gain otherwise rightfully theirs for support of the state. Rent taken would not represent a tax in this sense because of falling on a land-fertility advantage not rightfully because quasi-monopolistically held under private ownership. The policy bears against hereditary, monopolist, Unworking, Dedlock landlords, while encouraging non-monopoly industry and trade by lightening taxes on them.

Once again a colonial policy had implications at home. Here we see a particularly strong Indian component and one serving some particularly liberal developments. The language of Mill's *Political Economy* moves often and easily from East to West. In this case it moves from colonial India to colonial Ireland. Mill criticizes the permanent settlement of Bengal that flattered itself it would produce English landlords because it 'only created Irish ones' (ii. 321).

Irish rack-renting was an on-going economic scandal and political flashpoint. Going back to his 1825 'Ireland', Mill refuses to moderate his style to avoid 'exasperating animosities' over the Irish Question: 'If it be always a crime to excite animosities, it must be always a crime to expose abuse' (p. 72). This is the voice of 'impetuous eagerness' in the young Mill's Radical journalism noted by Ann and John Robson. Mill interrupted composition of his *Political Economy* in 1846–7 for further, still-radical journalism concerning Ireland in the *Morning Chronicle*. And there is a great deal about Irish cottiers as well as Indian *ryots* in the *Political Economy*. Cottiers present something of the mentality of the gift-beholden, being systematically thrall to unpayable debt to their landlords. (How intolerable Mr Tulliver would find this!) Cottiers cannot better themselves by work, saving, or 'moral restraint', for anything they gain is already wholly owed. Indolence, torpor, careless imprudence follow when 'the inducements of free human beings are taken away'. Carlyle is particularly responsive to a passage in the *Political Economy* that calls the landlords of Ireland the greatest burdens on the land. Daringly enough, he approves of their being bought out in a land redistribution scheme.[27] Mill states his position in uncompromising terms in a manuscript of 1848: 'It is of no use saying, that the fault is not in the laws of property or the customs related to landed tenure.... This laziness, this recklessness, this improvident multiplication, are themselves part and parcel of the evil of a bad social system; are a principle portion of the case against it' ('What Is to Be Done with Ireland?', 502). His chapter on 'Means of Abolishing Cottier Tenancy' is important enough to merit substantial updates in editions of *Political Economy* he prepared up to 1871. India provided a model for Ireland from first to last.

In 1868 comes Mill's virulent 'England and Ireland'. It reviews the history of England's despoliation of Ireland. While some disabilities had been lifted, Mill declares that land tenure remains the prime offence and feeder of a deadly hatred. He closely links the Irish and Indian agricultural economies and the characters of their peasant populations (p. 519, and see *Political Economy*, ii. 319–20). As regards Ireland, he blasts the conceit of the British in believing that their own institutions must set the universal norm. And he points to India as the place where Britons had learned otherwise. East India Company rule was not by the British Parliament or by home ministers but by men who passed their lives in India or made it their professional study at East India House, and accordingly they

reconciled themselves to the idea that their business was not to sweep away the rights they found established, or wrench and compress them into the similitude of something English, but to ascertain what they were; having ascertained them, to abolish only those which were absolutely mischievous; otherwise to protect them, and use them as a starting point for further steps in improvement.

India shows that 'Englishmen are not always incapable of shaking off insular prejudices' (p. 519).[28]

Mill then outlines an orderly plan for, in effect, expropriation or land transfer in Ireland, compulsory and non-gradual, commuting variable to fixed rent, providing a permanent holding to every working proprietor or tenant and an option to landlords for buyout of rent claims through government consoles. In these new conditions the worst of the absentee rack-renters would be likely to sell off their land altogether. The state would be landlord or else arbiter and subsidizer in a new landlord–tenant system, paying the difference between what an existing tenant could pay and what was due to an existing landlord for state-set fair compensation (pp. 526–7).

Mill says do this or lose Ireland. The essay argues for keeping the colonial relation and thus still serves the cause of liberal imperialism. But liberal imperialism moves in the direction of liberal anti-imperialism here. Abuse, outrage, and hatred explain Fenian terrorism, and however unproductive Fenianism may be, according to Mill's account, there is no point in expecting rational moderation from a country with such a history of oppression and suffering. Mill states all this in the strongest terms. That Irish patience should be nearing an end seems entirely understandable. In 'What Is to Be Done with Ireland?' and *Political Economy* (1857 edn.) Mill does not scruple to observe the 'great and salutary' gain to be had from revolution. He notes that after the French Revolution a great part of the soil passed to the peasants (p. 503; iii. 1004).

Mill's position proved to be radically consequential if short of directly revolutionary. It is likely to have influenced his Liberal admirer Gladstone. Other Liberals with Indian experience followed Mill in writing on Ireland, such as Sir George Campbell in his 1869 pamphlet *The Irish Land*, which informed Gladstone's first Irish Land Act of 1870 and the second one of 1881, the latter perhaps the most far-reaching Irish legislation of the nineteenth century (perhaps next to the 1829 Catholic Emancipation). By these liberal measures Gladstone set a direction towards his later more 'extreme' emancipatory cause of Home Rule.[29]

In his last years Mill made land tenure reform a British issue:

The absolute power of landlords over the soil is what political economy really condemns; and condemns in England as well as in Ireland, though its economic mischiefs are not, in England, so flagrant and unqualified. ('Leslie on the Land Question', 675)

He presents this issue as marking a threshold between a Utilitarian political economy that stops short in its development and one that takes a bold next step.[30]

Critical thinking on British ideas and institutions, learning from mistakes, taking lessons from foreign examples, innovation, and advance over time—colonies occasioned these for liberalism at home. So Ireland exposes the fact that certain universals 'are perhaps not universal at all, but merely English customs' ('Leslie on the Land Question', 672), as India had exposed the fact that, in Bentham's formulation, what is bad for Bengal in a British system might be 'bad everywhere', and, beyond that, that Indian ideas that are better for Bengal might prove better for Ireland, and for England herself.

Mill applauds Professor Leslie's ideas on land but wants even more radical change. He does not think it enough to increase the alienability of land by inheritance measures such as trenching on primogeniture, entail, and marriage settlements. He became a founding member of the Land Tenure Reform Association in 1869 and describes its programme in an 1871 pamphlet. Beyond supporting alienability, this tract especially calls for 'the right of laying peculiar taxation on land' ('Land Tenure Reform', 690). We should recognize here the Indian land revenue idea in its new confluence with rent theory flowing back through Ireland to England.

The Utilitarian political economy of James Mill's and Ricardo's day and after had looked sharply askance at great hereditary landlords, as does Dickens, as does Carlyle. Church endowments and perquisites often traced to land and landlord-class ties, as Trollope lays bare. Gaskell smiles at the rector's daughters of Cranford who are loath to lose their blue-blooded county style, and she shows their society gaining in prosperity and gender and class equity by accommodation to the 'vulgar' new economics of railways, the East–West tea and cotton trades, and the mill-town Drumble. Tagore upholds the rights of lowly sellers and buyers in the cloth economy not to be ruled in the market by their landlord *zemindar*. In England the most aggressive Utilitarian political-economic move against landlords was Corn Law Repeal. This cut their subsidy by protective tariffs. Reform of Chancery and other legal reforms in addition to Ecclesiastical and Charity Commission reforms represent more piecemeal parallel trimmings of the flow of wealth and power to affiliate elites of lawyers and clergy. But Corn Law Repeal did not cut landlords' deeper-laid monopolistic advantage, another subsidy, by rent. Mill advances the analysis and faces off against English landlords because 'the country belongs, at least in principle, to the whole of its inhabitants' ('Land Tenure Reform', 689). He advocates land valuation and levying of assessments on future increases of value, buyouts of landlords who prefer to sell than to be taxed on rent, also cessation of private enclosure of common lands and extension of common lands by their purchase by the state. State lands may be leased to farmers, preferably small farmers, with stipulations to benefit their labourers. And they may be used for experiments aimed at improving the general welfare such as development of cooperative farms, sanitary works, and public gardens. Might Mill be thinking of Panopticon-like pleasure gardens? He himself was a leading member of the Commons Preservation Society, which worked to protect open spaces and parks like Hampstead Heath.[31] In 'Land Tenure Reform' he calls for public access to places of 'wild natural beauty and freedom' and ends his tract by extolling what state-preserved places of historical, scientific, and artistic interest will offer the public in instruction and, yes, 'enjoyment' (pp. 693, 695).

The agenda is here liberal, and strikingly so, both in its critical derivation and its intentions. The upshot may be seen in 'New Liberal' Lloyd George's People's Budget of 1909, which aimed at redistribution of wealth and funding of what would become the welfare state—by a 20 per cent capital gains tax on the unearned increment of land value at sale, a levy on unused land, and taxes payable at expiration of leases and land's reversion to landlords. The People's Budget is a major marker of the decline of the landlord class in England.[32] Mill's liberalism in the last years of his life points towards it. This is a liberalism consonant with his posthumously published 'Chapters on Socialism', which asserts that 'all the land might be declared the property of the State, without interfering with the right of property in anything which is the product of human labor and abstinence' (p. 736). Mill still faults communism for underestimating the power of private ownership of the fruits of labour to provide incentive for work and saving, as well as the power of competition to enhance productivity and consumption by preventing monopoly and bringing down prices. But his attitude is experimental. He says communist experiments should be tried. His attitude had long been experimental, being based on a critical perspective. Thus 'Chapters on Socialism' points to possibilities that had been brought into view by contemplation of 'many countries of Asia, before European ideas intervened, [where] nothing existed to which the expression property in land, as we understand the phrase, is strictly applicable.... The government was part owner, having the right to a heavy rent' (p. 751).

Seen in India, tried in Ireland, to try in England. Among key policies, revenue and land tenure reform best shows a self-transformation of liberal imperialism into something like its opposite. For colonial Ireland, if not yet for India, it brings freedom from England into prospect, for England a prospect of liberalization so levelling as to be almost socialist in terms, and to be gained by trial of un-English ideas.

CONCLUSION

J. S. Mill's tradition from Bentham, Smith, Malthus, Ricardo, and James Mill proposes to maximize utility or each person's balance of pleasure over pain and the greatest happiness of the greatest number. The most fundamental principle is that of pleasure, while the pleasure principle is also inseparably related to that of pain. Indeed the tradition justifies pains of work and capital savings and investment, sometimes in association with sexual giving up and going without. But always there is to be delay or trade-off in satisfaction only, no self-sacrifice that outruns self-interest. Liberty comes to be cast in principle as a utility, as one of the pleasures of Benthamism. A temporal principle runs throughout the rest of the theory. This principle along with the others feeds the critical thinking of Utilitarian political economy that makes it open, dynamic, and developmental.

I have proceeded through chapters that take up principles in turn, setting them in the context of historical applications and tracing their powerful expression in theoretical/topical and literary texts. In the last two chapters I have increased attention to applications of massive significance in the economy of cloth and Britain's Indian empire. Throughout, I have underscored closer affinities than are commonly acknowledged between Utilitarians and political economists and other writers of the period—Dickens, Carlyle, Trollope, Eliot, Gaskell, and Tagore. Utilitarian political economy—Benthamism, capitalism, liberalism—this bourgeois tradition of industrial market culture, is more pleasure-seeking than 'dismal'. It is reformist and 'improving', favourable to freedom, and levelling vis-à-vis gender and class. Altogether, it is too important to an understanding of the period and its literature to be as confusedly known and as discredited as it is in Victorian literary and cultural studies.

Still, given its principles and especially that of liberty, the tradition comes to a point of apparent contradiction and impasse in its connection with empire. In this final chapter on writings on India by Bentham, with links to Smith, and by Macaulay and the Mills, I have returned once again to the critical thinking that does not disappear but actually finds stimulus in the imperial connection. I have considered policy rationales for equalization of persons; the penal code; education; and revenue collection and land tenure. I have done so always mindful of Gradgrindian, panoptical spectres, always asking the question, where is the liberalism in liberal imperialism? Scholarship on British rule in India increasingly directs attention to consequences for Britain as well as its colony, and I have looked at changes in both places and influences flowing not only West to East but East to West. In empire there are evident impositions and evident damages, but these do not dominate my analysis as is most often the case in studies of colonialism. I conclude with a paradox that holds room for credit. Though the illiberality of empire cannot but be present to mind, it is possible to recognize within colonial interactions liberal critical processes of cultural production, and contributions to utility, including liberatory trends. I believe I do Mill justice. I demonstrate how his liberal tradition of Utilitarian political economy—with its wide reach in Victorian literature and culture— developed *as* liberalism even alongside and partly *through* imperialism.

NOTES

1. Pitts, *A Turn to Empire*. Said considers Mill more enlightened than Carlyle or Ruskin re his efforts to bring Gov. Eyre to justice for his bloody quelling of the 1865 Jamaica uprising (*Culture and Imperialism*, 163). Dipesh Chakrabarty echoes Mehta in placing blame for empire on liberalism, with Mill as a key spokesman (*Provincializing Europe*, 7–8 n. 27). David Wayne Thomas contests Mehta's charge that an imperialist impulse is integral to liberalism (*Cultivating Victorians*, 16–25). He argues upon a philosophical basis that Burke, whom Mehta champions, uses normative standards to make judgements about India, no less so than Mill, whom Mehta denounces. Still Thomas lets Mehta's charge of Mill's illiberalism in the case of India stand (p. 17). Levin is in overall agreement with Mehta (*J. S. Mill on Civilization*, 56–7). Eileen Sullivan anticipates Pitts in arguing that Mill transforms liberalism from a dominantly anti-imperialist theory to a defence of empire ('Liberalism and Imperialism', 617). Her judgement concerns his backing of Edward Gibbon Wakefield's scheme for emigration to S. Australia. What made the difference here was Malthus's, then Ricardo's ideas, raising concerns about harm to Britain from population growth. Still, Mill sees population control rather than emigration as the longer-term solution (*Political Economy*, ii. 194–5; iii. 735, 747–9, 962–7). See also n. 2.

2. Schofield contests Donald Winch's account of Bentham's inconsistency on colonialism (*Utility and Democracy*, 199–200; Winch, *Classical Political Economy*, 25–39). He is in some agreement with Boralevi (200–2; Boralevi, *Bentham and the Oppressed*, 127–35) as well as Pitts. With Boralevi, he observes Bentham's sensitivity to particular circumstances, which might sometimes justify colonial regimes, within limits. He stresses Bentham's increasing engagement with Malthusian arguments for the utility of emigration, and his increasing attention to sinister interests and to various means of reining them in to reduce tolls on utility. For Schofield, these factors come together in Bentham's delicately balanced support of the Wakefield scheme for S. Australia, expressed in his 1831 'Colonization

Society Proposal' (pp. 219–20, citing Bentham, MS University College London, Box 8, fos. 150, 154, 171, 180–91). Bentham sees advantages— population relief for Britain, population transfer to more favourable conditions, etc.—and avoidance of disadvantages: curbs on sinister interests such as limiting home government patronage, rapid progress to independence, and expected hand-off to a representative political system. See also n. 1.

3. Peers ('Imperial Epitaph', 204) and D. G. Brown ('Millian Liberalism', 84) support this position, as does Levin to an extent, though without arguing that it substantially alters a perception of contradiction applicable to both Mills as liberals who were also committed to empire (*J. S. Mill on Civilization*, 38–41, 56–7).

4. See also Ch. 2 and nn. 26, 27, and Ch. 5.

5. Ronald Inden (*Imagining India*) urges us not to underestimate Indian agency in constructions of knowledge of India; C. A. Bayley (*Empire and Information*) shows the extent of intelligence-gathering from Indians informing British rule, and Eugene Irschick describes the development of South Indian revenue policy as an 'intensely collaborative, if not harmonious, project' (*Dialogue and History*, 11). Guari Viswanathan (*Masks of Conquest*) examines how the imperial power was acted upon as well as acting in its educational policy, and Said's *Culture and Imperialism* draws attention to ways in which the imperial experience of the East has been formative for British literature and culture.

6. I value Irschick's articulation (*Dialogue and History*, 9–12) of divergence from Nandy (*Intimate Enemy*, pp. xiv–xv, 32)—shifting emphasis from cultural damages to cultural *production* in imperial interactions. Zastoupil, compared to many, is less focused on damages. Priya Joshi critiques Viswanathan for scant attention to what the English language and English literature meant to Indians besides 'conquest', and critiques Bhabha for a theory of colonial 'mimicry' that minimizes the positive agency of the colonial who in part imitates discourses of the colonizer (*In Another Country*, 6–7, 24–5). Her stress is on creative Indian 'indigenization' of a British literary form that was popular in India, the novel (pp. 32–3). Niall Ferguson, the general historian of British imperialism, finds legacies to value as well as indict. He says: 'the difficulty with the achievements of empire is that they are much more likely to be taken for granted than the sins of empire' (*Rise and Demise*, p. xxi).

7. As Pitts acknowledges, Smith thought a call for the total emancipation of colonies would be politically futile, and Bentham ends 'Emancipate your Colonies!' wryly recommending to the French as a fallback that they sell their colonies to the British East India Co. (*Turn to Empire*, 55–6, 113–14).

8. Mehta (*Liberalism and Empire*, 99–100, 111), Pitts (*Turn to Empire*, 133, 138–9), also Chakrabarty (*Provincializing Europe*, 7–8), David Wayne Thomas (*Cultivating Victorians*, 17), Levin (*J. S. Mill*, 39, 57).

9. *Autobiography*, 227, 237. See also Ch. 2 and nn. 26, 27 and Ch. 5.

10. This is not a direct policy proposal, more a hypothetical exercise.

11. 'The Tree of Utility in India', 37; consistent with Boralevi (*Bentham and the Oppressed*, 127–35) and Schofield (*Utility and Democracy*, 200–2) on Bentham's attentiveness to particular circumstances in particular colonies.

12. *Ungoverned Imaginings*, 140; 'James Mill's *The History of British India*: A Reevaluation', 66; by contrast to Bannerji's charge of James Mill's total unselfconsciousness of his ideological position ('Beyond the Ruling Category', 11). Something like Majeed re James Mill, Engelmann stands out for noting critical self-consciousness in economic rationality, which he ties to Benthamism (*Imagining Interest*, 8).

13. Mehta (*Liberalism and Empire*, 90), Pitts (*Turn to Empire*, 123), by contrast to Majeed: 'the elder Mill's *History of British India* has unjustifiably suffered a bad press' ('James Mill's *The History of British India*', 66).

14. Cf. Majeed, *Ungoverned Imaginings*: 'It is important to stress that [James] Mill was not in any way racist' (p. 138). David Levy argues that capitalism stands in antithetical relation to racial slavery (*How the Dismal Science Got its Name*, 181). Pitts says J. S. Mill resists racial determinism but considerably qualifies this by saying he stereotypes national characters (p. 136).

15. See Mueller, *Bureaucracy, Education*.

16. *John Stuart Mill and India*, 30–47; 'India, J. S. Mill, and "Western" Culture', 111–14.

17. That Anglicist policy tended to estrange English-educated '*Babus*' from the masses has been acknowledged (Clive, *Macaulay*, 415; Viswanathan, *Masks of Conquest*, 159–63), while the policy was not without some usefulness, as indicated by its retention post-Independence. In the light of India's polyglossia, it had difficulty with Hindi as its official language after 1947, and the 1960s saw English brought back as an associate official language. In subsequent decades a three-language formula retained study of English in the schools and its prominence at institutions of higher learning (Chatterji, 'Landmarks of Official Educational Policy').

18. Eagleton sees something ideologically manipulative and illiberal in the rise of English studies in England (*Literary Theory*, 22–9). Court counters this by discussing the first English Literary Professorship, established in 1828 at University College London, which was founded by the liberal Reform Whig Henry Brougham in connection with Utilitarians like James Mill. Court considers the institution of English studies to be liberal, aimed at expanding literacy across class lines, and co-developmental

with the institution of English studies at Mechanics' Institutes, 'an endorsement of equal rights, in this case, the right to read and to have access to books'. According to Court, educational democratization was in view, 'not to pacify the populace' (*Institutionalizing English Literature*, 50–1). See also Ch. 2 and n. 30.

19. Winch's editorial commentary on Mill's economic writings, especially *History of British India* and *Elements of Political Economy* (Mill, *Selected Economic Writings*, 197–8), indicates Mill's prompting to Ricardo to push the implications of rent theory for land taxation. Ricardo's 'Notes on Mill's *Elements of Political Economy*' (pp. 132–3) speaks positively of his friend's land-taxation ideas, referring to the 'Asiatic mode', on which Mill's Indian expertise would make him the authority. Winch indicates Ricardo's interest, yet his holding back, while the economist J. R. McCulloch baulked even more. Mill went out in front on rent revenue on land based on what he learned from India.

20. Cf. Metcalf, who calls liberalism at heart Euro-Anglo-centric: 'No other cultures had any intrinsic validity' (*Ideologies of the Raj*, 34). Kinzer dismisses the notion of significant Indian influence on J. S. Mill's thinking on the revenue (*England's Disgrace?*, 57–9). Stafford is close to Kinzer (*John Stuart Mill*, 112). Levin, too, cites no Indian source (*J. S. Mill*, 41, 129–30).

21. See Moore's challenge ('John Stuart Mill and Royal India', 101) to Zastoupil's claim that J. S. shifted away from James to favour traditional elites and existing institutions re policy for the native states (*John Stuart Mill and India*, 110–27; 'India, J. S. Mill, and "Western" Culture', 131). Moore does not think J. S. leaned in the main towards maintenance of native states in quasi-independence.

22. It is Thomas Munro along with John Malcolm, Mountstuart Elphinstone, and Charles Metcalfe whom Zastoupil calls the 'empire-of-opinion' school, characterized by affinities with Burke and Romanticism. Zastoupil cites Stein on Munro's expressions of admiration for Burke (*John Stuart Mill and India*, 56; Stein, *Thomas Munro*, 56, 296). Eric Stokes describes Munro as belonging to a school of Romantic/Burkean 'paternal conservatism' but at the same time stresses Munro's link to Utilitarianism, for instance, in opposing Cornwallis's permanent settlement and promoting *ryotwar* (*English Utilitarians in India*, 13, xvi, 148). Zastoupil ultimately acknowledges a somewhat comparable linkage but in a way that is tardy and misleading, as I see it. He argues that empire-of-opinion respect for Indian traditions came together with Utilitarian backing of peasant property rights in Robert Bird's development of the village-community revenue system from 1834 to 1844 in the North-western Provinces, and that this gave

J. S. Mill occasion to better reconcile what had been two sharply divided streams of influence (*John Stuart Mill and India*, 133). I think the division is overdrawn and that much easier and earlier crossovers should be recognized. Bird was carrying forward from Holt Mackenzie's advocacy of the village-community system, which dated back to 1819, and Mackenzie was trained in Utilitarian political economy under Malthus and versed in Ricardian rent doctrine (Stokes, 95; also Rosselli, *Lord William Bentinck*, 251–3, notes Utilitarian influence on Mackenzie and Bird, though without supposing they were ruled by pure theory). Indeed the connection goes back to James Mill, who treats Munro's interest in Indian revenue traditions as highly welcome to Utilitarianism (*History*, 125). Irschick (*Dialogue and History*, 23–7) testifies to close investigation of existing arrangements and consultation with native informants in revenue innovations set in train by Munro and Read.

23. James Mill refers not only to Munro but also to Lionel Place and John Hodgson, who followed through from the Munro/Read investigations of *ryotwar* in the Baramahal district of Madras by investigating the village-community alternative in the Jagir district of Madras in the 1790s to 1802 (*History*, 125, Irschick, 117–23). Mill notes their reports considered by a Parliamentary committee in 1810.

24. I perceive active interest in taking on Indian influence here. I do not assume lack of engagement with things Indian as Kinzer does. Based on 'what may...be assumed', Kinzer locates what matters in the Mills' thinking on Indian revenue policy in British-based 'anti-landlord bias' prompting embrace of Ricardian rent theory (*England's Disgrace?*, 57–9). Nor am I satisfied to interpret the two Mills' attitude on the revenue in the way Moore interprets the younger Mill's attitude on native states and the way Levin interprets his attitude on Indians' role in administration. Moore characterizes Mill's sometime accommodation of native institutions in terms of 'expediency rather than justice' ('John Stuart Mill', 106, 104, 89). Levin speaks of 'prudential realism' motivating some cooperativeness and tolerance (*J. S. Mill*, 41) in Mill's backing for extensive inclusion of Indians even at high administrative levels. Neither Moore nor Levin perceives significant openness to merits of Indian contributions.

25. Stokes, *English Utilitarians and India*, 127–8, 137.

26. Metcalf, *Forging the Raj*, 48, 71.

27. Carlyle, 'In the Margins', 83 re *Political Economy*, ii. 229–31.

28. Pitts portrays Mill as more concerned about Ireland than India because he believes the Irish, unlike Indians, are not fixed in national character but able to gain from specific institutional reforms. She pronounces that

'Mill's critical eye toward British self-satisfaction in Ireland is largely absent from his writings on India' (*Turn to Empire*, 148). I think this overlooks a number of factors: the stress Mill puts on Irish–Indian similarity, the credit he gives to British experience in India for exposing complacency and widening critical awareness, the fact that the remedy for Ireland in this case is drawn from India.

29. Stokes, *English Utilitarians*, 122 n. 2; Metcalf, *Forging the Raj*, 44–5; Kinzer, *England's Disgrace?*, 213–14.

30. In *John Stuart Mill and India* Zastoupil takes some notice of the back-influence of land-revenue ideas developed in India upon Ireland and England. But in line with his general thesis, he declares that the thinking comes 'straight out of the [Burkean/Romantic/Coleridgean] empire-of-opinion book of administration' (p. 185), as opposed to Utilitarian political economy. To the contrary, the passage I cite shows Mill overtly identifying his position as belonging to political economy. Levin draws on Zastoupil re Mill's taking his own way, beyond his father, to accept Burkean/Romantic/Coleridgean influence, and he sees Mill's views on land tenure as a sign of some significant distancing from laissez-faire capitalism and movement towards Coleridge as a key source (*J. S. Mill*, 38–41, 129–30). It is true that in his essay on Coleridge Mill endorses some ideas from the *Second Lay Sermon* concerning the national and not only private interest attaching to property in land. Mill salutes Coleridge as the first philosopher to give sanction to land reform. He must not be considering his father to be the voice of philosophy on this matter, though he certainly would consider him to be the voice of Utilitarian political economy in addressing land reform in the *History*. Mill concludes his essay with a tip-off to its rhetorical/argumentative strategy. He says landlords as a class belong overwhelmingly on the Conservative side of the land question. They hold great power. How better to budge them than by promoting the Liberal-leaning ideas to be found *even* in the writings of one of their own like Coleridge? This represents an a fortiori strategy. That is, Mill proceeds not 'by the impracticable method of converting them from Conservatives into Liberals, but by their being led to adopt one liberal position after another, as a part of Conservatism itself' (pp. 157–8, 163). Kinzer contemplates some back-influence from India to Ireland re revenue and land tenure. Unlike Zastoupil and Levin, he points to no Burkean/Romantic/Coleridgean source. Rather he points to a source in James Mill and Utilitarian political economy. I am with him on this. But I am not with him in 'what may . . . be assumed'—that we should downplay anything learned by the Mills from the Indian system (*England's Disgrace?*, 57–9). I welcome Zastoupil's effort in 'India, J. S.

Mill, and "Western" Culture' to increase attention to 'the neglected story of the influence of the colonized on the colonizer' (p. 130). But it is not revenue/land-tenure policy out of India that Zastoupil presents as an instance of such influence. Rather he instances Indian voices that entered into Anglo-Indian educational debates and debates on policy for the native states. In neither case does he trace influence on the colonizer in the sense of influence on British policy *for Britain*. Zastoupil also looks at a footnote in Mill's 'Subjection of Women' and a letter to Charlotte Speir Manning concerning Indian examples of female rulers (pp. 138–9). This may have some relevance for developing feminism back in Britain. Still, any influence by the colonized on the colonizer is on a very small scale here. It is *far* from small in the matter of revenue/land tenure. See Riley for a strong statement on the importance of the Millian concept of taxation of rent for social justice under capitalism, yet without noting any Indian component ('Justice under Capitalism', 139–41).

31. Owen, *English Philanthropy*, 492; Parry, *Rise and Fall*, 235.
32. Fraser, *Evolution of the British Welfare State*, 145, Benson, *Rise of Consumer Society*, 23–4.

Bibliography

Adams, James Eli, *Dandies and Desert Saints: Styles of Victorian Masculinity* (Ithaca: Cornell University Press, 1998).

Altick, Richard, *Victorian People and Ideas: A Companion for the Modern Reader of Victorian Literature* (New York: Norton, 1973).

Alton, Ann Hiebert, 'Education in Victorian Fact and Fiction: Kay-Shuttleworth and Dickens' *Hard Times*', *Dickens Quarterly*, 9 (1992), 67–80.

Amariglio, Jack, 'Give the Ghost a Chance! A Comrade's Shadowy Addendum', in Mark Osteen (ed.), *The Question of the Gift: Essays across Disciplines* (London: Routledge, 2002), 266–79.

Anderson, Amanda, *The Powers of Distance: Cosmopolitanism and the Cultivation of Detachment* (Princeton: Princeton University Press, 2001).

—— *Tainted Souls and Painted Faces: The Rhetoric of Fallenness in Victorian Culture* (Ithaca: Cornell University Press, 1993).

Armstrong, Nancy, *Desire and Domestic Fiction: A Political History of the Novel* (Oxford: Oxford University Press, 1987).

—— *Fiction in the Age of Photography: The Legacy of British Realism* (Cambridge: Harvard University Press, 1999).

Ashton, Rosemary. *The German Idea: Four English Writers and the Reception of German Thought 1800–1860* (Cambridge: Cambridge University Press, 1980).

Atkins, Stuart. *Essays on Goethe*, ed. Jane K. Brown and Thomas P. Saine (Columbus, SC: Camden House, 1995).

—— *Goethe's Faust: A Literary Analysis* (Cambridge, Mass.: Harvard University Press, 1958).

Auerbach, Nina, 'Alluring Vacancies in the Victorian Character', *Kenyon Review*, 8 (Summer 1986), 36–48.

—— 'The Power of Hunger, Demonism and Maggie Tulliver', *Nineteenth-Century Fiction*, 30 (1975), 150–71.

Baker, William, and Womack, Kenneth (eds.), *A Companion to the Victorian Novel* (Westport, Conn.: Greenwood, 2002).

Bannerji, Himani, 'Beyond the Ruling Category to what Actually Happens: Notes on James Mill's Historiography in *The History of British India*', *Jadavpur Journal of Comparative Literature*, 32 (1994–5), 5–21.

Barlow, Paul, 'Thomas Carlyle's Grotesque Conceits', in Colin Trodd, Paul Barlow, and David Amigoni (eds.), *Victorian Culture and the Idea of the Grotesque* (Aldershot and Brookfield, Vt.: Ashgate, 1998).

Battacharya, Malini, '*Gora* and *The Home and the World*: The Long Quest for Modernity', in Datta (ed.), *Rabindranath Tagore's* The Home and the World, 127–42.

Baudrillard, Jean, 'For a Critique of the Political Economy of the Sign' and 'The Mirror of Production', in *Selected Writings*, ed. Mark Poster, trans. Charles Levin and Mark Poster (Stanford: Stanford University Press, 1988), 57–118.

Baum, Bruce, *Rereading Power and Freedom in J. S. Mill* (Toronto: University of Toronto Press, 2000).

Baumgarten, Murray, *see* Carlyle, 'In the Margins', 66–129.

Bayley, C. A., *Empire and Information: Intelligence Gathering and Social Communication in India, 1780–1870* (Cambridge: Cambridge University Press, 1996).

Bean, Susan S., 'Gandhi and Khadi, the Fabric of Indian Independence', in Annette Weiner and Jane Schneider (eds.), *Cloth and Human Experience* (Washington, DC: Smithsonian Institute Press, 1989), 355–76.

Benson, John, *The Rise of Consumer Society in Britain, 1880–1980* (London: Longman, 1994).

Bentham, Jeremy, *Chrestomathia* (1817, 1843), ed. M. J. Smith and W. H. Burston (*CW*; 1983).

—— *The Collected Works of Jeremy Bentham*, gen. ed. J. H. Burns, J. R. Dinwiddy, F. Rosen, Philip Schofield (London: Athlone Press, 1968–77; Oxford: Clarendon Press, 1983–) (abbreviated as *CW*).

—— *Constitutional Code* (1830), ed. F. Rosen and J. H. Burns (*CW*; 1983).

—— 'Defence of Usury in Letters to a Friend, to which is Added a Letter to Adam Smith' (1787) (*Works*, iii).

—— 'Equity Dispatch Court Proposal' (1830) (*Works*, iii).

—— 'Emancipate your Colonies!' (1893, 1830), in *Rights, Representation, and Reform: Nonsense upon Stilts and Other Writings on the French Revolution*, ed. Philip Schofield, Catherine Pease-Watkin, and Cyprian Blamires (*CW*; 2002).

—— 'Essay on Language' (*c.*1813–15) (*Works*, viii).

—— 'Essay on Logic' (*c.*1813–15) (*Works*, viii).

—— *First Principles Preparatory to Constitutional Code* (1822), ed. Philip Schofield (*CW*; 1989).

—— *A Fragment on Government* (1776, 1823), ed. J. H. Burns and H. L. A. Hart (1977), intro. by Ross Harrison (Cambridge: Cambridge University Press, 1988).

—— 'A Fragment on Ontology' (*c.*1813–15) (*Works*, viii).

—— 'Indications Respecting Lord Eldon', in *Official Aptitude Maximized; Expense Minimized* (1830; pamphlet version, 1825), ed. Philip Schofield (*CW*; 1993).

Bentham, Jeremy, *An Introduction to the Principles of Morals and Legislation* (1789), ed. J. H. Burns and H. L. A. Hart, interpretive essay by Hart (1982), intro. by F. Rosen (1996) (*CW*; 1970, 1996).

—— 'Manual of Political Economy' (1793 f.) (*Works*, iii).

—— *Memoirs and Correspondence* (1843) (*Works*, x–xi).

—— *Not Paul, but Jesus* (pseud. Gamaliel Smith) (London: John Hunt, 1823).

—— *Not Paul, but Jesus*, Notes for Part III, Doctrine (1816–18), unpublished MS, Bentham Library, University College London.

—— 'On the Influence of Time and Place in Matters of Legislation' (*c.*1780) (*Works*, i).

—— 'Pannomial Fragments' (1843) (*Works*, iii).

—— 'Panopticon; or, the Inspection House' (1791) (*Works*, iv).

—— *Rationale of Judicial Evidence* (1827) (*Works*, vi–vii).

—— 'The Rationale of Reward' (1825) (*Works*, ii).

—— 'Sextus' (1817), unpublished MS, Bentham Library, University College London.

—— 'A Table of the Springs of Action' (1817), in *Deontology, together with a Table of the Springs of Action and Article on Utilitarianism*, ed. Amnon Goldworth (*CW*; 1983).

—— *Works*, ed. John Bowring (Edinburgh: Tait, 1838–43) (abbreviated as *Works*).

Bhabha, Homi K. (ed.), *Nation and Narration* (London: Routledge, 1990).

Bigelow, Gordon, *Fiction, Famine, and the Rise of Economics in Victorian Britain and Ireland* (Cambridge: Cambridge University Press, 2003).

—— Blake, Kathleen, and Goodlad, Lauren, Papers for 'Political Economy and Empire' session; Commentator David Wayne Thomas (North American Conference on British Studies, Boston, Nov. 2006).

Bizup, Joseph, *Manufacturing Culture: Vindications of Early Victorian Industry* (Charlottesville: University of Virginia Press, 2003).

Blainey, Ann, *Immortal Boy: A Portrait of Leigh Hunt* (London: Croom Helm, 1985).

Blake, Kathleen, 'George Eliot: The Critical Heritage', in Levine (ed.), *The Cambridge Companion to George Eliot*, 202–25.

Blumberg, Ilana M., ' "Unnatural Self-Sacrifice": Trollope's Ethic of Mutual Benefit', *Nineteenth-Century Literature*, 58 (2004), 506–46.

Bonaparte, Felicia, *Will and Destiny: Morality and Tragedy in George Eliot's Novels* (New York: New York University Press, 1975).

Boralevi, Lea Campos, *Bentham and the Oppressed* (Berlin: Walter de Gruyter, 1984).

Bose, Sugata, and Jalal, Ayesha, *Modern South Asia: History, Culture, Political Economy* (New York: Routledge, 2004).

Bourdieu, Pierre, 'Symbolic Capital', in *The Logic of Practice* (1980), trans. Richard Nice (Stanford: Stanford University Press, 1990), 112–21.

Boyer, George R., 'Living Standards, 1860–1939', in Roderick Floud and Paul Johnson (eds.), *The Cambridge History of Modern Britain*, ii: *Economic Maturity 1860–1939* (Cambridge: Cambridge University Press, 2004), 280–313.

Brantlinger, Patrick, *Fictions of State: Culture and Credit in Britain, 1694–1994* (Ithaca: Cornell University Press, 1996).

—— and Thesing, William (eds.), *A Companion to the Victorian Novel* (Oxford: Blackwell, 2005).

Brink, David O., 'Mill's Deliberative Utilitarianism', in Lyons (ed.), *Mill's Utilitarianism*, 149–83.

Brown, D. G., 'Millian Liberalism and Colonial Oppression', in Catherine Wilson (ed.), *Civilization and Oppression* (Calgary: University of Calgary Press, 1999), 79–97.

Brown, James M., *Dickens: Novelist in the Marketplace* (London: Macmillan, 1982).

Budd, Donna, 'Language Couples in *Bleak House*', *Nineteenth-Century Literature*, 49 (1994), 196–220.

Butwin, Joseph, 'The Paradox of the Clown in Dickens', *Dickens Studies Annual*, 5 (1976), 115–32.

Caine, Michael (ed.). *A Cultivated Mind: Essays on J. S. Mill Presented to John M. Robson* (Toronto: University of Toronto Press, 1991).

Cannadine, David, *The Decline and Fall of the British Aristocracy* (New Haven: Yale University Press, 1990).

Capaldi, Nicholas, *John Stuart Mill: A Biography* (Cambridge: Cambridge University Press, 2004).

Carlyle, Thomas, 'Corn-Law Rhymes' (1832) (*Works*, xxviii).

—— 'Death of Goethe' (1832) (*Works*, xxvii).

—— 'Goethe' (1828) (*Works*, xxvi).

—— 'Goethe's Helena' (1828) (*Works*, xxvi).

—— 'Goethe's Works' (1832) (*Works*, xxvii).

—— 'In the Margins: Carlyle's Markings and Annotations in his Gift Copy of Mill's *Principles of Political Economy* of 1848', ed. and transcribed Murray Baumgarten, with 'Parameters of Debate: A Reading of Carlyle's Annotations of Mill's *Principles of Political Economy*', in *Carlyle: Books and Margins* (University Library: University of California at Santa Cruz, 1980), 66–106, 107–29.

—— 'Jean Paul Friedrich Richter' (1827) (*Works*, xxii).

—— 'Jean Paul Friedrich Richter' (1827) (*Works*, xxvi).

—— 'The Nigger Question' (1849) (*Works*, xxix).

Carlyle, Thomas, *Past and Present*, ed. Richard D. Altick (New York: New York University Press, 1965).

—— *Reminiscences* (1881), ed. James Anthony Froude (New York: Charles Scribner's, 1881).

—— *Sartor Resartus: The Life and Opinions of Herr Teufelsdröckh* (1834), ed. Charles Frederick Harrold (New York: Odyssey, 1937).

—— 'Schiller' (1831) (*Works*, xxvii).

—— 'State of German Literature' (1827) (*Works*, xxvi).

—— *Wilhelm Meister's Travels*, trans. from Goethe (1827) (*Works*, xxiv).

—— *Works*, ed. H. D. Traill, Centenary Edition (1899) (New York: AMS, 1969) (abbreviated as *Works*).

Carroll, David (ed.) *George Eliot: The Critical Heritage* (New York: Barnes & Noble, 1971).

Cass, Jeffrey, 'The Scraps, Patches, and Rags of Daily Life: Gaskell's Oriental Other and the Conservation of Cranford', *Papers on Language and Literature*, 35 (1999), 417–33.

Cazamian, Louis, *Carlyle* (1913), trans. E. K. Brown (New York: Macmillan, 1932).

—— *The Social Novel in England 1830–1850: Dickens, Disraeli, Mrs. Gaskell, Kingsley* (1903), trans. Martin Fido (London: Routledge & Kegan Paul, 1973).

Chakrabarty, Dipesh, *Provincializing Europe: Postcolonial Thought and Historical Difference* (Princeton: Princeton University Press, 2000).

Chapman, Sydney J., *The Lancashire Cotton Industry: A Study in Economic Development* (1904) (repr. Clifton, NJ: Augustus M. Kelley, 1973).

Chatterji, Lola, 'Landmarks of Official Educational Policy: Some Facts and Figures', in Rajeswari Suder Rajan (ed.), *The Lie of the Land: English Literary Studies in India* (Delhi: Oxford University Press, 1992).

Chaudhuri, Nupur, 'Shawls, Jewelry, Curry, and Rice', in Chaudhuri and Margaret Strobel (eds.), *Western Women and Imperialism* (Bloomington: Indiana University Press, 1992), 231–46.

Cheadle, Brian, 'The Late Novels: *Great Expectations* and *Our Mutual Friend*', in Jordan (ed.), *The Cambridge Companion to Charles Dickens*, 78–91.

Cheal, David, *The Gift Economy* (London: Routledge, 1988).

Clive, John, *Macaulay: The Shaping of the Historian* (New York: Knopf, 1973).

Colby, Robin, *'Some Appointed Work to Do': Women and Vocation in the Fiction of Elizabeth Gaskell* (Westport, Conn.: Greenwood, 1995).

Coles, Nicholas, 'The Politics of *Hard Times*: Dickens the Novelist versus Dickens the Reformer', *Dickens Studies Annual*, 15 (1986), 145–77.

Colligan, Collette, 'Raising the House-Tops: Sexual Surveillance in Charles Dickens' *Dombey and Son*', *Dickens Studies Annual*, 29 (2000), 99–123.

Collins, Philip (ed.), *Dickens: The Critical Heritage* (New York: Barnes & Noble, 1971).

Connell, Philip, *Romanticism, Economics, and the Question of 'Culture'* (Oxford: Oxford University Press, 2001).

Connor, Steven (ed.), *Charles Dickens* (Harlow, Essex: Addison Wesley Longman, 1996).

Coovadia, Imraan, 'George Eliot's Realism and Adam Smith', *Studies in English Literature 1500–1900*, 42 (2002), 819–35.

Corbett, Edward, *Classical Rhetoric for the Modern Student*, 3rd edn. (New York: Oxford University Press, 1990).

Court, Franklin E., *Institutionalizing English Literature: The Culture and Politics of Literary Study 1750–1900* (Stanford: Stanford University Press, 1992).

Crimmins, James E., *Secular Utilitarianism: Social Science and the Critique of Religion in the Thought of Jeremy Bentham* (Oxford: Clarendon Press, 1990).

Crompton, Louis, *Byron and Greek Love: Homophobia in 19th-Century England* (Swaffham, Norfolk: Gay Men's Press, 1998).

Crosby, Christina, ' "A Taste for More": Trollope's Addictive Realism', in Woodmansee and Osteen (eds.), *The New Economic Criticism*, 293–306.

Dale, Peter Allan, '*Sartor Resartus* and the Inverse Sublime: The Art of Humorous Deconstruction', in Morton W. Bloomfield (ed.), *Allegory, Myth, and Symbol* (Cambridge, Mass.: Harvard University Press, 1981), 293–312.

Daly, Suzanne, 'Kashmir Shawls in Mid-Victorian Novels', *Victorian Literature and Culture*, 30 (2002), 237–56.

Danahay, Martin A., 'Housekeeping and Hegemony in *Bleak House*', in Dickerson (ed.), *Keeping the Victorian House*, 3–25.

Datta, P. K. (ed.), *Rabindranath Tagore's* The Home and the World: *A Critical Companion* (Delhi: Permanent Black, 2003).

Daunton, M. J., *Progress and Poverty: An Economic and Social History of Britain 1700–1850* (Oxford: Oxford University Press, 1995).

David, Deirdre, 'Imperial Chintz', *Victorian Literature and Culture*, 27 (1999), 569–77.

Davidoff, Leonore, and Hall, Catherine, *Family Fortunes: Men and Women of the English Middle Class, 1780–1850* (London: Hutchinson, 1987).

DeLacy, Margaret, *Prison Reform in Lancashire 1700–1850* (Stanford: Stanford University Press, 1986).

Delany, Paul, *Literature, Money, and the Market from Trollope to Amis* (Houndsmill, Basingstoke: Palgrave, 2002).

Dickens, Charles, *Bleak House* (1853), intro. by Morton Zabel (Riverside edn.; Boston: Houghton Mifflin, 1956).

—— *Dickens' Journalism*, iii: *'Gone Astray' and Other Papers from Household Words 1851–59*, ed. Michael Slater (London: Dent, 1998).

Dickens, Charles, *Hard Times* (1854), ed. George Ford and Sylvère Monod, 2nd edn. (New York: Norton, 1996).

—— *Household Words, A Weekly Journal 1850–1859: Table of Contents, list of contributors and contributions based on* Household Words *Office Book. Morris Parrish Collection of Victorian Novelists, Princeton University Library*, comp. Ann Lohri (Toronto: University of Toronto Press, 1973).

—— *The Mystery of Edwin Drood*, ed. Arthur Cox, intro. by Angus Wilson (Harmondsworth: Penguin, 1946).

Dickerson, Vanessa D. (ed.), *Keeping the Victorian House: A Collection of Essays* (New York: Garland, 1995).

Dinwiddy, J. R., 'Bentham's Transition to Political Radicalism', *Journal of the History of Ideas*, 35 (1975), 683–700.

Dodsley, Robert, *The Economy of Human Life*, attrib. to the Earl of Chesterfield as trans. of an Indian MS within a fictional letter dated 1749 (Dodsley b. 1703, d. 1764) (Philadelphia: Edward Earle, 1817).

Dolin, Kieran, *Fiction and the Law: Legal Discourse in Victorian and Modernist Literature* (Cambridge: Cambridge University Press, 1999).

Dolin, Tim, *George Eliot* (Oxford: Oxford University Press, 2005).

—— *Mistress of the House: Women of Property in the Victorian Novel* (Aldershot: Ashgate, 1997).

Donner, Wendy, 'Mill's Theory of Value', in West (ed.), *Mill's Utilitarianism*, 117–38.

—— 'Mill's Utilitarianism', in Skorupski (ed.), *The Cambridge Companion to Mill*, 255–92.

Dowling, Linda C., *The Vulgarization of Art: The Victorians and Aesthetic Democracy* (Charlottesville: University of Virginia Press, 1996).

Dube, Allison, 'The Tree of Utility in India: *Panace* or Weed?', in Moir, Peers, and Zastoupil (eds.), *J. S. Mill's Encounter with India*, 34–52.

Dupree, Marguerite, 'Foreign Competition and the Interwar Period', in Rose (ed.), *The Lancashire Cotton Industry*, 265–95.

Durey, Jill Felicity, *Trollope and the Church of England* (Houndsmill, Basingstoke: Palgrave, 2002).

Dworkin, Gerald (ed.), *Mill's* On Liberty*: Critical Essays* (Lanham, Md: Rowman & Littlefield, 1997).

Eagleton, Terry, 'Critical Commentary', in Charles Dickens, *Hard Times* (London: Methuen, 1987).

—— *Criticism and Ideology: A Study in Marxist Literary Theory* (London: Humanities Press, 1976).

—— *Literary Theory: An Introduction* (Oxford: Blackwell, 1983).

Eisenach, Eldon J. (ed.), *Mill and the Moral Character of Liberalism* (University Park: Pennsylvania State University Press, 1999).

Eliot, George, *Impressions of Theophrastus Such* (1880), ed. Nancy Henry (London: William Pickering, 1994).

—— 'The Influence of Rationalism' (1865), in *Essays of George Eliot*, ed. Thomas Pinney (London: Routledge & Kegan Paul, 1963).

—— *The Mill on the Floss* (1860), ed. Gordon S. Haight (Clarendon edn. of the *Works of George Eliot*; Oxford: Clarendon Press, 1980).

Engelmann, Stephen G., *Imagining Interest in Political Thought: Origins of Economic Rationality* (Durham, NC: Duke University Press, 2003).

Engels, Friedrich, *The Condition of the Working Class in England* (1845), trans. W. O. Henderson and W. H. Chaloner (Stanford: Stanford University Press, 1958).

Erickson, Lee, *The Economy of Literary Form: English Literature and the Industrialization of Publishing 1800–1850* (Baltimore: Johns Hopkins University Press, 1996).

Ermarth, Elizabeth, 'Maggie Tulliver's Long Suicide', *Studies in English Literature 1500–1900*, 14 (1974), 587–601.

Esty, Joshua, 'Nationhood, Adulthood, and the Ruptures of Bildung: Arresting Developments in *The Mill on the Floss*', in Yousaf and Maunder (eds.), *The Mill on the Floss and Silas Marner*, 101–21.

Federico, Annette, '*David Copperfield* and the Pursuit of Happiness', *Victorian Studies*, 46 (2003), 69–95.

Ferguson, Frances, 'Beliefs and Emotions (from Stanley Fish to Jeremy Bentham and John Stuart Mill)', in Victoria Kahn, Neil Saccamano, and Daniel Coli (eds.), *Politics and the Passions, 1500–1850* (Princeton: Princeton University Press, 2006), 231–50.

—— 'Envy Rising', in James Chandler and Kevin Gilmartin (eds.), *Metropolis: The Urban Scene of British Culture* (Cambridge: Cambridge University Press, 2005), 132–48.

—— *Pornography, the Theory: What Utilitarianism Did to Action* (Chicago: University of Chicago Press, 2004).

Ferguson, Niall, *The Rise and Demise of the British World Order and the Lessons for Global Power* (New York: Basic Books, 2004).

Fichte, Johann Gottlieb, *The Vocation of Man* (1800), ed. and trans. Roderick M. Chisholm (New York: Macmillan, 1956).

Fielding, K. J., and Smith, Anne, '*Hard Times* and the Factory Controversy: Dickens vs. Harriet Martineau', in Ada Nisbit and Blake Nevius (eds.), *Dickens Centennial Essays* (Berkeley: University of California Press, 1971), 22–45.

Finn, Margot C., *The Character of Credit: Personal Debt in English Culture, 1740–1914* (Cambridge: Cambridge University Press, 2003).

Flint, Kate, *The Victorians and the Visual Imagination* (Cambridge: Cambridge University Press, 2000).

Floud, Roderick, *The People and the British Economy, 1830–1914* (Oxford: Oxford University Press, 1997).

Foucault, Michel, *Discipline and Punish: The Birth of the Prison* (1975), trans. Alan Sheridan (New York: Vintage, 1979).

—— 'Governmentality', in Graham Burchell, Colin Gordon, and Peter Miller (eds.), *The Foucault Effect: Studies of Governmentality* (Chicago: Chicago University Press, 1991), 87–104.

—— 'The Subject and Power', in Michel Foucault, *Beyond Structuralism and Hermeneutics*, ed. Herbert L. Dreyfus and Paul Rabinow (Chicago: University of Chicago Press, 1983), 208–26.

—— *Technologies of the Self: A Seminar with Michel Foucault*, ed. Luther H. Martin, Huck Gutman, and Patrick H. Hutton (Amherst: University of Massachusetts Press, 1988).

Fraiman, Susan, 'The Mill on the Floss, the Critics, and the Bildungsroman', in Yousaf and Maunder (eds.), *The Mill on the Floss and Silas Marner*, 31–56.

Franklin, J. Jeffrey, 'Anthony Trollope Meets Pierre Bourdieu: The Conversion of Capital as Plot in the Mid-Victorian Novel', *Victorian Literature and Culture*, 31 (2003), 501–21.

Fraser, Derek, *The Evolution of the British Welfare State: A History of Social Policy since the Industrial Revolution* (New York: Barnes & Noble, 1973).

Freedgood, Elaine, *Victorian Writing about Risk: Imagining a Safe England in a Dangerous World* (Cambridge: Cambridge University Press, 2000).

—— (ed.), *Factory Production in Nineteenth-Century Britain* (Oxford: Oxford University Press, 2003).

Gagnier, Regenia, *The Insatiability of Human Wants: Economics and Aesthetics in Market Society* (Chicago: University of Chicago Press, 2000).

—— 'Money, the Economy, and Social Class', in Brantlinger and Thesing (eds.), *A Companion to the Victorian Novel*, 48–66.

—— and John Dupré, 'Reply to Amariglio and Ruccio's "Literary/Cultural 'Economies', Economic Discourse, and the Question of Marxism"', in Woodmansee and Osteen (eds.), *The New Economic Criticism*, 401–7.

Gallagher, Catherine, *The Body Economic: Life, Death, and Sensation in Political Economy and the Victorian Novel* (Princeton: Princeton University Press, 2006).

—— *The Industrial Reformation of English Fiction: Social Discourse and Narrative Form 1832–1867* (Chicago: University of Chicago Press, 1985).

Gardner, Peter, 'Liberty and Compulsory Education', in Griffiths (ed.), *Of Liberty*, 109–29.

Gaskell, Elizabeth, *Cranford* (1853), with *Cousin Phillis*, ed. Peter Keating (London: Penguin, 1976).

—— *North and South* (1855), ed. Patricia Ingham (London: Penguin, 1995).

Gilbert, Sandra, and Gubar, Susan, *The Madwoman in the Attic: The Woman Writer and the Nineteenth-Century Literary Imagination* (New Haven: Yale University Press, 1979).

Gillooly, Eileen, *Smile of Discontent: Humor, Gender, and Nineteenth-Century British Fiction* (Chicago: University of Chicago Press, 1999).

Gillow, John, and Barnard, Nicholas, *Traditional Indian Textiles* (London: Thames & Hudson, 1991).

Gilmour, Robin, 'The Gradgrind School: Political Economy in the Classroom', *Victorian Studies*, 11 (1967), 207–24.

—— *The Idea of the Gentleman in the Victorian Novel* (London: Allen & Unwin, 1981).

—— *The Victorian Period: The Intellectual and Cultural Context of English Literature 1830–1890* (London: Longman, 1993).

Goethe, Johann Wolfgang von, *Faust*, 2nd Part (1832), ed. Albrecht Schöne (*Sämtliche Werke*; Frankfurt: Klassischer Verlag, 1994).

—— *Wilhelm Meister's Travels* (1821), *see* Carlyle, trans.

Goldberg, Michael, *Carlyle and Dickens* (Athens: University of Georgia Press, 1972).

Goodlad, Lauren M. E., *Victorian Literature and the Victorian State: Character and Governance in a Liberal Society* (Baltimore, Md.: Johns Hopkins University Press, 2003).

Graver, Suzanne, *George Eliot and Community: A Study in Social Theory and Fictional Form* (Berkeley: University of California Press, 1984).

—— 'Writing in a "Womanly Way" and the Double Vision of *Bleak House*', *Dickens Quarterly*, 4 (1987), 3–15.

Griffiths, A. Phillips (ed.), *Of Liberty* (Cambridge: Cambridge University Press, 1983).

Gutmann, Amy, 'What's the Use of Going to School? The Problem of Education in Utilitarianism and Rights Theories', in Lyons (ed.), *Mill's Utilitarianism*, 67–84.

Guy, John, *Woven Cargoes: Indian Textiles in the East* (New York: Thames & Hudson, 1998).

Guy, Josephine M., *The Victorian Social-Problem Novel: The Market, the Individual, and Communal Life* (New York: St. Martin's Press, 1996).

—— (ed.), *The Victorian Age: An Anthology of Sources and Documents* (London: Routledge, 1998).

—— and Ian Small, *Oscar Wilde's Profession: Writing and the Culture Industry in the Late Nineteenth Century* (Oxford: Oxford University Press, 2000).

Halévy, Elie, *The Growth of Philosophic Radicalism* (1901–4), trans. Mary Morris (Boston: Beacon, 1960).

Hamburger, Joseph, *John Stuart Mill on Liberty and Control* (Princeton: Princeton University Press, 1999).

Hardy, Barbara, *Particularities: Readings in George Eliot* (London: Peter Owen, 1982).

Harrison, Ross, *Bentham* (London: Routledge & Kegan Paul, 1983).

Harrold, Charles Frederick, *Carlyle and German Thought, 1819–1834* (New Haven: Yale University Press, 1934).

Haslam, Jason, and Wright, Julia (eds.), *Captivating Subjects: Writing Confinement, Citizenship, and Nationhood in the Nineteenth Century* (Toronto: University of Toronto Press, 2005).

Henderson, W. O., *The Lancashire Cotton Famine* (Manchester: University of Manchester Press, 1934).

Henry, Nancy, *George Eliot and the British Empire* (Cambridge: Cambridge University Press, 2002).

—— '"Ladies do it?": Victorian Women Investors in Fact and Fiction', in O'Gorman (ed.), *A Concise Companion to the Victorian Novel*, 111–31.

Herbert, Christopher, *Culture and Anomie: Ethnographic Imagination in the Nineteenth Century* (Chicago: University of Chicago Press, 1991).

—— *Trollope and Comic Pleasure* (Chicago: University of Chicago Press, 1987).

Hilton, Boyd, *The Age of Atonement: The Influence of Evangelicalism on Social and Economic Thought, 1795–1865* (Oxford: Clarendon Press, 1988).

Himmelfarb, Gertrude, 'The Haunted House of Jeremy Bentham', in *Victorian Minds* (New York: Knopf, 1968).

Hinderer, Drew, 'Bentham on Poetry, Push-pin, and the Arts', *Michigan Academician*, 27 (1995), 57–64.

Holdsworth, William S., *Charles Dickens as a Legal Historian* (New Haven: Yale University Press, 1928).

Hollander, Samuel, *The Economics of John Stuart Mill*, 2 vols. (Toronto: University of Toronto Press, 1985).

Holloway, John, '*Hard Times*: A History and a Criticism', in John Gross and Gabriel Pearson (eds.), *Dickens and the Twentieth Century* (London: Routledge & Kegan Paul, 1962), 159–74.

Holstrom, John, and Lerner, Laurence (eds.), *George Eliot and her Readers: A Selection of Contemporary Reviews* (London: Bodley Head, 1966).

Homans, Margaret, 'Dinah's Blush, Maggie's Arm, Class, Gender, and Sexuality in George Eliot's Early Novels', *Victorian Studies*, 36 (1993), 155–78.

House, Humphrey, *The Dickens World* (London: Oxford University Press, 1941).

Houston, Gail Turley, *From Dickens to Dracula: Gothic, Economics, and Victorian Fiction* (Cambridge: Cambridge University Press, 2005).

Hume, L. J., *Bentham and Bureaucracy* (Cambridge: Cambridge University Press, 1981).

Ignatieff, Michael, *A Just Measure of Pain: The Penitentiary in the Industrial Revolution 1750– 1850* (New York: Pantheon, 1978).

Inden, Ronald, *Imagining India* (Oxford: Blackwell, 1990).

Irschick, Eugene F., *Dialogue and History: Constructing South India, 1795–1895* (Berkeley: University of California Press, 1994).

Irwin, John, and Brett, Katharine B., *Origins of Chintz* (London: Her Majesty's Stationery Office, 1970).

Jacobus, Nancy, 'The Question of Language: Men of Maxims and *The Mill on the Floss*', in Elizabeth Abel (ed.), *Writing and Sexual Difference* (Chicago: University of Chicago Press, 1982), 37–52.

Jaffe, Audrey, 'Modern and Postmodern Theories of Fiction', in Brantlinger and Thesing (eds.), *A Companion to the Victorian Novel*, 424– 41.

Jahn, Karen, 'Fit to Survive: Christian Ethics in *Bleak House*', *Studies in the Novel*, 18 (1986), 367–80.

James, Henry, 'The Novels of George Eliot', *Atlantic Monthly*, Oct. 1866, in *The Mill on the Floss*, ed. Carol Christ (New York: Norton, 1994), 464–5.

Jessop, Ralph, *Carlyle and Scottish Thought* (Houndsmill, Basingstoke: Macmillan, 1997).

Jevons, William Stanley, 'John Stuart Mill's Philosophy Tested', in *Pure Logic and Minor Works*, ed. Robert Adamson and Harriet Jevons (London: Macmillan, 1890), 197–299.

—— *The Theory of Political Economy* (1871), 5th edn. (New York: Kelley & Millman, 1957).

Johnson, Edgar, *Charles Dickens: His Tragedy and Triumph*, rev. abr. edn. (Harmondsworth: Penguin, 1979).

Johnson, Patricia, '*Hard Times* and the Structure of Industrialism: The Novel as Factory', *Studies in the Novel*, 21 (1989), 128–37.

Jordan, John O. (ed.), *The Cambridge Companion to Charles Dickens* (Cambridge: Cambridge University Press, 2001).

Joshi, Priya, *In Another Country: Colonialism, Culture, and the English Novel in India* (New York: Columbia University Press, 2002).

Joyce, Patrick, and Kent, Christopher, 'Victorian Studies Now: The State of the Discipline', paper delivered at 'Locating the Victorians', Interdisciplinary Conference for the Sesquicentenary of the Great Exhibition, Science and Victoria & Albert Museums, London, July 2001.

Kaufmann, David, *The Business of Common Life: Novels and Classical Economics between Revolution and Reform* (Baltimore, Md.: Johns Hopkins University Press, 1995).

Keep, Christopher, 'Technology and Information: Accelerating Developments', in Brantlinger and Thesing (eds.), *A Companion to the Victorian Novel*, 137–54.

Kelly, P. J., *Utilitarianism and Distributive Justice: Jeremy Bentham and the Civil Law* (Oxford: Clarendon Press, 1990).

Ketabgian, Tamara, ' "Melancholy Mad Elephants": Affect and the Animal Machine in *Hard Times*', *Victorian Studies*, 45 (2003), 649–76.

Kincaid, James, 'Resist Me, You Sweet Resistible You', *PMLA* 118 (2003), 1325–33.

Kinzer, Bruce L., *England's Disgrace?: J. S. Mill and the Irish Question* (Toronto: University of Toronto Press, 2001).

Klaver, Claudia C., *A/Moral Economics: Classical Political Economy and Cultural Authority in Nineteenth-Century England* (Columbus: Ohio State University Press, 2003).

Knezevic, Borislav, *Figures of Finance Capitalism: Writing, Class, and Capital in the Age of Dickens* (New York: Routledge, 2003).

Knoepflmacher, U. C., *George Eliot's Early Novels* (Berkeley: University of California Press, 1968).

Koljian, Kathleen, ' "Durga—for whom I would redden the earth with sacrificial offerings": Mythology, Nationalism, and Patriarchal Ambivalence in *The Home and the World*', in Patrick Colm Hogan and Lalita Pandit (eds.), *Rabindranath Tagore, Universality and Tradition* (Madison, NJ: Fairleigh Dickinson University Press, 2003), 119–28.

Kreisel, Deanna, 'Superfluity and Suction: The Problem with Saving in *The Mill on the Floss*', *Novel: A Forum on Fiction*, 35 (2001), 69–103.

Kucich, John. *The Power of Lies: Transgression in Victorian Fiction* (Ithaca: Cornell University Press, 1994).

—— *Repression in Victorian Fiction: Charlotte Brontë, George Eliot, and Charles Dickens* (Berkeley: University of California Press, 1987).

Landa, José Angél Garcia, 'The Chains of Semiosis: Semiotics, Marxism, and the Female Stereotypes in *The Mill on the Floss*', in Yousaf and Maunder (eds.), *The Mill on the Floss*, 73–100.

Langland, Elizabeth, *Nobody's Angels: Middle-Class Women and Domestic Ideology in Victorian Culture* (Ithaca: Cornell University Press, 1995).

Lanham, Richard, *A Handlist of Rhetorical Terms* (Berkeley: University of California Press, 1968).

Lansbury, Coral, *The Reasonable Man: Trollope's Legal Fiction* (Princeton: Princeton University Press, 1981).

Laqueur, Thomas W., 'Sexual Desire and the Market Economy during the Industrial Revolution', in Donna C. Stanton (ed.), *Discourses of Sexuality from Aristotle to AIDS* (Ann Arbor: University of Michigan Press, 1992), 185–215.

Leadbeater, S. R. B., *The Politics of Textiles: The Indian Cotton-Mill Industry and the Legacy of Swadeshi, 1900–1985* (New Delhi: Sage, 1993).

Leavis, F. R., *The Great Tradition* (1948) (New York: New York University Press, 1973).

—— ' "Hard Times": The World of Bentham' (1947), incorporated in *The Great Tradition* (1973), 227–48.

Lemire, Beverly, *Fashion's Favourite: The Cotton Trade and the Consumer in Britain: 1660–1800* (Oxford: Pasold Research Fund Oxford University Press, 1991).

Lerner, Laurence, and Holstrom, John (eds.), *George Eliot and her Readers* (London: The Bodley Head, 1966).

Levin, Michael, *J. S. Mill on Civilization and Barbarism* (London: Routledge, 2004).

Levine, George, 'Intelligence as Deception: *The Mill on the Floss*', *PMLA* 80 (1965), 402–9.

—— (ed.), 'Introduction: George Eliot and the Art of Realism', in *The Cambridge Companion to George Eliot* (Cambridge: Cambridge University Press, 2001), 1–19.

Levitt, Sarah, 'Clothing', in Rose (ed.), *The Lancashire Cotton Industry*, 154–86.

Levy, David M., *How the Dismal Science Got its Name: Classical Economics and the Ur-Text of Racial Politics* (Ann Arbor: University of Michigan Press, 2001).

Levy, Eric P., 'Property Morality in *The Mill on the Floss*', *Victorians Institute Journal*, 31 (2003), 173–85.

Lewis, Charles R., *A Coincidence of Wants: The Novel and Neoclassical Economics* (New York: Garland, 2000).

Lindert, P., and Williamson, J. G., 'English Workers' Living Standards during the Industrial Revolution: A New Look', *Economic History Review*, 36 (1983), 1–25.

Lloyd, Trevor, 'John Stuart Mill and the East India Company', in Caine (ed.), *A Cultivated Mind*, 44–79.

Logan, Thad, *The Victorian Parlor* (Cambridge: Cambridge University Press, 2001).

Long, Douglas G., *Bentham on Liberty: Jeremy Bentham's Idea of Liberty in Relation to his Utilitarianism* (Toronto: University of Toronto Press, 1977).

Lyons, David (ed.), *Mill's Utilitarianism: Critical Essays* (Lanham, Md.: Rowman & Littlefield, 1997).

Macaulay, Thomas Babington, *Complete Writings* (Boston and New York: Houghton, Mifflin, 1900) (abbreviated as *CW*).

—— From *The Edinburgh Review*, Mar., June, Oct. 1829: (1) 'Mill's Essay on Government'; (2) 'Westminster Reviewer's Defense of Mill'; (3) 'Utilitarian Theory of Government' (*CW*, xii).

Macaulay, Thomas Babington, 'Government of India' (10 July 1833) (*CW,* xvii).

—— *Indian Penal Code* (1837) (*CW,* xviii).

—— 'Minute on Indian Education', 2 Feb. 1835, in *Macaulay, Prose and Poetry,* selected by G. M. Young (London: Rupert Hart-Davis, 1952).

McClintock, Anne, *Imperial Leather: Race, Gender, and Sexuality in the Colonial Context* (New York: Routledge, 1995).

McDermott, Jim, 'New Womanly Man: Feminized Heroism and the Politics of Compromise in *The Warden*', *Victorians Institute Journal,* 27 (1999), 71–90.

McDonagh, Josephine, 'The Early Novels', in Levine (ed.), *The Cambridge Companion to George Eliot,* 38–56.

McLaughlin, Kevin, 'Losing One's Place: Displacement and Domesticity in Dickens's *Bleak House,* in Tambling (ed.), *Bleak House,* 228–45.

Majeed, Javed, 'James Mill's *The History of British India*: A Reevaluation', in Moir, Peers, and Zastoupil (eds.), *J. S. Mill's Encounter with India,* 53–71.

—— *Ungoverned Imaginings: James Mill's* The History of British India *and Orientalism* (Oxford: Clarendon Press, 1992).

Malthus, Thomas Robert, *An Essay on the Principle of Population* (1798), ed. Antony Flew (London: Penguin, 1985).

—— *An Essay on the Principle of Population* (1803), selections, intro. by Donald Winch, based on the text prepared by Patricia James (Cambridge: Cambridge University Press, 1992).

—— *Principles of Political Economy Considered with a View to their Practical Application* (1820) (Boston: Well & Lilly, 1821).

Manning, D. J., *The Mind of Jeremy Bentham* (London: Longmans, 1968).

Martineau, Harriet, 'Female Industry' (1859), in Susan Hamilton (ed.), '*Criminals, Idiots, Women, and Minors': Nineteenth-Century Writing by Women on Women* (Petersborough, Ont.: Broadview Press, 1995), 29–70.

—— *A History of the Thirty Years' Peace, A.D. 1816–1846* (1849–50), 4 vols. (London: George Bell, 1907).

Marx, Karl, *Capital: A Critique of Political Economy* (with Preface, 1st German edn., 1867), trans. Samuel Moore and Edward Aveling, ed. and intro. by C. J. Arthur (Student edn.; London: Lawrence & Wishart, 1992).

Mauss, Marcel. *The Gift: Forms and Functions of Exchange in Archaic Societies* (1925), trans. Ian Cunnison, intro. by E. E. Evans-Pritchard (New York: Norton, 1967).

Mehta, Uday Singh, *Liberalism and Empire: A Study in Nineteenth-Century British Liberal Thought* (Chicago and London: University of Chicago Press, 1999).

Mellor, Anne K., *English Romantic Irony* (Cambridge, Mass.: Harvard University Press, 1980).

Metcalf, Thomas R., *Forging the Raj: Essays on British India in the Heyday of Empire* (New Delhi: Oxford University Press, 2005).

—— *Ideologies of the Raj: The New Cambridge History of England*, iii, pt. 4 (Cambridge: Cambridge University Press, 1994).

Mill, James, *Elements of Political Economy* (1826), in *Selected Economic Writings*, ed. Donald Winch (Chicago: University of Chicago Press, 1966).

—— *The History of British India* (1818), abr., intro. by William Thomas (Chicago: University of Chicago Press, 1975).

—— 'Liberty of the Press', in *Essays on Government, Jurisprudence, Liberty of the Press, and Law of Nations*, written for the Supplement to the *Encyclopedia Britannica* (1816–23) (New York: Augustus M. Kelley, 1967).

—— 'Schools for All, in Preference to Schools for Churchmen Only (1812), in *James Mill on Education*, ed. W. H. Burston (Cambridge: Cambridge University Press, 1969).

Mill, John Stuart, *Autobiography*, ed. John M. Robson and Jack Stillinger (1873) (*CW*, i, 1981).

—— 'Bentham' (1838), in *Essays on Ethics, Religion and Society* (*CW*, x, 1969).

—— 'Coleridge' (1840), in *Essays on Ethics, Religion and Society* (*CW*, x, 1969).

—— 'Chapters on Socialism' (1879), in *Essays on Economics and Society* (*CW*, v, 1967).

—— *Collected Works*, ed. John M. Robson et al. (Toronto: University of Toronto Press, 1963–) (abbreviated as *CW*).

—— 'Considerations on Representative Government' (1861), in *Essays on Politics and Society* (*CW*, xix, 1977).

—— 'Corporation and Church Property' (1833), in *Essays on Economics and Society* (*CW*, iv, 1967).

—— 'The East India Company's Charter' (1852), in *Writings on India* (*CW*, xxx, 1990).

—— 'Endowments' (1869), in *Essays on Economics and Society* (*CW*, iv, 1967).

—— 'England and Ireland' (1868), in *Essays on England, Ireland and the Empire* (*CW*, vi, 1982).

—— 'Ireland' (1825), in *Essays on England, Ireland and the Empire* (*CW*, vi, 1982).

—— 'Land Tenure Reform' (1871), in *Essays on Economics and Society* (*CW*, iv, 1967).

—— 'Leslie on the Land Question' (1870), in *Essays on Economics and Society* (*CW*, iv, 1967).

—— 'Memorandum of the Improvements in the Administration of India during the Last Thirty Years' (1858), in *Writings on India* (*CW*, xxx, 1990).

—— 'Minute on the Black Act' (1836), in *Writings on India* (*CW*, xxx, 1990).

Mill, John Stuart, 'The Negro Question' (1850), in *Essays on Equality, Law and Education* (*CW*, xxi, 1984).

—— 'On Liberty' (1859), in *Essays on Politics and Society* (*CW*, xviii, 1977).

—— 'Penal Code for India' (1838), in *Writings on India* (*CW*, xxx, 1990).

—— 'The Petition of the East-India Company' (1858), in *Writings on India* (*CW*, xxx, 1990).

—— 'Previous Communication 1828' (1836), in *The Great Indian Education Debate: Documents Relating to the Orientalist–Anglicist Controversy, 1781–1843*, ed. Lynn Zastoupil and Martin Moir (Richmond, Surrey: Curzon, 1999).

—— *Principles of Political Economy with Some of their Applications to Social Philosophy* (1848) (*CW*, ii–iii, 1965).

—— 'Reform of the Civil Service' (1854), in *Essays on Politics and Society* (*CW*, xviii, 1977).

—— 'The Subjection of Women' (1869), in *Essays on Equality, Law and Education* (*CW*, xxi, 1984).

—— *A System of Logic, Ratiocinative and Inductive* (1843) (*CW*, vii–viii, 1973–4).

—— 'Utilitarianism' (1861), in *Essays on Ethics, Religion and Society* (*CW*, x, 1969).

—— 'What Is to Be Done with Ireland?' (1848?), in *Essays on England, Ireland and the Empire* (*CW*, vi, 1982).

—— *Writings on India*, ed. John M. Robson, Martin Moir, and Zawahir Moir, 'Introduction' by Martin Moir (*CW*, xxx, 1990).

Miller, Andrew H., *Novels behind Glass: Commodity Culture and Victorian Narrative* (Cambridge: Cambridge University Press, 1995).

Miller, D. A., *The Novel and the Police* (Berkeley: University of California Press, 1988).

Miller, J. Hillis, 'Moments of Decision in *Bleak House*', in Jordan (ed.), *The Cambridge Companion to Charles Dickens*, 49–63.

Miller, Nancy K., 'Emphasis Added: Plots and Plausibilities in Women's Fiction', in Elaine Showalter (ed.), *The New Feminist Criticism: Essays on Women, Literature and Theory* (London: Virago, 1986), 339–60.

Moir, Martin I., Peers, Douglas M., and Zastoupil, Lynn (eds.), *J. S. Mill's Encounter with India* (Toronto: University of Toronto Press, 1999).

Moore, Robin, 'John Stuart Mill and Royal India', in Moir, Peers, and Zastoupil (eds.), *J. S. Mill's Encounter with India*, 87–110.

Morgan, Carol E., *Women Workers and Gender Identities 1835–1913: The Cotton and Metal Industries in England* (London: Routledge, 2001).

Morris, Pam, '*Bleak House* and the Struggle for the State Domain', *ELH* 68 (2001), 679–98.

Mueller, Hans-Eberhard, *Bureaucracy, Education, and Monopoly: Civil Service Reforms in Prussia and England* (Berkeley: University of California Press, 1984).

Murphy, Margueritte, 'The Ethics of the Gift in George Eliot's *Daniel Deronda*', *Victorian Literature and Culture*, 34 (2006), 189–207.

Nandy, Ashis, *The Illegitimacy of Nationalism: Rabindranath Tagore and the Politics of Self* (Delhi: Oxford University Press, 1994).

—— *Intimate Enemy: Loss and Recovery of Self under Colonialism* (Delhi: Oxford University Press, 1983).

Nardin, Jane, *Trollope and Victorian Moral Philosophy* (Athens, Ohio: Ohio University Press, 1996).

Neff, Emory, *Carlyle and Mill: Mystic and Utilitarian* (New York: Columbia University Press, 1924).

Nelson, James G., 'The Victorian Social Problem Novel', in Baker and Womack (eds.), *A Companion to the Victorian Novel*, 189–207.

Newsom, Robert, 'Administrative', in Tucker (ed.), *A Companion to Victorian Literature and Culture*, 212–24.

—— *Charles Dickens Revisited* (New York: Twayne, 2000).

Newsome, David, *The Victorian World Picture: Perceptions and Introspections in an Age of Change* (New Brunswick, NJ: Rutgers University Press, 1997).

Newton, Judith Lowder, *Women, Power, and Subversion: Social Strategies in British Fiction 1778–1860* (Athens, Ga.: University of Georgia Press, 1981).

Nunokawa, Jeff, *The Afterlife of Property: Domestic Security and the Victorian Novel* (Princeton: Princeton University Press, 1994).

Nussbaum, Martha C., 'The Literary Imagination in Public Life', *New Literary History*, 22 (1991), 877–910.

—— *Poetic Justice* (Boston: Beacon, 1995).

Ogden, C. K., *Bentham's Theory of Fictions* (New York: Harcourt Brace, 1932).

O'Gorman, Francis (ed.), *A Concise Companion to the Victorian Novel* (Malden, Mass.: Blackwell, 2005).

—— (ed.), *Victorian Literature and Finance* (Oxford: Oxford University Press, 2007).

Otis, Laura, 'Nineteenth-Century Webs: The Exchange between Literature and Science', paper delivered at 'Locating the Victorians' Conference for the Sesquicentenary of the Great Exhibition, Science and Victoria & Albert Museums, London, July 2001.

Owen, David, *English Philanthropy, 1660–1960* (Cambridge, Mass.: Harvard University Press, 1964).

Parry, Jonathan, *The Rise and Fall of Liberal Government in Victorian Britain* (New Haven: Yale University Press, 1993).

Paxton, Nancy L., *George Eliot and Herbert Spencer: Feminism, Evolutionism, and the Reconstruction of Gender* (Princeton: Princeton University Press, 1991).

Peers, Douglas M., 'Imperial Epitaph: John Stuart Mill's Defense of the East India Company', in Moir, Peers, and Zastoupil (eds.), *J. S. Mill's Encounter with India*, 198–220.

Peltason, Timothy, 'Esther's Will', in Tambling (ed.), *Bleak House*, 205–27.

Pettitt, Clare, 'Legal Subjects, Legal Objects: The Law and Victorian Fiction', in O'Gorman (ed.), *A Concise Companion to the Victorian Novel*, 71–90.

—— *Patent Inventions, Intellectual Property and the Victorian Novel* (Oxford: Oxford University Press, 2004).

Pitts, Jennifer, *A Turn to Empire: The Rise of Imperial Liberalism in Britain and France* (Princeton: Princeton University Press, 2005).

Polhemus, Robert, *The Changing World of Anthony Trollope* (Berkeley: University of California Press, 1968).

Polloczek, Dieter Paul, *Literature and Legal Discourse: Equity and Ethics from Sterne to Conrad* (Cambridge: Cambridge University Press, 1999).

Poovey, Mary, *Genres of the Credit Economy: Mediating Value in Eighteenth- and Nineteenth-Century Britain* (Chicago: University of Chicago Press, 2008).

—— *A History of the Modern Fact: Problems of Knowledge in the Sciences of Wealth and Society* (Chicago: University of Chicago Press, 1998).

—— *Uneven Developments: The Ideological Work of Gender in Mid-Victorian England* (Chicago: University of Chicago Press, 1988).

—— 'Writing about Finance in Victorian England: Disclosure and Secrecy in the Culture of Investment', *Victorian Studies*, 45 (2002), 17–37.

—— (ed.). *The Financial System in Nineteenth-Century Britain* (New York: Oxford University Press, 2003).

Porter, Roy, *Mind-Forg'd Manacles: A History of Madness in England from the Restoration to the Regency* (London: Athlone, 1987).

Postema, Gerald, 'Mill's Utilitarianism', in West (ed.), *Mill's Utilitarianism*, 26–44.

Pratt, Mary Louise, *Imperial Eyes: Travel Writing and Transculturation* (London: Routledge, 1992).

Price, Margaret Joan, from 'Selected Design Techniques from Indian Textiles in the Costume and Textile Study Collection' in the (Ph.D. diss., University of Washington, 1966).

Ray, Sangeeta, *Engendering India: Woman and Nation in Colonial and Postcolonial Narratives* (Durham, NC: Duke University Press, 2000).

Rees, John C., *John Stuart Mill's On Liberty*. (Oxford: Clarendon Press, 1985).

Ricardo, David, 'Notes on James Mill's *Elements of Political Economy*', 18 Dec. 1821 (*Works*, ix).

—— *On the Principles of Political Economy and Taxation* (1817) (*Works*, i).

——Ricardo–Malthus letter exchange, 24, 26 Jan. 1817 (*Works*, vii).

—— *Works and Correspondence*, ed. Piero Sraffa with M. H. Dobb (Cambridge: Cambridge University Press, 1951–) (abbreviated as *Works*).

Riley, Jonathan, 'Justice under Capitalism', in *Markets and Justice*, ed. John W. Chapman and J. Roland Pennock. (NOMOS, 31; New York: New York University Press, 1989), 122–62.

—— *Mill on Liberty* (London: Routledge, 1998).

Robson, Ann P. and John M., ' "Impetuous Eagerness": The Young Mill's Radical Journalism', in Joanne Shattock and Michael Wolff (eds.), *The Victorian Periodical Press: Samplings and Soundings* (Leicester: Leicester University Press, 1982), 59–77.

Rose, Jonathan, 'Was Capitalism Good for Victorian Literature?', *Victorian Studies*, 46 (2004), 489–501.

Rose, Mary B., 'Introduction: The Rise of the Cotton Industry in Lancashire to 1830', in ead. (ed.), *The Lancashire Cotton Industry*, 1–28.

—— (ed.), *The Lancashire Cotton Industry: A History since 1700* (Preston: Lancashire County Books, 1996).

Rosen, F., 'Eric Stokes, British Utilitarianism, and India', in Moir, Peers, and Zastoupil (eds.), *J. S. Mill's Encounter with India*, 18–33.

—— *Jeremy Bentham and Representative Democracy: A Study of the Constitutional Code* (Oxford: Clarendon Press, 1983).

Rosenthal, Rae, 'Gaskell's Feminist Utopia: The Cranfordians and the Reign of Goodwill', in Jane Donawerth and Carol Kolmerten (eds.), *Utopian and Scientific Fiction by Women: A World of Difference*, foreword by Susan Gubar (Syracuse: Syracuse University Press, 1994), 73–92.

Rosselli, John, *Lord William Bentinck: The Making of a Liberal Imperialist* (Berkeley: University of California Press, 1974).

Rothschild, Emma, *Economic Sentiments: Adam Smith, Condorcet, and the Enlightenment* (Cambridge, Mass.: Harvard University Press, 2001).

Roy, Tirthankar, *The Economic History of India 1857–1947* (New Delhi: Oxford University Press, 2000).

Rubinstein, W. D., *Britain's Century: A Political and Social History 1815–1905* (London: Arnold, 1998).

Ryan, Alan (ed.), 'Introduction', in *Utilitarianism and Other Essays: J. S. Mill and Jeremy Bentham* (Harmondsworth: Penguin, 1987).

Said, Edward W., *Culture and Imperialism* (New York: Knopf, 1993).

—— *Orientalism* (New York: Pantheon, 1978).

Sarkar, Sumit, '*Ghare Baire* in its Times', in Datta (ed.), *Rabindranath Tagore's The Home and the World*, 143–73.

Sawicki, Joseph, ' "The mere truth won't do it": Esther as Narrator in *Bleak House*', *Journal of Narrative Technique*, 17 (1987), 209–24.

Schiller, Friedrich von, *On the Aesthetic Education of Man, in a Series of Letters* (1795), trans. Reginald Snell (New York: Ungar, 1965).

Schoeser, Mary, '"Shewey and Full of Work": Design', in Rose (ed.), *The Lancashire Cotton Industry*, 187–209.

Schofield, Philip, *Utility and Democracy: The Political Thought of Jeremy Bentham* (Oxford: Oxford University Press, 2006).

Schor, Hilary, 'Novels of the 1850's: *Hard Times, Little Dorrit*, and *A Tale of Two Cities*', in Jordan (ed.), *The Cambridge Companion to Charles Dickens*, 64–77.

—— *Scheherazade in the Marketplace: Elizabeth Gaskell and the Victorian Novel* (New York: Oxford University Press, 1992).

Schramm, Jan-Melissa, *Testimony and Advocacy in Victorian Law, Literature, and Theology* (Cambridge: Cambridge University Press, 2000).

Schumpeter, J. A., *History of Economic Analysis* (New York: Oxford University Press, 1954).

Searle, G. R., *Morality and the Market in Victorian England* (Oxford: Clarendon Press, 1998).

Seed, John, 'Unitarianism, Political Economy, and the Antinomies of Liberal Culture in Manchester, 1830–50', *Social History*, 7 (1982), 1–25.

Semple, Janet, *Bentham's Prison: A Study of the Panopticon Penitentiary* (Oxford: Clarendon Press, 1993).

Seville, Catherine, *Literary Copyright Reform in Early Victorian England: The Framing of the 1842 Copyright Act* (Cambridge: Cambridge University Press, 1999).

Sharpe, Pamela, *Adapting to Capitalism: Working Women in the English Economy, 1700–1850* (Basingstoke: St. Martin's Press, 1996).

Shatto, Susan, *The Companion to Bleak House* (London: Unwin Hyman, 1988).

Showalter, Elaine, *A Literature of their Own: British Women Novelists from Brontë to Lessing* (Princeton: Princeton University Press, 1977).

Sinfield, Alan, *Literature, Politics and Culture in Postwar Britain* (Oxford: Blackwell, 1989).

Skorupski, John, 'The Place of Utilitarianism in Mill's Philosophy', in West (ed.), *Mill's Utilitarianism*, 45–59.

—— (ed.), 'Introduction: The Fortunes of Liberal Naturalism', in *The Cambridge Companion to Mill* (Cambridge: Cambridge University Press, 1998), 1–34.

Smelser, Neil J., *Social Paralysis and Social Change: British Working-Class Education in the Nineteenth Century* (Berkeley: University of California Press, 1991).

Smith, Adam, *An Inquiry into the Nature and Causes of the Wealth of Nations* (1776), ed. R. H. Campbell, A. S. Skinner, and W. B. Todd, 2 vols. (Oxford: Clarendon Press, 1976).

—— *The Theory of Moral Sentiments* (1759), ed. D. D. Raphael and A. L. Macfie (Oxford: Clarendon Press, 1976).

Smith, Grahame, 'Comic Subversion and *Hard Times*', *Dickens Studies Annual*, 18 (1989), 145–60.

—— *Dickens, Money, and Society* (Berkeley: University of California Press, 1968).

Specker, Konrad, 'Madras Handlooms in the Nineteenth Century', in Tirthankar Roy (ed.), *Cloth and Commerce: Textiles in Colonial India* (New Delhi: Sage, 1996), 218–41.

Stafford, William, *John Stuart Mill* (Houndsmill, Basingstoke: Macmillan, 1998).

Stein, Burton, *Thomas Munro: The Origins of the Colonial State and his Visions of Empire* (Delhi: Oxford University Press, 1989).

Stephen, Leslie, *George Eliot* (1902) (London: Macmillan, 1919).

Stillinger, Jack, 'John Mill's Education: Fact, Fiction, and Myth', in Caine (ed.), *A Cultivated Mind*, 19–43.

Stokes, Eric, *The English Utilitarians and India* (Oxford: Clarendon Press, 1959).

Stokes, Peter, 'Bentham, Dickens, and the Uses of the Workhouse', *Studies in English Literature 1500–1900*, 41 (2001), 711–27.

Stone, Marjorie, 'Dickens, Bentham, and the Fictions of the Law: A Victorian Controversy and its Consequences', *Victorian Studies*, 29 (1985), 125–54.

Sullivan, Eileen, 'Liberalism and Imperialism: John Stuart Mill's Defense of the British Empire', *Journal of the History of Ideas*, 44 (1983), 599–617.

Sussman, Herbert, 'Industrial', in Tucker (ed.), *A Companion to Victorian Literature and Culture*, 244–57.

—— *Victorians and the Machine: The Literary Response to Technology* (Cambridge, Mass.: Harvard University Press, 1968).

Tagore, Rabindranath, *The Home and the World* (1916), trans. Surendranath Tagore, intro. by Anita Desai (London: Penguin, 1985).

—— 'Nationalism in India', in *Nationalism* (New York: Macmillan, 1917).

—— 'Woman', in *Personality* (New York: Macmillan, 1917).

Tambling, Jeremy, *Dickens, Violence and the Modern State: Dreams of the Scaffold* (Houndsmill, Basingstoke: Macmillan, 1995).

—— 'Prison-Bound: Dickens and Foucault (*Great Expectations*)', in Connor (ed.), *Charles Dickens*, 117–34.

—— (ed.) *Bleak House: New Casebooks* (Houndsmill, Basingstoke: Macmillan, 1998).

Thale, Jerome, *The Novels of George Eliot* (New York: Columbia University Press, 1959).

Thomas, D. A. Lloyd, 'Rights, Consequences, and Mill on Liberty', in Griffiths (ed.), *Of Liberty*, 167–80.

Thomas, David Wayne, *Cultivating Victorians: Liberal Culture and the Aesthetic* (Philadelphia: University of Pennsylvania Press, 2004).

Thomas, William, *The Philosophic Radicals: Nine Studies in Theory and Practice, 1817–1841* (Oxford: Clarendon Press, 1979).

Thomas à Kempis, *The Imitation of Christ* (1503; 1st English translation), trans. Leo Sherley-Price (London: Penguin, 1952).

Thompson, E. P., *The Making of the English Working Class* (London: Victor Gollancz, 1963).

Thoms, Peter, *Detection and its Designs: Narrative Power in 19th-Century Detective Fiction* (Athens, Ohio: Ohio University Press, 1998).

Timmins, Geoffrey, 'Technological Change', in Rose (ed.), *The Lancashire Cotton Industry*, 29–62.

Trevelyan, George Macaulay, *British History in the Nineteenth Century (1782–1901)* (1922) (London: Longmans, Green, 1934).

Trollope, Anthony, *An Autobiography* (1883), intro. by Bradford Allen Booth (Berkeley: University of California Press, 1947).

—— *The Warden* (1855), ed., intro. by Robin Gilmour (London: Penguin, 1982).

Tucker, Herbert F. (ed.), *A Companion to Victorian Literature and Culture* (Malden, Mass.: Blackwell, 1999).

Ulrich, John, *Signs of their Times: History, Labour, and the Body in Cobbett, Carlyle, and Disraeli* (Athens, Ohio: Ohio University Press, 2002).

Vanden Bosche, Chris R., *Carlyle and the Search for Authority* (Columbus: Ohio State University Press, 1991).

—— 'Class, Discourse, and Popular Agency in *Bleak House*', *Victorian Studies*, 47 (2004), 7–31.

Veblen, Thorstein, *The Theory of the Leisure Class* (1912), intro. by John Kenneth Galbraith (Boston: Houghton Mifflin, 1973).

Vida, Elizabeth M., *Romantic Affinities, German Authors and Carlyle: A Study in the History of Ideas* (Toronto: University of Toronto Press, 1993).

Viswanathan, Gauri, *Masks of Conquest: Literary Study and British Rule in India* (New York: Columbia University Press, 1989).

Voth, Hans-Joachim, 'Living Standards and the Urban Environment', in Roderick Floud and Paul Johnson (eds.), *The Cambridge Economic History of Modern Britain*, i: *Industrialization, 1700–1860* (Cambridge: Cambridge University Press, 2004), 268–94.

Vrettos, Athena, 'Victorian Psychology', in Brantlinger and Thesing (eds.), *A Companion to the Victorian Novel*, 67–83.

Waterman, A. M. C., *Revolution, Economics, and Religion* (Cambridge: Cambridge University Press, 1991).

Waters, Catherine, *Dickens and the Politics of the Family* (Cambridge: Cambridge University Press, 1997).

—— 'Gender, Family, and Domestic Ideology', in Jordan (ed.), *The Cambridge Companion to Charles Dickens*, 120–35.

Webb, Igor, *From Custom to Capital: The English Novel and the Industrial Revolution* (Ithaca: Cornell University Press, 1981).

Weber, Max, *The Protestant Ethic and the Spirit of Capitalism* (1904–5), trans. Talcott Parsons, intro. by Anthony Giddens (Gloucester, Mass.: Peter Smith, 1988).

Weiss, Barbara, *The Hell of the English: Bankruptcy and the Victorian Novel* (Lewisburg, Pa.: Bucknell University Press, 1986).

Welsh, Alexander, *Dickens Redressed: The Art of Bleak House and Hard Times* (New Haven: Yale University Press, 2000).

West, Henry R., *An Introduction to Mill's Utilitarian Ethics* (Cambridge: Cambridge University Press, 2004).

—— (ed.), *Mill's Utilitarianism* (Malden, Mass.: Blackwell, 2006).

West Surrey College of Art & Design, Towner Art Gallery and Museums, *Five Centuries of Lace* (Guildford: West Surrey College of Art & Design, 1983).

Whale, John, *Imagination under Pressure, 1789–1832: Aesthetics, Politics, and Utility* (Cambridge: Cambridge University Press, 2000).

Wicke, Jennifer, 'Commercial', in Tucker (ed.), *A Companion to Victorian Literature and Culture*, 258–75.

Williams, John R., *Goethe's Faust* (London: Allen & Unwin, 1987).

Williams, Raymond, *Culture and Society 1780–1950* (1958) (Harmondsworth: Penguin, 1963).

—— 'Dickens and Social Ideas', in Michael Slater (ed.), *Dickens 1970* (London: Chapman & Hall, 1970).

Williford, Miriam, 'Bentham on the Rights of Women', *Journal of the History of Ideas*, 36 (1975), 167–76.

Winch, Donald, *Classical Political Economy and Colonies* (Cambridge, Mass.: Harvard University Press, 1965).

Winstanley, Michael, 'The Factory Workforce', in Rose (ed.), *The Lancashire Cotton Industry*, 121–53.

Wisdom, A. S., *The Law of Rivers and Watercourses* (London: Shaw & Sons, 1970).

Woodmansee, Martha, and Osteen, Mark (eds.), *The New Economic Criticism: Studies at the Intersection of Literature and Economics* (London: Routledge, 1999).

Yousaf, Nahem, and Maunder, Andrew (ed.), *The Mill on the Floss and Silas Marner: New Casebooks* (Houndsmill, Basingstoke: Palgrave, 2002).

Zastoupil, Lynn, 'India, J. S. Mill, and "Western" Culture', in Moir, Peers, and Zastoupil (eds.), *J. S. Mill's Encounter with India*, 111–48.

—— *John Stuart Mill and India* (Stanford: Stanford University Press, 1994).

Zlotnick, Susan, *Women, Writing, and the Industrial Revolution* (Baltimore, Md.: Johns Hopkins University Press, 1998).

Zwerdling, Alex, 'Esther Summerson Rehabilitated', *PMLA* 88 (1973), 429–39.

Index